Behavior-Based
Land Planning

Incentive-Based Strategies for the Achievement of Sustainable Growth Management in the United States

Donald R. Chance, Ph.D.

Copyright © 2009 Donald R. Chance

Behavior-Based Land Planning

Copyright © 2009 by Donald R. Chance. All rights reserved.
Except as permitted by the United States Copyright Act of 1976, no part of this publication may be reproduced or distributed in any form or by any means, or stored in a database or retrieval system, without the written permission of the author and publisher.

ISBN-13: 978-0-9800596-4-9

Sustainable Land Development International (SLDI), the publisher, and the author make no implied or expressed representation, warranty or guarantees of materials provided in this book and are not responsible for any errors or omissions or the results obtained from the use and/or implementation of such information.

Books produced by Sustainable Land Development International are available at special quantity discounts. Refer to SLDI Catalog Number: BBL01.

Sustainable Land Development International
275 East 10th Street, Suite 201
Dubuque, Iowa 52001
www.SLDI.org
563-690-2020

Project Editor: Greg Yoko
Copy Editor: Phyllis Bittinger
Composition and Cover Design: Bob Buss

Dedication

This book is dedicated to the land planners of rural and small town America – the most politically exposed, under appreciated, poorly financed, and challenging positions in our profession. Stumble into my base camp and I'm good for the first beer.

Acknowledgements

I owe a particular heartfelt thank you to ten individuals associated with Virginia Tech, many of whom are cherished working associates and friends. Dr. John Randolph, Dr. Diane Zahm, Mr. Jesse Richardson, and Dr. Ted Koebel of the College of Architecture have all made immeasurable contributions, often hammered-out over hundreds of miles of hiking together on far-flung trails. Without their support and compass bearings, I have no doubt that I would have found myself hopelessly lost. Dr. Rachel Holloway, program chair for the Virginia Tech Communications Program, and Dr. Scott Geller, Virginia Tech's renowned behavioral psychologist, both contributed critical insights and review for which I am deeply appreciative. Dr. Catherine Eckles, an experimental and behavioral economist, previously with Virginia Tech and now with the University of Texas, provided a fundamental linkage in the development of the book. Finally, Dr. Richard Vasey, retired Associate Dean of the Virginia Tech College of Natural Resources who has been a close confidant for nearly four decades, continues to affect my thinking in all things professional.

I also owe a debt of gratitude to three other long-time colleagues who assisted in the constructive review of the work – Dr. Gordon Bradley, Associate Dean of Forestry at the University of Washington, Ms. Enid Layes of the Washington State Legislature, and Mr. Robert Hanson, a professional planning peer and close associate for nearly 40 years. Also of criteria assistance and support was the specialized publishing division of Sustainable Land Development International with Greg Yoko, project editor, and Phyllis Bittinger, the copy editor.

But for all the debts I owe, I owe none greater than that to my wife of 33 years, Joanne Chance, who has put-up with and supported my interest in this project over the last seven years despite promises of retirement. Her only reward in all of this is that it is now completed whereby I promptly went back to work as a real planner on the frontlines, something that she justifiably detests but good naturedly supports. Sorry Dear.

TABLE OF Contents

Dedication v
Acknowledgements vii
Preface viii
Introduction xvii

SECTION I ~ *The Need for a Course Correction*

Chapter 1 ~ American Growth Management ~ The Need for a Course Correction 3

The Test of Performance
Performance Measures
Planning Performance in America
The Quantitative Evidence
The Qualitative Evidence

Chapter 2 ~ The Politics of Growth Management ~ The Limiting Factor 33

Political Sustainability
Chain of Requirements
Current Political Prospects

SECTION II ~ *The Model and Techniques of CBIP*

Chapter 3 ~ Culture-Based Incentive Planning 57

Regulatory Reform
Regulation Strategies
CBIP
CBIP and Planning Theory
A Question of Ethics and the Public Interest
What is the Nature of the Public Interest?
What is the Proper Relation of Planning to
  Politics and Power?

Chapter 4 ~ Culture and Planning 93
    Grid-Group Typology and Cultural Theory
    Grid-Group Typology and Planning
    Grid-Group Typology and a Cross-Cultural
      Perspective of Planning

Chapter 5 ~ Applied Behavior Analysis and
          Planning 119
    Applied Behavior Analysis
    The ABC Model
    Basic Conclusions in ABA Research
    Antecedent Strategies
    Consequence Strategies

Chapter 6 ~ The Design of Incentive Programs . . .147
    Incentive Theory
    Incentive Design Under CBIP
    Types of Incentives
        Economic Incentives
        Social Incentives
        Behavioral Incentives

SECTION III ~ CBIP In Application

Chapter 7 ~ Private Forestlands and Community
          Planning 213
    Forest Fragmentation
    The Cultural Matrix
    Existing Programs and the Test of Performance
      under CBIP
    Delineation of the Planning Objective
    Incentive Program Design and ABI Analysis
    Incentive Design

Bibilography 261

Preface

Fate can be so very strange. After decades of professional wanderlust as a planner, I found myself returning to the university scene for a boot-camp style intellectual retrofit and a Ph.D. at the age of 55. It was a little like volunteering for Ranger paratrooper school three decades late ~ it made absolutely no sense at my age. What drove me back to academia was a long simmering dissatisfaction with the results of American planning.

I can still mark the moment ~ over 30 years ago ~ that I started to suspect that much of what I had been initially taught as a planner wasn't particularly effective in the American culture and had ethical overtones in practice. What had started as a nagging professional unease early in my career progressed over the years to a combination of disgust and despair. For validation or the invalidation of my instincts, or perhaps to make sure I hadn't lost all perspective of my professional purpose, I returned to the environment of the research university. For the next seven years I dedicated myself to the search for potential new tools better suited to the American culture. What evolved from that personal intellectual journey was the synthesis of a reflective practitioner with a newly trained reflective researcher. A strange beast indeed that resulted in a different kind of book ~ a crossover that blends applied theory with new techniques in actual practice.

This manuscript is virtually my exact and completed doctoral dissertation specifically written and reviewed from inception as a potential book ~ a book that my doctorial committee informed me I would write if I ever wanted to escape their grasp. It has undergone the rigorous review of six senior Ph.D. faculty members at Virginia Tech over two years with specializations in planning, land-use law, behavioral economics, behavioral psychology, and communications. It has also been subjected to review by outside academics in natural resource management, and professional planners and legislative affairs specialists. No portions of the manuscript have been used in journal publications, and the dissertation has been restricted to only electronic access by members of the Virginia Tech campus. In short, as applied to planning it is largely new material.

My Professional Perspective

My experience as a planner is much more extensive than my academic pursuits. In fact, I would never make the claim to be a true planning academic, far from it, although I spent years as a researcher and lecturer. Instead, I have synthesized the clever basic research and theoretical contributions of some wonderfully talented people, largely outside the discipline of planning, with my own professional insights into an applied model of practice for American planners.

While uncomfortable to me personally, I recite here my professional and academic background in the interest of full disclosure, and at the insistence of my publisher, so that you may understand my perspective and where it originates.

My resume includes 33 years of urban planning, including current and advanced planning functions, commercial and residential site design and development, municipal ordinance development and administration, and environmental assessment. This includes 18 years of management experience in the administration of local government planning agencies, housing and natural resource industry trade associations, and planning consulting firms.

In addition, my professional time has also painfully included 16 legislative sessions in the states of Washington and Montana, as well as Washington, D.C. representing various clients groups. I dealt with governmental and legislative affairs on a broad range of land planning, property development and natural resource management issues with an emphasis on collaboration and consensus building in complex political and economic environments.

Finally, interspersed with my practical experience were my years as a university professor and researcher in the fields of environmental design and planning with a specialization in small cities and incentive-based planning formats. These days I have returned to my roots in the name of intellectual honesty and as a nostalgic conclusion to my career, serving once again as a local government planning director for an isolated small city in eastern Oregon.

Introduction

For more than a century, neo-classical economists took comfort in the belief that people would act in their own economic self-interest, so much so, that most economic theory rests on the fundamental assumption that people will strive for utility maximization, which drives concepts of efficiency, equilibrium, and ultimately human welfare. Then came the behavioral economists.

A little over two decades ago, a creative cadre of mavericks began to challenge orthodoxy in their own discipline with experiments in such areas as happiness research, altruistic behavior and risk preferences. Why, for instance, doesn't wealth, over and above basic levels of comfort and security, have a direct correlation with increased levels of happiness? Or why will someone engage in economically self-destructive behavior, forgoing as much as several months' wages in a laboratory experiment, to punish a stranger? The answers lie in human psychology.

Elsewhere in academia, behavior analysts and marketing researchers have been exploring, for more than six decades, human decision-making and how to influence it. Their findings complement the results of the behavioral economists. Do our underlying values determine what choices we make? Unlikely, according to substantial research, which is why many public information campaigns fail to permanently change behavior in such areas as public health or conservation.

As every planner has observed, it is quite possible to sincerely hold strong environmental values and yet live on a large exurban estate and drive 60 miles to work in a 5,000-pound sport utility vehicle. Conversely, a champion of private property rights is just as likely to speak against a subdivision proposal next door as his communitarian-minded neighbors. Values, it appears, have limited impact on much of our behavior, but perceived consequences and incentives do - incentives that often have nothing to do with economic well-being. Moreover, incentives can be managed and manufactured with deliberate purpose. They also can be framed with the right type of language or marketing approach to elicit the desired behavioral response, which politicians, industrial psychologists, and marketers have known for years.

Planners and Behavioralism

Land planners work within systems, both natural and man-made, but they devise and execute public policy at the human level. Our professional training almost exclusively relates to applied systems management, from transportation considerations and subdivision design to command and control regulation. Yet, most of us spend our careers as intermediaries in neighborhood controversy, personality conflicts, and dealing with the effects of human behavior on the natural and the human-made environment. We are in the people business yet rarely do we relate to our profession in those terms.

For example, when attempting to manage some element of growth, we do not say to ourselves, "What consequences or incentives can be devised that are politically acceptable and culturally effective to establish the desired behavioral response?" Instead we ask, "What regulation can be legislatively imposed at the state or local level?" An analogy that every novice whitewater canoeist learns applies here. The current (culture and marketplace forces) is too strong to be out-muscled in a direct confrontation (culturally insensitive planning approaches). Harness that power with better technique (culture-sensitive design) to achieve the desired objective, or crash and burn. This book contends that as a profession, we have been smashing up canoes all across the American landscape for decades, but a better way exists other than constantly sacrificing ourselves to the cultural current.

A New Model

This book introduces a new model of practice for land planning in America based on behavioralism. It is called, Cultural-Based Incentive Planning or CBIP. The model and its associated techniques draw upon a number of disciplines with which planning has no substantial heritage of collaboration: applied behavior analysis, environmental psychology, social biology, behavioral economics, cultural anthropology, and the communication and marketing sciences. Observations from these fields are adapted to growth management practices and regulatory reform. They also are extended to a private sector orientation for the profession. The basic premise of the approach is to plan based on human nature and the American culture, not ignore them.

CBIP offers planners in the public and private sectors a politically realistic alternative, adaptable to both existing tools and new approaches. The approach was specifically created to reduce the current contentiousness between America's culture of competitive individualism and planning's egalitarian objectives. While applicable to a broad range of planning fields from transportation to housing, the text focuses on examples in growth management and traditional land planning applications. Planners, resource managers, and policy analysts operating in more conservative environments will find the approach particularly helpful in the fight for relevancy and effectiveness.

The CBIP model and techniques are based on four pillars: cultural sensitivity, behavior analysis, engineered incentive regimes, and the tools of persuasion.

The cultural pillar of CBIP is concerned with how a society operationalizes issues such as freedom, equality, and security, which in turn affect land-use behaviors in the areas of privacy, autonomy, and mobility. The book explores these and other American cultural traits and their implications for planning practice by contrasting them against other world cultures. By exposing these differences, a foundation is developed for a culturally sensitive planning format better suited to American circumstances.

The second pillar of CBIP is the mechanics of how to engineer effective interventions for behavior change, whether housing decisions by consumers or development deliberations by landowners. It is based on half a century of practice and research in applied behavior analysis. The conclusions and basic principles are deceptively simple, but they have powerful implications for planners searching for more effective approaches.

The third pillar of the model is the design and application of incentives, both positive and negative. When planners hear the word incentives, they tend to think economic inducements through such mechanisms as density bonuses. But, by combining an understanding of cultural tendencies with the psychological quirks of human decision-making, the role of incentives can be greatly expanded for planning application. Process, lifestyle, social, behavioral, and technical assistance incentives can be created for various stakeholder groups in the land-use equation. This book considers many incentive strategies.

These strategies draw upon, among other areas, the fourth pillar ~ communication theory and the psychological underpinnings of influence and persuasion and incentive theory.

Rethinking the Role of Planners

Many will find CBIP to be provocative, which is a polite way of saying that it challenges directly some of the traditions of the American planning profession. Know that such positions are not taken out of dogmatic ideology, imprudence, or a desire to provoke controversy. Instead they come from pragmatism and a deep commitment to obtain results. This book suggests, among other things, that the future of American planning must shift in both sector orientation and approach if it is to regain societal relevance. It promotes unapologetically an advocacy role and associated techniques that would supplant the assumed position of neutral interpreters of the public interest. The book also directs a spotlight on our own attitudes as planners, asking questions about ethics and the moral appropriateness of CBIP as a practical model.

It is argued that to approach an understanding of the American land-use experience is to approach an understanding of American culture. Our man-made environment and land-use practices are a publicly driven, bottom-up creation ~ the embodiment of a set of behaviors and values. Some of these behaviors, such as consumerism, have been specifically manufactured using tools of influence, while others, like automobile dependence and single-family detached housing preferences, likely arise from values of independence and security that are then reinforced in public policy. The end result is a cultural lifestyle embodied in a landform. America is a metaphor ~ its developed environments are a reflection of our own collective behaviors and motivations.

To provoke a different development pattern in a market-driven society in which individualism dominates, requires manufacturing a different set of lifestyle preferences with products to match. It also requires aligning personal self-interest with broader public policy objectives through the use of various incentive strategies. Neither will be accomplished in most of America by regulatory fiat. What is fair game, however, in our culture is the application of the tools of influence, marketing, persuasion, and profit motive in the pursuit of goals. Planners' aggressive application of these tools requires far more than a rethinking of technique. It requires introspection into how we have defined our relationship with society and in how we have designed planning institutions. This book does not shy away from these repercussions, asking and offering an answer to the implications of CBIP.

So Does it Work?

The practice of American planning is too difficult an enterprise and too painful an experience to sustain a field professional over a forty-year career unless it can provide justifiable results. I know one planner who half-jokingly says that the highlight of his career is successfully changing a proposed KFC color scheme. Acknowledgement is growing, reflected in research, that traditional planning practice is failing in America. But in general, very little research is directed at assessing the specific nature of these failures as it relates to a given tool or to the design of new or retrofitted tools for the field professional. A commitment to the observable and testable truth has gradually led this planner over the decades to first question and to later reject a number of standard planning approaches as largely ineffectual when applied in American culture. Consider me a slow learner. Culture-based incentive planning represents a quest to improve the performance of land planning practice through a behaviorist approach.

CBIP, as you might guess, finds its origin in other disciplines. Planning has always had a rich history as an applied management profession, drawing upon the contributions of many other fields, and CBIP continues that heritage. Will it work to improve field performance? Yes, substantial evidence in both research and application suggest that these techniques are highly effective. But, be forewarned that CBIP as a specific model of planning practice is in its infancy.

This book is intended to introduce a potentially powerful approach, and in so doing, provoke debate, experimentation, and refinement. But,

I do not claim the ultimate solution to America's land use dilemma. Both successes and failures will abound as we gain experience in how best to apply the concepts. The validity of these behavioral concepts has been confirmed in exhaustive experimentation and other forms of research in applied behavior analysis, behavioral economics, marketing, and communications science for decades. These principles work without question in applications from political campaigns to improving safety behavior in the workplace. Our challenge is to best apply these concepts and techniques to planning practice. To date, they have found their greatest planning application in transportation, but only future field experimentation combined with applied research will tell us how best to maximize their potential in other realms of planning.

As a final note, this book attempts to straddle several divides, often awkwardly so. The first is the different worlds of planning academia and professional field practice. Both are critical components to the advancement of knowledge in the discipline, but they constitute distinct experiences. The second divide is the natural compartmentalization of disciplines related to the CBIP model ~ behavioral economics, applied behavior analysis, the communication and marketing sciences, and land planning. The translation from one discipline to another can be, shall we say, sloppy, even unknowingly offensive. Those steps, however, must be taken otherwise useful knowledge is not transferred and perfected in practice. Behavioral-Based Land Planning strives to initiate a new transfer of information between previously segregated disciplines for direct application, but I would like to apologize for those strained moments when the belay is set up across the crevasse.

Organization of the Book

This book is organized in three sections. The first section provides context, while the second section presents the model and techniques of CBIP in some detail. The final section of the book is a case study.

Section I is comprised of two chapters. Chapter One explores the performance of American planning and, in particular, growth management, suggesting that a course correction is required in both technique and outlook if the profession is to regain constructive influence in our culture. Chapter Two provides further context for CBIP by extending the consideration of political culture into the realm of planning performance. To fully comprehend the strategic options for the improvement of growth management practice, state legislative realities must be addressed. These political realities are the limiting factors in establishing traditional models of regional command and control planning systems, forcing the consideration of other modified approaches with a higher degree of political consensus.

Section II of the book directly addresses the model and techniques of CBIP in four chapters. Chapter Three introduces and describes the fundamental structure and principles of Culture-Based Incentive Planning. Chapter Four addresses the first structural pillar of CBIP, the consideration of culture and its implications in planning practice. Chapter Five presents the second pillar of CBIP ~ applied behavior analysis (ABA). Chapter Six approaches CBIP from the tactical level and addresses its third pillar - specific techniques for the construction of incentive-based strategies.

Section III of the book is a demonstration of CBIP principles and process in application. Chapter Seven presents a recent CBIP-based analysis conducted for the U.S. Forest Service and Virginia Department of Forestry concerning private forestland fragmentation trends. While a rural lands example, the CBIP principles and process are equally applicable to suburban or urban practice.

Behavior-Based Land Planning

SECTION One

The Need for a Course Correction

CHAPTER One

American Growth Management – Noble Endeavor and Painful Reality

When many East Coast planners think of Oregon, they imagine mist, majestic Douglas Fir forests, and, of course, Portland. While the images are all accurate, two-thirds of the state is predominantly arid high plains, interspersed with isolated mountain ranges, such as the Blues, Strawberries, and Eagle Caps. Located in this rugged landscape is Malheur County with the kind of hauntingly beautiful sagebrush country and high timber that you'd expect in a Clint Eastwood western. The amazingly large and desolate jurisdiction served as a killing ground on the Oregon Trail where livestock and people would finally give out. With 94 percent in rangeland, and two-thirds in federal ownership, Malheur County is one of the locations where the American government located internment camps for Japanese Americans in a fit of national hysteria in World War II. To this day, it remains largely an isolated and sparsely populated landscape.

In 1977, Malheur County paid me the princely sum of $12,000 a year to assist in bringing the gospel of Oregon's newly-minted growth management program to the state's back forty. The assignment was to develop first generation comprehensive plans, zoning codes, and subdivision ordinances for both the county and four small incorporated towns, two of which had populations under 300. To meet the state-imposed deadline, the planning director, buttressed by a handful of planners on short-term contract, had one year to accomplish the task after the initial Land Conservation and Development Commission guidelines were published. Having just spent several years attempting to sell zoning in the darkest recesses of southern Appalachia as a local planner, I figured how bad could it get? As a former planner with the USDA Forest Service in the South and then as a local government planner in western North Carolina, I had become moderately accustomed to having law enforcement protection at public hearings. My previous salary had been $9,000 so I assumed that the position was a great opportunity, and it was located in a progressive state, no less. Consider the experience innocence lost.

Thirty years later I can still mark the moment that I started to realize that much of what I had been taught as a planner wasn't particularly effective in the American culture and had ethical overtones in practice. It happened one night at a particularly ugly public hearing in Malheur County. The Oregon state growth management law mandated that every incorporated hamlet in the state have an adopted plan with ordinances to match in accordance with state guidelines. This even applied to isolated jurisdictions like Adrian and Jordan Valley, Oregon, with populations less than 200. Neither had seen any development in 20 years and now, 30 years later, they still have shown virtually no population growth.

Part of the original concept behind Oregon's Senate Bill 100, in fact, a major factor in how it was politically promoted to local governments, was that the program expected a partnership between local and state governments. It was argued that community self-determination through public involvement was not going to be replaced by state mandate. Instead, broad goals at the state level would guide local performance matched with state financial assistance. Yes, state approval was required of plans and ordinances, but local planners and elected officials would still have the ability to respond to local circumstances and find consensus within their communities through any number of approaches. That was the original political concept, but not the eventual reality.

Sitting isolated at that public hearing in 1978, I was called a communist, a Nazi, and a long-haired college subversive from the 1960s, which struck me as odd since I was a short-haired moderate from conservative Virginia. During the course of this shellacking, I was reminded how the county had received its name. Malheur is French for "bad hour." But I didn't blame the citizens for their anger. In fact, I privately shared it. In the previous nine months, a painstaking community involvement process had been conducted to construct a neighborhood consensus, jurisdiction by jurisdiction, to comply with the state's new planning mandates. These mandates made little sense for remote desert hamlets of 150 people, but working together, people had found reasonable solutions in both plan and ordinance that matched the social and land-use fabric of the area. These micro-communities were proud of the approaches they had engineered, including their first zoning code, a simply administered 20-page document with only three districts. It wasn't much, but it certainly made sense for the circumstances.

The controversy had come in the reaction from the state, and Malheur's citizens and elected officials were furious. State reviews summarily bashed draft plans as wave after wave of local government guidance was informally suggested. Across Oregon, local planners begged for a state presence in the brutal public hearings to explain the positions being taken in Salem. Threats of state imposed building permit moratoriums were being made against local governments throughout eastern Oregon and ultimately imposed in some cases. It slowly became obvious to local elected officials and rural planners that local discretion was to be seriously restricted, and ultimately nearly eliminated, in the interpretation and compliance with the then broad planning goals of the new law. Over time, minimum lot size requirements mandated from the state would climb from 20 acres to 40 acres and eventually reach sizes of as much as 160 acres. Ultimately, 12 years were required before all local jurisdictions were found in compliance with the 1973 law, as regulatory guidance became increasingly autocratic. Fifteen percent of the state's local jurisdictions had refused to even submit plans and ordinances for review seven years after enactment of the law (DeGrove, 1984).

It was in Oregon that I recognized the ethical dilemma of American planning practice and the limited effectiveness of many of our basic tools in a society steeped in competitive individualism. If you truly believed in the principles of community self-determination through various forms of public involvement, how did you reconcile the imposition of a rigorous top-down approach? Moreover, if planners were desperate for results in their land-use planning practice, would anything but the most restrictive command and control regulatory format work? And in how many states could such a demanding system be politically imposed and sustained?

By any number of measures, Oregon has the most effective, and, some would argue, the only effective, statewide growth management program in the nation. It is the only state with a rigorous enough regulatory format to render a physical difference over time in how the regional landscape actually looks, principally because the program has curtailed rural sprawl. But the achievement has come with a number of limitations and undesirable side effects; not the least of which is that the citizens of the state have twice effectively voted to emasculate the program. While results are measurable and obvious to the experienced planner's eye, they are still modest by comparison, to say, the results of British planning practice, which is exponentially more regulatory in places like the Yorkshire Dales or Lake District.

The pattern is clear in Western European and British planning practice. Aggressive regulatory control does work. How could it not, particularly when applied uniformly across large regions the size of most states? It is a wonderfully easy shortcut to results, if you can get away with it. But, it is only effective in achieving some, not all, planning objectives. It also has serious political, cultural, and economic limitations in America. You cannot control demand by limiting supply, a fundamental flaw in many growth management strategies. Nor can you order farming or forestry to be economically viable through exclusive use zoning. You can't regulate housing to be affordable. And avoiding exaggerated market psychology responses is difficult with even a whiff of enhanced regulation. Most importantly, forcing a narcissistic and fiercely independent society like America to adopt and sustain the highly rigorous land planning controls necessary to achieve real results is nearly impossible, except in communities with elite socio-economic characteristics, or in circumstances where the horse has long since bolted from the barn, as in the case of jurisdictions where the majority of damage has already occurred.

Consider the application of zoning. Many of the aging generation of planners now approaching retirement spent much of their early careers fighting for the establishment of zoning, jurisdiction by painful jurisdiction. The tool was originally designed to separate incompatible land-uses in a time of filthy industries and deplorable air quality, not guide growth, and in the former capacity, it has been highly effective. Some argue convincingly that it has been too effective (Duany, Plater, Zyberk, & Speck, 2000; Jacobs, 1961; Kendig, Connor, Byrd, & Heyman, 1980). As land-use practices have changed with predominately clean industries and office parks, planners have slowly come to understand the role that traditional zoning practice has played in creating separation and sterility. New urbanism is a response to that mistake and a potential extension of it because it locks in rigidity. The basic provisions and institutions of today's American planning regimes come from and are designed for a world that to a significant extent no longer exists. They are largely designed for the culture and land-use dynamics of the 1920s, not the 21st century.

Unfortunately, planners now find themselves in the same situation that the forestry profession finds itself. For 60 years professional foresters, in conjunction with the Ad Council, promoted the evils of forest fires through Smokey Bear. The effective campaign went as far as incidentally restricting the management options of foresters to use fire as a tool. As knowledge has advanced with the benefit of hindsight, forest management professionals now understand that they have to reintroduce fire back into the western forest ecosystem and engage in certain harvesting regimes to avoid catastrophic burns. That's not an easy sell to Smokey's disciples, the general public.

By comparison, zoning has been embraced across most American communities. Its principal support comes from its power to exclude different socio-economic elements not identical to one's own. Public endorsement of the tool has, at its roots, power to maintain and enhance a privileged status quo, a strong human behavioral preference. Neighborhoods have become sophisticated regarding how to use zoning to protect and enhance private economic investment, while local governments use it as a tool to enhance revenue. These exclusionary zoning themes have now become so prevalent that they are the foundation of the public's support for planning. In short, exclusionary zoning and punitive subdivision requirements now masquerade as growth management.

Consider this pattern of public behavior. Established neighborhoods will nearly always support downzoning below existing densities in their area. They will resist up-zoning efforts to implement a variety of growth management strategies from transit-oriented developments to infill. Voters in small suburban governments, where they have the most political clout, will force excessively low-density residential zoning within their jurisdiction (Fischel, 1995). Rural landowner interests will typically resist extremely large-lot-size zoning themes and restrictions on family exemptions or occasional sales. Recent exurban move-ins will endorse punitive large lot requirements, the more exclusive the better. Both groups will challenge rural clustering themes because they can't relate to the market segment, one seeing it as a reduction in its development potential and the other perceiving it as development that it doesn't want. The inevitable outcome of this tug-of-war is a rural minimum lot size of 5, 10, or 20 acres, the worst possible format among the choices.

Culture-based incentive planning (CBIP) finds its roots in that Oregon public hearing back in 1978. In a very real sense, its origin comes from the frustration of American planners hungry for meaningful results. CBIP rests on the fundamental assumption that current planning practice in America is underperforming, so much so that planners must be willing to experiment with alternative models or risk complete irrelevance as a profession in today's evolving culture. To accept the need for CBIP or any other alternative model of practice is to accept the assumption that current technique is failing, or at least seriously flawed. The remainder of this chapter addresses that assumption. It asks how do we judge effectiveness of planning programs, and then applies those tests to the evidence of the last three decades.

The Test of Performance

Planners, like lobbyists, tend to measure success as the adoption of a new program, not the long-term results generated from that plan, ordinance, or new statute. This natural emotional reaction for those down in the trenches attempting to scratch out a victory can distort open-minded assessments of what has been accomplished. When you spend years completely committed to the development of a new state growth management statute, and you actually accomplish enactment of a bill against all odds, it is difficult not to feel success has been achieved regardless of all those political compromises and field realities that may ultimately emasculate the effort in future years. When you sacrifice yourself for the passage of a controversial ordinance, not transcribing community adoption as planning performance is almost asking too much. The harsh reality is that passage of any plan, ordinance, or statute is not success except in the most temporal time frame, confusing effectiveness with the occasional political triumph.

Psychologists have long recognized a human behavioral trait that they refer to as "lock-in and lock-out." Once a person has formed an opinion she or he will have a strong tendency to cognitively defend that position in internal thought processes. Since we don't want to seem inconsistent to ourselves, our minds conveniently oblige by filtering incoming information without our awareness. Information that is perceived as supporting an established opinion will be quickly recognized. In other words, we will take notice of it. Information that may challenge that established opinion often won't be noticed in our reflective thoughts, and even if it is, we tend to quickly reject it. In short, we lock-in positions and then lock-out information that contradicts those opinions.

Advertisers and political operatives have recognized this tendency for years. Major consumer manufacturers spend much of their advertising dollars in branding efforts aimed at the young, knowing that once committed, customers are likely to maintain a purchasing pattern for years, if not life. Political campaigns focus on influencing undecided voters and reinforcing the views of voters already committed to a candidate. They rarely attempt to change voters' minds. Political attack ads infuriate voters who are committed to the candidate under attack, reinforcing their commitment, but that is not who those ads are aimed at.

To make matters worse, opinions have a tendency to perpetuate. Humans often fabricate new evidence and reasons in support of opinions by inventing social proof. So what does this have to do with land planning and the perception of performance? Objectivity is hard to maintain in the immediate pressure and pains of a planner's life. The ability to judge performance is complicated by the long time frames and complex systems in which planners operate. They share this dilemma of lack of rapid feedback with several other disciplines, such as forest management and preventative health. Trial-and-success learning by the individuals in these disciplines can take decades or lifetimes and is always suspect due to the influence of so many potential confounding factors.

Planners face a similar situation. The complexity of factors that can influence the outcome of any given planning policy and the ability to anticipate the un-anticipatable can make a mockery of the term planner. Older planners have the advantage of being able to periodically revisit jurisdictions where they have previously worked. It can be a sobering experience to see the market or political response to a regulatory mechanism put into place decades earlier.

One personal example is the unintended destructive consequences of rural large-lot zoning schemes that I was responsible for establishing. A second example is the sheer insignificance of many thoughtfully developed comprehensive plans. Few things are so depressing as seeing a stack of old comprehensive plans on the shelf in a jurisdiction, each representing a different planning effort, and realizing upon review that they all basically say the same thing and bear little resemblance to what actually occurred.

But even reflective observation taken in a historic context can have serious limitations for the planner. Questions always arise about market shifts that have occurred over the horizon beyond immediate comprehension. Nor is it necessarily possible to fathom all of the other potential realities evoked or missed in the planning effort. What was the true impact, if any, on the quality of life in the neighborhood? Was social equity advanced or retarded by previous program elements? To what extent did the development pattern reflect planning intervention or natural market trends? To speculate on effectiveness, you have to consider the counterfactual – what would have happened without the planning intervention (Burby & May, 1997)? Planning is often not an easy business in which to judge performance, even with visual and quantitative clues.

Performance Measures

The academic literature on growth management regulatory regimes is largely devoid of any specific discussion of design and application criteria. That is, by what standards should we judge any potential planning tool that we are capable of inventing? Or put another way, what should our design criteria be in planning implementation schemes? What does exist in the literature are proposed objectives for growth management from which you can generally deduce the implied criteria of a given author (Downs, 1989; Knaap & Nelson, 1992; Nelson & Dawkins, 2005). The common thread is a heavy emphasis on the perspectives of local or state government. The prevailing orientation is the assumption that the public interest is essentially the same as the government interest. Hence, the purpose of growth management springs forth from the perspective of traditional governmental objectives and programs. Areas of emphasis include public utility and transportation efficiencies, along with tax policy and local finance concerns. Also included are social service concerns – particularly, affordable housing, issues of gentrification, and economic or racial segregation. Urban form and development practices are a concern, primarily as they relate to the considerations of infrastructure efficiency, public finance, and capturing environmental externalities. These are all areas of the public interest, but it is the public interest narrowly defined as the traditional areas of government concern.

Others challenge the paradigm. They argue that growth management should reflect American culture and strive to enhance a full range of lifestyle options, lending institutional support to market driven preferences (Center, 2000; Garreau, 1995; PERC, 2000; Shaw & Utt, 2000; Staley, 2001; Webster & Wai-Chung, 2003). Under their outlook, the intention of planning is not so much to control markets and engage in visioning, but to enable markets to serve as the organizing force and expression of societal objectives. The perspective is that government interventions should largely be limited to creating market institutions, where possible, to manage public goods and externalities.

Both perspectives, public interest and market enabling, obliquely suggest appropriate criteria by which a planning program can be judged. CBIP blends these considerations in a pragmatic outlook. Under the CBIP model of planning practice that is introduced later in the book, five broad performance criteria are recognized as central concerns: social validity, market sensitivity, technical performance, ethical appropriateness, and the availability of implementation resources. These criteria are value neutral in that they don't assume a certain set of planning objectives. Instead, I suggest that regardless of the goals that you are trying to obtain, the tools that you design should be judged by the following five tests:

1) Social Validity and Political Acceptance

As considered in some detail in the next chapter, social validity and political acceptance comprise the first strategic test. While closely related, the two criteria are not identical. Social validity, a concept of behavior analysis, requires that the target audience embrace, as significant, the goals of the planning intervention and the procedures used in the intervention. It also requires willingness to participate to achieve a successful outcome (Winett, Moore, & Anderson, 1991). All three are required. This is not to say that social validity cannot be manufactured through active issue management. In fact, through the tools of influence, marketing, and public relations campaigns, we engage in manufacturing social validity all the time. CBIP as an activist model encourages the manufacturing of social validity to achieve planning objectives.

In a planning context, supporting the goals without supporting the means is not sufficient. One behavior analyst defines social invalidity as, "the behaviors of consumers who not only disapprove of some component in the ongoing program but are going to do something about it," including not participating or seeking policy change (Baer, 1987). While any planning strategy may have selective acceptance under just the right circumstances, approaches with broad-based social validity are the real objective. Planners can't all work in liberal enclaves such as a university town. Sufficient behavioral change in the target population has to occur, the interventions continually supported, for it to represent a sustainable solution.

One reason social validity is of paramount importance in planning interventions is the behavioral implications of getting it wrong. Every rule-based constraint that is not widely endorsed will stimulate many individuals to engage in dedicated efforts to circumscribe the system (Geller, 2001a; Jensen, 1998; Levitt & Dubner, 2005). The resistance response stimulates the powers of human ingenuity to find substitutes for what is constrained by going over, under, around, or through the limitation, often inventing new alternatives that did not previously exist or simply by cheating. It generates creative compliance in which rules are not technically broken, but the spirit and scope of the rules are circumvented – the bane of planners everywhere. While such reactions can be expected even in incentive-based formats of regulation, dampening the resistance response is far better than taunting it by ignoring cultural preferences.

Political acceptability is the second branch of this validity test. It is quite possible to have a planning intervention with a high degree of social validity that is not politically acceptable to the legislative or administrative branches of government. It is also common to have the inverse. As important as these considerations are, what may be even more significant is political endorsement at one level of government with rejection at another. This is, of course, a major consideration in land-use planning because local governments derive both their powers and mandates from a state legislature.

Consider, as an example, the latitude of planners and elected officials within the political culture of their local setting. American planners can only be as effective as the local political climate allows them to be. It's not a matter of political courage but of operational reality if you are to maintain effectiveness and credibility. Planners in general do not make decisions; they make recommendations. Local elected officials are influenced in day-to-day project review and zoning deliberations by the political culture of their jurisdiction far more than state mandate. These individuals, as elected representatives, are not only subject to community pressure; they embody the local political culture of their area. One example is a 1980 Oregon study in which 1,046 applications for residential development in state-mandated exclusive-use farm zones were analyzed. Researchers found that 90 percent of the applications in the 12 counties reviewed were approved, and 81 percent of the approvals were illegal under existing state law (DeGrove, 1984). These results occurred in a state that has the most restrictive farm and forestland provisions in the nation.

While social validity and political acceptability are often not aligned, in American culture both normally have to be present for a successful planning intervention. Without political acceptance, few planning programs can be initiated. Without social validity in our market-based economy, too many opportunities arise to circumvent program elements. Housing consumers can simply cross jurisdictional lines to meet their desires, gated communities can become the norm, and drivers can sit in horrendous congestion rather than give up their independence and lifestyle preferences. In the final analysis, if you believe in the concept of sustainability, planning programs must have both broad social validity and political acceptance to be effective.

2) Market Sensitivity

The second of the five tests by which to judge a planning approach is market sensitivity. Market sensitivity as a design criterion in planning programs, involves two considerations. The first is that market response must be anticipated in the design of any planning strategy. To ignore and not legitimately accommodate a range of market preferences in some effective format, invites planning failure. That is not to imply, however, that preferences can't be either strengthened or weakened through a variety of mechanisms, including the employment of behavioral incentives that constitute the foundation of CBIP.

Among industrialized nations, American society has embraced the model of an unfettered modern market economy more strongly than any other. Jeremy Rifkin, in his comparative analysis with European cultures, claims that, "Americans may be the only pure capitalists left in the world" (Rifkin, 2005a). The concepts of neoclassical economics are now so deeply embedded in the culture that they have been adopted as the principal organizing paradigm for the society. Regardless of the degree to which you accept this current guiding paradigm, it is embedded in the beliefs and values of the culture, so much so that market economy principles have permeated nearly every realm of public policy deliberation from health care delivery to Social Security.

One of the fundamental weaknesses of today's command-and-control growth management model in America is community and market response. In a culture accustomed to market choice and the largely unrestricted exercise of personal freedom, American society is reluctant to accept and enforce the kind of absolute regulatory restrictions necessary to make current growth management models work. Unanticipated market responses to growth management practice are legendary, as are regulatory attempts to correct the problem.

When Montana imposed a 20-acre threshold for subdivision review, rural subdivision activity in the state took a decided preference toward 20-acre lots. As legislators were finally preparing to eliminate this aberrant incentive, the state had a land rush of speculative subdivision activity that created a multi-decade supply of 20-acre lots in some jurisdictions.

The Portland growth management boundary partially provoked growth to migrate across state lines into Vancouver, Washington. Builders responded to consumer preferences by continuing to build at low densities within the growth boundary, consuming land at a faster pace than anticipated and creating an exclusionary cost effect. The city reacted by imposing minimum density standards and waiving public hearings to circumvent neighborhood opposition to the imposed density increases.

One documented measure of market performance in American planning can be found in a myriad of hedonic econometric housing studies. These studies have investigated the relationship of land-use controls to price impacts, homeownership rates, market shifts, development industry response and political fragmentation. Most scholars recognize that all land-use controls affect in some way the cost, availability, and spatial pattern of housing (Fischel, 1990; Kelly, 2004; Luger & Temkin, 2000; Malpezzi, 1996; Phillips & Goodstein, 2000). William Fischel, in his meta-analysis of hedonic studies, concluded:

> "Land use controls, especially overall growth control programs, are important constraints on the land market. This in turn affects housing values, especially in suburban and exurban communities. Growth controls and other aggressive extensions of land use regulations probably impose costs on society that are larger than the benefits they provide. The higher housing prices associated with communities that impose growth controls are more likely the result of wasteful supply constraints than benign amenity production" (Fischel, 1990).

Stephen Malpezzi sums up one of the key dilemmas in surveying the current literature with its various methodologies and potential agendas when he states, "No one would be, or should be surprised at a finding that regulations raise housing prices. What is at issue is how much they raise prices, compared with any benefits they confer" (Malpezzi, 1996). Some spatial and price impacts are intentional, such as exclusionary zoning, while others are unintended consequences of growth management techniques gone awry. Of particular concern in the design of the next generation of growth management programs is the impact of program elements on the residential housing market since it comprises a major share of the nation's built environment (Danielsen, Lang, & Fulton, 1999; Koebel, 1990). As Danielsen, Lang, and Fulton comment, "There exists tough social equity issues that remain mostly unresolved by the Smart Growth movement." Those difficult issues of social equity and spatial development have a rich heritage in the literature.

Various studies have cataloged the different cost factors that land-use regulation represents in housing costs (Downs, 1991; Luger & Temkin, 2000; U.S. Department of Housing and Urban Development, 1991). Anthony Downs classified costs into three broad categories: direct restrictions on housing supply, direct cost increases, and delay-causing requirements. In a recent study conducted by the Center for Urban Policy Research at Rutgers University for the New Jersey Department of Community Affairs, researchers devised a methodology that separated excessive requirements from those necessary to achieve basic community goals (Luger & Temkin, 2000). Utilizing a combination of builder surveys and an economic regression model examining 70 communities, they determined that excessive regulation in New Jersey added an average of 8 percent ($10,000 to $20,000) to the cost of a new house. However, when finance and builder-related multipliers were included, the cost increase rose to $40,000 to $80,000 per house.

Similar findings have been replicated in a significant number of other studies in which a variety of econometric models have been tested (Katz & Rosen, 1987; Knaap, 1985; Malpezzi, 1996; Pollakowski & Wachter, 1990; Schwartz, Hansen, & Green, 1984; Schwartz & Zorn, 1988; Segal & Srinivasan, 1985; Shilling, Sirmans, & Guidry, 1991; Vaillancourt & Luc, 1985). Katz and Rosen analyzed 64 communities in the San Francisco Bay area, finding that housing in growth controlled communities was 17 to 38 percent more expensive than comparable communities in the same market with more moderate regulatory structures (Katz & Rosen, 1987). In a 1990 Montgomery County, Maryland, growth management study, Pollakowski and Wachter found similar price effects on the housing market of 10 to 30 percent (Pollakowski & Wachter, 1990).

In addition to the direct cost implications of growth management to housing affordability, there are also questions of the interconnectedness of market components, regional governance, and growth shifting.

It has long been known that urban residential growth is a migratory phenomena (Nelson, 1988; Rusk, 1999). In one representative California study, scholars concluded that 500,000 housing units were either not built or displaced to another jurisdiction as a result of growth management policies (Levine, 1999).

When reviewed collectively, the hedonic econometric housing studies, along with planner experience, raise a number of fundamental problems with current growth management practices. The literature clearly infers that new home costs directly influence other segments of the housing market, including rents and the price of pre-existing homes. The empirical literature also indicates that in closed markets with high regulatory barriers, competition declines among housing construction interests. Small builders are driven from the market and large, well-capitalized firms increase their market share (Luger & Temkin, 2000). While many factors can contribute to affordability, including interest rates, finance mechanisms, and input costs, the role of any given planning scheme has to be considered. Market sensitivity faults documented in research are not likely to be resolved without a shift in growth management design strategy.

The second and related consideration for planners, as relates to market sensitivity, concerns the design of market-based planning institutions. Scholars widely acknowledge that markets fail in the provision of public goods and the management of externalities (Dolsak & Ostrom, 2003; Laffont & Martimort, 2002; Olson, 1965). Externalities, the inability of the marketplace in a given circumstance to reflect all costs or benefits of a given action or project, can dramatically distort individual and institutional decision-making. Regulatory reform, as discussed in detail in Chapter Six, suggests that planning institutions can in some circumstances be redesigned to provide price feedback where traditional markets' mechanisms are now failing. One important design challenge for planners is to attempt to align the incentives that drive self-interested behavior in individuals with community-wide goals. Planners are capable of both influencing existing market outcomes through incentive-based strategies and in creating new market-oriented mechanisms for the management of public goods and externalities.

Another way to characterize this consideration is that planners don't have to be passive bystanders to perceived market forces. They are capable of competing with other societal interests and forces, but are subject to the same market tests as every other interest in a free-market oriented economy. To make that transition requires a shift in self-image from referees of market transactions involved with regulatory controls to just another team in competition in an open market economy. Superior product and creative institutional design can transform markets and human behavior when they capture the preference of consumers in an environment of choice. The exercise is both one of advanced design and marketing.

Planners must compete in both idea and product in a market-oriented environment. It is a legitimate test. To achieve sustainability, a given planning strategy must ultimately have social validity, and such validity is difficult to accomplish in America through top-down regulatory fiat. Consumer choice in America is now considered near sacrosanct, almost a basic human right. Planning schemes that attempt to restrict or deny market preferences are pitting themselves against powerful and unrelenting social forces. The alternative is to compete in the open marketplace with superior product and lifestyle visions aggressively marketed. Creative design of planning institutions must also incorporate market mechanisms. For sure, it is a different way of thinking for the profession. Planners currently see themselves in the role as a sort of social and environmental protectorate, the land-use conscience of a society, attempting to manage for externalities in a market economy. But what if we played by a different orientation, an orientation readily accepted in society as manufacturers and marketers of a certain line of products and services?

3) Technical Performance

Technical performance is the third test for planning programs. Scores of potential growth management goals exist from issues of community character, urban form, and housing choice, to public service delivery and environmental management. A given tool needs to be effective and the explanation for its application accepted as legitimate. Too often, planning interventions do not accomplish their intended purposes, or they are imposed, at best, under questionable logic.

Serious technical performance issues exist in a broad variety of planning tools. Most of these tools have their place when matched to a specific set of circumstances supported by careful design. However, the widespread indiscriminate application of traditional planning mechanisms with little beneficial effect needs to be challenged. Barry Cullingworth, the recently deceased preeminent British planner, noted in his comparative analysis of American, British, and Canadian planning models that after years of residence in America he "could see little that was common between the standard descriptions of American planning and what was happening" (Cullingworth, 1993).

Consider, for instance, the standard planning approach taken to conserve rural resource lands and open space character. Large-lot zoning formats and exclusive-use districts are often producing the inverse of desired results (Arendt, 1994, 1999). Another example of technical mischief are street standards that are often generating sterile community environments, restricting design innovation, and resulting in unnecessary environmental consequences (Duany et al., 2000; Jacobs, 1961; Kendig et al., 1980).

It is becoming more apparent that flaws in technical performance are resulting in certain policy failures beyond issues of social validity and market sensitivity. Recent interview research by Helen Jarvis in Portland, Seattle, and San Francisco illustrates the limits of purely design-based thinking, planning strategies based on the concept of compact, self-contained neighborhoods as a structural solution to reduce automobile dependence and other common planning objectives (Jarvis, 2003). Jarvis interviewed 60 randomly selected dual worker married couples with children in the three cities. Half resided in the suburbs, and the other half lived in mixed-use, pedestrian-friendly, urban village configurations near the central core.

Her conclusions challenge conventional thinking. The complexity of accommodating a two-career family with children ultimately overrides localized living for urban villagers. Even when people have a stated preference for and select compact, self-contained neighborhoods, their travel behavior is significantly influenced by both the demands and desires of modern life. When jobs change or children attend off-site private schools and activities, both common occurrences, house location stays the same, but travel patterns adjust. The pedestrian features of the urban village are used primarily, often exclusively, as a weekend amenity. These effects, along with market resistance, are the dynamics that are undermining the effectiveness of the urban village design strategies like those of Portland, Oregon. Jarvis concludes that design can undoubtedly affect human behavior, but planning strategies based primarily on community configuration ignore numerous social and behavioral considerations that may be more effectively approached in other ways.

4) Ethical Appropriateness

The fourth test for any planning program is ethical appropriateness. Economic success has its privileges and should be recognized in planning practice, but ethical limits exist. Arguably, planners should not engage in the design or management support of highly exclusionary growth management regimes, an increasingly common practice in a number of local jurisdictions. Such regulatory regimes can exist in the traditional areas of race or economic class, but also in urban and suburban policy actions taken against rural interests. Imposing development requirements with the unstated agenda of simply making development more expensive so as to retard residential growth is difficult to justify with a straight face and clear conscience.

State-imposed growth management policies that extract open space values from rural landowners in the name of protecting agricultural or forestry resources are also ethically questionable forms of urban elitism. Rural open space and recreation values are, in fact, a far more salient issue in most settings than the protection of commodity production values. But we need to be clear about the true values under consideration and the issue of who pays and who benefits. Planning tools should and can constitute equitable approaches for such societal objectives without imposing an unfair burden on the politically weak. In an ethical sense, the test of a technique is its equitability and social justifiability, not whether it's a "taking." The American Planning Association and many planners celebrated the 2005 Kelo v. City of New London U.S. Supreme Court case conclusion on condemnation practice.(Kelo v. City of New London 545 U.S. 469). The cultural response to that decision has been overwhelmingly negative with federal and state condemnation statutes being legislatively amended across the nation. The issue is the perception of fairness, not legal authority.

At a deeper level, the planning profession faces a more fundamental ethical conflict. How does it rectify a commitment to the public's right to self-determination in a participatory democracy with a rigorous top-down planning regime? Unless the community at-large truly supports both the goals and the regulatory approach, an ethical dilemma exists. Planning regimes need to be designed to avoid this and other ethical conflicts.

5) Implementation Resources

The final test of any planning program format is the adequacy of implementation resources. Often, advocated growth management tools are impractical for large segments of the local planner community. The majority of the American land base falls under the planning purview of small town and rural county planning offices. Growth management tools for these jurisdictions must be designed for their particular circumstances, including formats that are embraced by lay planning boards, widely accepted within the rural culture, and capable of implementation within the technical and monetary restraints of the planning office.

Across America these front-line planning offices are generally understaffed and underfunded, commonly filled by individuals from other disciplines called upon to serve multiple duties. They tend to be highly vulnerable and controversial positions in the community. We perform no favors for the capable individuals who fill these positions when we offer them transfer of development rights programs and complex form-based development codes as the solutions to their dilemma. Effective planning schemes for the majority of the American land base need to be as simple and cost-efficient as possible, with strategies that lend themselves to self-implementation. Culturally sensitive approaches that rely on behavioral tendencies and market preferences are potential formulations.

Planning Performance in America

Five design criteria have now been suggested to judge the performance and appropriateness of a given planning intervention. The remainder of this chapter and the next will consider American land planning outcomes against these stated design criteria as a context for the CBIP model that is introduced in Chapter Three.

The effectiveness of growth management programs and even basic planning tools have been criticized for some time (Altshuler, 1965; Jacobs, 1961). John Friedmann, one of America's preeminent planning theorists, may have expressed the feelings of many planners when he wrote, "Speaking as an American, I would say that official planning in my own country is largely a farce" (Friedmann, 1997). As the empirical evidence mounts, the suspicions of a growing number of field professionals are being increasingly validated – outcomes do not reflect planning objectives.

The single most surprising result of a thorough literature review in planning performance is that little empirical research has been conducted, until quite recently, to measure program effectiveness against stated program goals (Anthony, 2004; Carruthers, 2002; Kelly, 2004; Nelson & Dawkins, 2005). And these limited results, in general, are certainly depressing. Only in the areas of housing cost impacts, jurisdictional fragmentation, and market shifts have there been substantial research. While individual issue studies exist and personal speculation and observation abound in the literature, rigorous analysis of broader system performance has only recently been attempted. Eric Kelly, who arguably provides the most comprehensive analysis of growth management practice in America, noted this in his 2004 edition of *Managing Community Growth*:

> "What has been surprisingly missing from later literature is any sort of comprehensive policy examination of growth management programs in general and how those programs affect the communities that adopt them. That deficiency was noted repeatedly in papers offered at a conference on research needs in the field." (Kelly, 2004)

Nelson and Dawkins also note the lack of comprehensive program analysis. Recent review of 131 growth management programs around the nation uncovered that, "only three included a detailed examination of the land value impact of the urban containment boundary, and only 12 included a detailed analysis of housing price effects"(Nelson & Dawkins, 2005).

It may be that rigorous quantitative analysis will never be capable of providing the system-wide assessments that we seek beyond specific questions such as housing mix, cost, or density impacts. Highly complex systems that can vary widely across jurisdictions and time, elements such as the quality of urban form and lifestyle satisfaction that are difficult to quantify, and limited data sets all handicap quantitative research in planning program effectiveness. These studies do contribute, however, to a broader mosaic of understanding. In particular, three areas of quantitative analysis helpfully illuminate the larger picture: spatial analysis studies on rates of sprawl, housing related hedonic regression analysis that was cited earlier, and survey research.

Qualitative evaluations can also contribute to an assessment of planning performance. In some capacities they may be superior to their quantitative counterparts because they can often capture important nuisances that do not lend themselves to rigorous measurement. Qualitative feedback can also be much quicker. An observant field planner will sense the response of the development community and political review process long before it appears in analytic data. Equally, the development community often possesses a hypersensitivity to consumer preferences and market response that defies formalized market research and delayed data analysis. Sometimes those gut judgments are wrong, but more often, they will be an accurate predictor.

Donald Schon identifies this consideration in his argument that practitioners possess "knowledge-in-practice," but that knowledge is difficult to capture, as the competent practitioners usually know more than they can articulate. He later identifies a crisis of confidence in professional planning knowledge, a crisis which he attributes in part to the way in which universities view knowledge, suggesting a marriage of the reflective researcher with the reflective practitioner (Schon, 1983). John Forester's communicative planning theory also finds its roots in trying to extract the essence of the practitioner's world (Forester, 1989). Case studies, planner observations, and visual assessment likely offer a clearer picture of what may or may not work in many circumstances.

The Quantitative Evidence

The rate of sprawl is one broad measure of land planning effectiveness. Between 1982 and 1997 the amount of urbanized land in the U.S. increased 47 percent, but the nation's population grew only 17 percent (Fulton, Pendall, Nguyen, & Harrison, 2001). Metropolitan density declined 15.7 percent during this time period with the rate of decentralization accelerating. This same study found that only 6 percent of the nation's 281 metropolitan areas became denser during the study period, largely metropolitan areas with high rates of foreign-born residents repopulating urban cores or areas hemmed in by natural features, such as mountain ranges or coastlines and federal lands, such as the national forests. Interestingly, regression analysis shows that states that had required growth management programs suffered a greater loss of density during the 15-year period. Metropolitan areas in California, Nevada and Arizona, all non-growth management states, dominated the list of those that gained density during the period.

In a similar study, Jerry Anthony utilized National Resources Inventory data from the USDA to analyze sprawl rates in 49 states at three time points: 1982, 1992 and 1997 (Anthony, 2004). His findings, while slightly different from the Fulton study, revealed and confirmed similar results. In the 11 growth management states, urban land increased by an average of 49 percent, while urban densities decreased by 9.5 percent. In states without growth management programs, urban land increased by 37 percent, and densities decreased by an average of 16 percent. Neither the presence nor duration of growth management programs had a statistically significant effect in reducing urban sprawl. Georgia, Florida, Washington, and Oregon, all growth management states, increased urban land by 30 to 75 percent, and with the exception of Washington, all experienced declines in urban density. In contrast, Nevada, Arizona, Utah, Colorado, Idaho, Kansas and Nebraska all had modest increases in urban density while increasing the urban land base.

Pendall, in an earlier study, found that only three states, California, Maryland and Arizona, maintained or increased their historic population density during the '80s and '90s (Pendall, 1999). All other states had a density decline in their metropolitan areas as growth occurred. He found that the population density of the average acre of land converted to urban use during the 10-year period was only 40 percent of the existing urban average in 1982. If the 1982 average density had been maintained during the ensuing decade, a 25 percent reduction in rural land conversion nationwide would have been realized.

In a similar vein, John Carruthers studied 283 metropolitan counties in 15 states from 1982 through 1997 (Carruthers, 2002). The comparative analysis looked at the performance of various state growth management programs. The study concluded that California's planning mandate had led to lower overall urban densities and higher property values with no effect on the total spatial extent of land urbanized. Florida's program had suffered a significant increase in the spatial extent of urbanized land, as had Georgia's, which has also resulted in a decrease in urban density and an increase in property values adjusted for other factors. Washington's program had no significant statistical effect in any parameter studied. Only Oregon's program has led to greater densities, but it has not successfully reduced the spatial extent of urbanized land over the study period.

Lopez and Hynes developed a national sprawl index that measures rates of decentralization in 330 metropolitan areas between 1990 and 2000. They found a 2-1 ratio of urban areas increasing in rates of sprawl over the decade (Lopez & Haynes, 2003). Their study also identified that 88.6 percent of U.S. metropolitan land area qualified as low-density tracts under their definition. John Landis, in an assessment of the effectiveness of growth controls, analyzed seven mid-sized California cities during the 1980s. His conclusion was that the programs were largely irrelevant, suggesting that in the long run, "careless growth control may be much worse than no growth control" (Landis, 1992). Similar conclusions are surfacing from growth management research aimed at the rural and farm sectors. In other words, ineffectual large-lot planning formats, the traditional approach to rural growth management, have fueled the spatial extension of residential development further into the landscape (Diaz & Green, 2001; Esrza & Carruthers, 2000; Richardson, 2000).

The significance of these studies is that they reflect a time period nationwide during which growth management efforts and basic planning controls became far more widespread and rigorous. If current planning formats were working reasonably well in the American culture, the conclusions from these studies should reflect it. They do not. They suggest the opposite, at least in the context of controlling sprawl and increasing densities. One potential explanation is that widely advocated growth management practices don't function technically. Examples of highly rigorous regulatory formats performing well in the context of development, both from America and overseas, render this an unlikely explanation if you dismiss cost impacts in the housing market. A second explanation is that political and social acceptance of programs rigorous enough to work is not widespread in the American culture. Existing research and observations from the field suggest that this later explanation is more likely, requiring alternative design of effective growth management tools that are politically acceptable and socially valid.

Another area of quantitative analysis that provides insight into the current state of planning performance is survey research. Public perception of planners, the planning process, and attitudes toward growth are all instructive, as are surveys related to housing preferences and neighborhood selection when considering likely market response. Surveys also help document the public inconsistencies between values and behaviors that planners routinely observe.

A nationwide survey that the Center for Economic and Civic Opinion at the University of Massachusetts conducted in 2006 indicates that Americans are fundamentally unhappy with today's planning results, but they are conflicted between a strong commitment to private property rights on the one hand and a desire for planning controls. Some 83 percent of suburban Americans do not want new development in their communities. Over 60 percent believe that their local government does only a fair-to-poor job regarding planning and zoning issues, while 70 percent believe that the relationships between elected officials and developers render the approval process unfair. This later result is, among other things, a strong indication that most Americans understand little of either the planning process or legal restraints under land-use law. It also reflects American's suspicion of government, a cultural trait that will be explored in Chapter Four.

It would be a mistake to interpret these results as a growing commitment by the general public to support sustainable planning strategies. Instead, they appear to support rigorous land-use control of their neighbors driven by self-interest, not a broader understanding and commitment to communitarian objectives that includes a wholehearted endorsement of restrictions on their own personal behavior for the greater public benefit. Combined with other cultural findings, an emerging picture represents a key dilemma for planners. American society continues to fiercely protect private property rights while at the same time pushing more strongly for personal entitlement in the name of the public interest. The sense of community obligation deteriorates as the learned and reinforced behavior of reciprocation continues to decline in the culture. At this junction, one must remember that one of the key tests for effective planning programs is social validity, which requires willing and direct participation in the planning intervention. If public support for a given planning regime is based on restricting others so that some may have exclusive enjoyment of a given land-use experience, the strategy is inherently conflicted. As Jonathan Levin notes in his analysis of exclusionary zoning, it restricts the ability of urban areas to transform themselves over time and perpetuates the forces of sprawl in both urban and rural settings (Levine, 2006).

Surveys on housing preferences further illustrate this conundrum. Survey research in both America and Europe shows a preference for low-density, single-family detached housing, particularly in small town and rural settings within striking distance of larger metropolitan resources, but it also shows a desire to protect rural landscapes. By way of example, one survey conducted in Great Britain associated with the House Beautiful New Homes Awards program determined that 63 percent of respondents felt that new homes should go in redeveloped urban areas. However, only 11 percent of the 500 respondents said they would choose such a town center location (NOP, 1997).

The results from location preference studies have been relatively consistent on both sides of the Atlantic. A Florida-based study considering the market acceptance rate of New Urbanist designs found a distinct preference for less centralized and less dense locations when adjusting for family status, income, age, and education (Audirac & Smith, 1992). Single-family home occupants are less likely to want to move than apartment occupants are, and attached unit occupants show a decided preference to move into single-family detached housing in decentralized locations.

Similar results have been found in two recent British studies, but transferability of results must be tempered due to different cultural experiences with terms such as single-family residence. The English are accustomed to far higher suburban densities than the average American and have less aversion to attached housing. Having said that, residential preferences trend toward suburban locations, larger lots, and larger homes. Higher density central locations and their associated public amenities do appeal to a significant minority of the marketplace in these English studies, averaging 20 to 25 percent of the population (Heath, 2001; Senior, Webster, & Blank, 2004). Such locations and project configurations appeal most to the young, childless, and single.

American survey research in New Urbanist designs also offers some hope that while the marketplace currently shows a decided preference for low density, single-family formats, a significant market segment desires more land-use friendly designs. Moreover, once exposed to the well-conceived alternatives, the market can be moved. Research indicates that residents have a stronger sense of community in urban village formats than traditional subdivision designs based on 17 specific physical characteristics. Likewise homes in neo-traditional projects appreciate 20 percent faster than comparable neighborhoods of traditional design (Carlton, 2006; Kim & Kaplan, 2004). Many factors indicate that market demand for higher density formats is, in fact, greater than generally believed and that supply has been artificially constrained (Levine, 2006).

From a planning strategy perspective it must be remembered that housing preferences are not necessarily fixed. Preferences can change over a person's lifecycle. They can also be marginally modified by personal experience, project exposure and marketing. Achieving the desired results, however, will require a fundamental change in both strategy and tactic. Consider that exurban areas are the fastest growing development format in America, and the fundamental reason people choose such a living experience, as determined by survey research, is that they desire to live in a rural environment. Other structural factors, such as cost, employment, or safety, have little effect (Crump, 2003b).

The Qualitative Evidence

If one dares to rely on simple observation to suggest that current planning formats are failing, then it is hard to escape reaching certain conclusions from the evidence of the last 50 years. One thing above all else has struck me, and a number of my aging colleagues, about our multistate experiences as planners. Taking into account differences in regional architecture, growth pressures, and native landscapes, we can't see any significant difference in the land development patterns from state to state, regardless of the planning system in place. Only in Oregon does a discernable visible difference exist on a large regional basis, and that difference is subtle and not always beneficial.

In my lifetime, almost every regionally important American landscape and metropolitan area that I know with some intimacy has undergone and continues to undergo a destructive transformation. Effective planning could have mitigated many of these impacts while still accommodating growth. This failure is not for lack of effort. A small army of dedicated planners, wave after wave, has been undertaking the task in nearly all of these regions. But our strategies and tools, it would appear, have been poorly suited to the culture and market forces.

The Washington, D.C. metropolitan area and northern Virginia, including such areas as Fairfax County with one million in population, have become a transportation and land-use nightmare, almost unrecognizable in less than a lifetime. Areas that were vacation destinations for Washingtonians during the 1950s are now commuter communities for the metropolitan area. Virtually no rural visual separation exists from Richmond, Virginia, to Portland, Maine, as suburban expansion feathers to exurban development and back to urban concentration.

The Chesapeake Bay and rich farmlands of the Delmarva Peninsula have been hammered with the Eastern Shore hanging in the balance. Further south, the Carolinas have badly sprawled, both in urban and rural contexts. Their magnificent coastal shoreline is a mere shell of its former wild self. The baby boom retirement wave, when it hits, will likely finish off all but the preserved national seashores and wildlife refuges of this coastal resource. All of Florida and the sprawl juggernaut of Atlanta, Georgia, are painful visual reminders of ineffectual growth management practices.

The Puget Sound basin has oozed from the Canadian border to Portland, Oregon, constrained only by the national forests and corporate timberlands of the Cascades. Even the mighty Cascade crest has not stopped the sprawl that has long since slipped over the passes into eastern Washington. Seattle is in transportation gridlock, a mere memory of its compact and demure past urban glories. Today, the area approaches transportation lockdown nearly 24 hours a day from Olympia to Everett, an all-too-common experience in metropolitan areas across America.

The Texas Transportation Institute's 2005 Urban Mobility Report analyzed 85 metropolitan areas across the nation concluding that between 1982 and 2003 every area studied, regardless of population size and transportation investment, experienced more severe congestion lasting a longer period of time. The same report found that only four metropolitan areas (Anchorage, Pittsburgh, New Orleans, and Tulsa) had succeeded in growing highway capacity at a faster rate than travel growth over the 21-year time period.

California's growth experience of the last half-century can only be described as heartbreaking. Even the wild and open landscapes of the inner mountain west are being vigorously transformed by exurban and recreational home development. The rural expanses of Montana, Utah, Idaho, Colorado, New Mexico, and Arizona have all undergone fundamental and uncomplimentary conversions in the last two decades. The Colorado front-range has seen low-density suburban sprawl extend from Denver to Fort Collins, and only the Douglas County land conservation effort has prevented a complete merging to the south with Colorado Springs. Across the nation only the better designed large-scale planned communities constitute an improvement in growth accommodation.

When planning is making a contribution, whether public or private sector, it contributes to the generation of compact villages and thriving urban areas that are stimulating, diverse, and support the human spirit. Open space resources compliment the daily living experience, and the built environment is pedestrian friendly and developed at a human scale. The housing experience is affordable, attractive, and integrated across incomes. The delivery of public services is efficient, and a strong sense of community prevails. When planning is underperforming, bordering on the irrelevant, it would appear that you get America.

Land planning in America, both town and county, is arguably the only significant category of environmental management in which major advancements in a system-wide context have not been achieved in the past 35 years. Since 1970, the nation's population has grown 45 percent, yet significant empirical improvements have been achieved in air quality, water quality, hazardous waste management, and applied natural resource management in most, but not all subcategories of concern (EPA, 2000a, 2000b, 2000c; Lomborg, 2001). In contrast, land planning measures of performance in America, both in a quantitative and qualitative context, have suffered major declines as the population has expanded at increasingly lower densities (Carruthers, 2002; Duany et al., 2000; Fulton et al., 2001; Orfield, 2002; Urban Land Institute, 1999). America in the next 45 years can anticipate the addition of 125 million people, the fastest growth rate among major industrialized nations. The challenges that the planning profession faces are nothing short of Herculean. Meeting that challenge will require new planning institutions and implementation models that address issues of social validly, market sensitivity, technical performance, and ethical application.

Chapter Two

The Politics of Growth Management - The Limiting Factor

One of the utilitarian management principles of the natural sciences is the concept of the limiting factor. Every living organism, fauna or flora, has a set of requirements necessary to survive, thrive, and reproduce. Under the limiting factor concept, whatever single component is in shortest supply among that list of requirements will set the limits of survival and success. The limiting factor for the current command-and-control planning paradigm in America is the broad-based social validity necessary for sustained political support. While field professionals know how to design programs that work technically, what is missing from the toolbox of American planners are effective program formats that are culturally endorsed and politically acceptable across a broad spectrum of public interests. Applied political and social acceptance research in growth management is a neglected area, yet it is the central strategic issue.

For the current paradigm of command-and-control growth management to succeed, it must: 1) be practiced on a regional basis across political boundaries; 2) be comprehensive in character, integrating policy and action across all three levels of government; and 3) be accommodating, or at least tolerated, by a variety of publics. Additionally, it must impose strict regulations on a continuous basis, with ironclad implementation and responsible oversight. The inherent political limitations of this current growth-management model in America – that is, the model that actually works, not the cosmetic version – are extensive. This chapter will explore these limiting factors to provide a better understanding and rationale for the CBIP model.

Political Sustainability

The concept of sustainability in planning is more than creating and maintaining a natural ecosystem, human environment, and supporting economy in balance. It is also inherently tied to social validity and sustained political consensus. One has difficulty conceiving how to achieve sustainability without accommodating these two critical elements in a freewheeling, market-based democracy like the United States. The test of political sustainability for different regional growth-management strategies begins on the battleground of state legislatures. Their significance for planning is that they are the headwaters of any coherent growth-management program. Local governments derive their powers, the necessary regional coordination authority, and often the funding for planning, from the state capital.

States also constitute the most logical geo-political entity among the three levels of government for enacting public planning policy. The national scale in America is too physically overwhelming and politically diverse. One should not be confused by the successful national-scale planning efforts of Europe and Britain, where culture tends to be more homogeneous internally and national policy programs operate at a management scale the size of a typical U.S. western state. Great Britain is approximately the size of California, while Germany is the size of Oregon, and Ireland is approximately the size of West Virginia.

Collaborative governance, the backbone of political sustainability, is the gold standard that we seek. But it is not enough to achieve consensus - consensus must be for a program that is actually effective. Achieving that combination in growth management has proven to be devilishly elusive. Until an alternative political formula better suited to the American culture is generated, field results based on current models will continue to prove disappointing.

During my planning career I somehow allowed myself to be pressed into service in legislative affairs, specialized in land-use and natural resource issues. For twenty legislative sessions, I represented a broad array of Fortune 500 companies, associations, conservation organizations, and local government interests in a number of state legislatures and at the national level. The lessons learned regarding the true nature of state legislative affairs and the dynamics of political sustainability fundamentally shaped my views on the strategic and tactical route to improved planning performance. One of those conclusions is that the interest groups with the greatest potential to mold land-use practices in the legislative arena are simultaneously miles apart and much closer together than many would assume. What prevents true collaboration is largely ideological focus that reinforces group identity. Collaborative solutions exist, we just can't get past our respective biases to entertain them.

Assumed identities in the legislature by both lobbyists and interest groups, quickly become internalized, fueled by group dynamics and social pressure. Egos and emotions quickly trump rationality as self-identity dictates behavioral response. Groups would rather take a hit to their self-interest than engage in collaborative solutions that require a change in problem definition and self-perception. The problem is that nearly all interests feel that they have compromised their principles if they engage in the kind of creative rethinking that true collaboration requires. Pragmatic results count less than personal ideology. Righteousness trumps reason.

In state legislatures, grassroots clients are much closer to their issue managers than at the national level. As a result, in state legislatures the top-tier issue managers of the lobbyist community associated with planning issues are, by and large, true believers, not glorified sales staff. They are trusted with the full power, and often leadership, of the interests they represent. Many are unpaid volunteers or receive nominal compensation. They often are the embodiment of the interest, unilaterally influencing and implementing policy with a quiet power unseen even by their own association memberships or company clients. It is common for them to spend more effort influencing policy within their own ranks, in short, lobbying their own constituency, than they expend in the legislatures. The more powerful of these individuals engage in far more than legislative affairs. They also focus on the rule-making process at the agency level, employ court strategies and coordinate media and public relations campaigns.

In state-level land-use policy, this dynamic directly undermines collaborative potential, which is critical to success since many interests are capable of subverting implementation over time. Weak lobbyists, those who do not have the stature of leadership within their own client groups, dare not stray into unconventional collaborative discussions that may threaten group beliefs. Strong lobbyists tend to be icons of the interests they represent, reflecting closely the beliefs and prejudices of their client group. It is rare to find a legislative affairs professional that is both powerful enough and progressive enough to lead their interests into the uncharted territory necessary for collaborative solutions in growth management. Beyond these considerations, there are two other political realties in state-level legislative affairs that impact growth-management potentials.

The first is the power of concentrated interests in state legislatures. Groups of people who are strongly motivated by immediate or common business interests for instance, landowners concerned with future development potential or builders concerned with business prospects, will have an organizational advantage over those with more diverse or vague future interests. That motivational power overcomes free-rider problems in political activism, whether in campaign contributions or interest group mobilization (G. J. Stigler, 1971). The better organized interests in a state legislature tend to be commonly aligned business interests ranging from cattleman's associations to chiropractors, not because of money, but because of behavioral motivation driven by a concentrated incentive. As William Fischel suggests, this phenomena of the power of concentrated interests applies best to political jurisdictions that are physically large with substantial populations, like the representative arena of state legislatures more than local governments (Fischel, 2005). In the growth management debate, who has more personal motivation, members of the general public with a diffuse interest in planning and environmental policy, or the small business person who may have his or her entire livelihood and personal worth at stake?

The second reality to be factored into the search for political sustainability is that opportunities always exist to overturn, amend, or otherwise subvert contentious elements of growth management statutes. Competent issue managers with a reasonable – not exorbitant – amount of resources, have a nearly endless number of ways to modify or circumvent growth management provisions. You just need to be persistent, which is one of the hallmarks of concentrated interests. Such circumvention is not limited to interest groups with clever issue managers, it is also widely present in the behaviors of the general public when social validity is lacking in imposed public policy. One of the truisms of political gamesmanship is that when powerful interests collide and one side succeeds in a power play due to a momentary political advantage, the conflict is not resolved. It has simply been postponed – and likely intensified – to the next available political opportunity.

Not to pick on Oregon, but it provides a typical example of this dynamic. On numerous occasions the Oregon growth-management statute has come under serious legislative attack. In a 1982 statewide referendum that would have largely eliminated the program, a narrow come-from-behind victory retained the statute. In 1995 a stringent property rights bill was passed by the legislature and was vetoed by the governor. Since the 1995 legislative effort, the statute has twice been effaced by statewide referendums, requiring compensation for reductions in property value caused by land-use regulation. The first referendum was overturned by the courts. The second amended referendum, Measure 37, passed in a statewide election in 2004 and was upheld by the Oregon Supreme Court in 2006.

Some have argued that Oregon's electors didn't know what they were voting for. A more likely explanation is that the general public didn't fully comprehend the implications of the initial Act, but came to understand them. Based on that evolving history, they supported both of the recent referendums. Given the years of public debate and media coverage that the issue received, the election results likely did not reflect misunderstanding. What they did reflect was public disagreement over some aspects of program goal implementation, and a latent political pressure that would resurface periodically, to correct a program that lacked sustainability with concentrated special interests.

Chain of Requirements

For state-level growth-management efforts to be successful, a chain of requirements must be met. If any link in the chain fails or underperforms, the entire system suffers. The higher the political dissonance, cultural conflict, or implementation complexity in any of the required links, the more suspect the underlying approach. This chain of performance includes five major links.

- The first link is the legislative bill draft. Is it technically sound and statutorily integrated with other programs in the state?
- The second is bill passage and gubernatorial support. Can the bill survive the rigors of the legislative obstacle course and still maintain its structural integrity without damaging modifications, and has it been appropriately funded?
- The third link is state agency competency, resources, and commitment to implementation after passage.
- Link four is local government. Will local governments, both staff and elected officials, enthusiastically commit to the program, and do they have the resources necessary?
- The final link is market response and public support. Is the program socially valid? Will the market respond as anticipated, and are there any unintended consequences? Does the general public support both politically and in personal action, the components of the program?

The following subsections will consider the dynamics of each of these five links in growth management and the probability of success in each link. These speculative individual probabilities are then combined under the mathematical rules of sequential probability analysis to convey the odds that each link in the chain of requirements will perform as a collective whole to achieve program objectives.

Program Formulation and Bill Drafting

Lobbyists tell an old joke to clients who are outraged by the law-making process: there are two things in life that you don't want to know how they are made, sausage and laws. It's true. One would think that given the potential impact, landmark legislation would be the product of years of research, integrated by a team of highly competent legislative specialists, toiling over an extended time period to get it just right.

Nothing could be further from the truth when you cut away the façade of deliberative process. Instead, imagine the following two scenarios that are the most common formats for bill preparation.

A handful of legislative affairs specialists representing clients with aligned interests are thrown together to develop a major new regulatory reform initiative in land-use. These individuals are expected to handle a broad array of issues for their employers, whether they represent the Association of Counties or Atlantic Richfield. They likely are involved in half-a-dozen similar efforts on other issues and may only have six months to prepare all the bill prototypes, while also maintaining a full range of other political responsibilities. While they are specialists in legislative affairs and a few may even have some general background in planning, they will not be single-focus experts in growth-management legislation. Some of the people on the working group are inevitably inexperienced, and may only be in their late twenties or early thirties. It is extremely rare that any of them would have true multi-state experience in the topic, meaning that they had firsthand legislative and field experience in state growth-management programs in more than one state, much less a grounded national perspective.

In drafting a bill, issue managers rely on similar statutes in other states, conjecture, rumor, and creativity. Some individuals in the drafting group may have access to national affiliates with land-use specialists, but their value may be limited by time, budget, or the quality of advice being given. The group must also cater to the preferences of the key legislative sponsor or sponsors they are working with in the House and Senate. Sponsors with enough clout to potentially see the bill to passage likely have strong opinions about the bill's content that can jeopardize the theoretical cohesiveness of the approach under design. Legislative staff, both policy and political, are also always at the drafting table at some point to protect their respective interests, and legislators listen to them more than they listen to outside interests, public or private sector.

Also at issue are the existing statutes in the state. Drafting teams rarely have the luxury of working from a clean slate. Existing law always creates constituencies with a vested interest in the old system. The result is that new program design that might make more sense is constrained by the political realities of existing statutes. There is, in addition, a concern about throwing existing land-use case law in the state into turmoil, something that generates uncertainty for all interests. The working group, undoubtedly, incorporates provisions that are already failing in other state programs partially out of ignorance, and partially because the states that they have extracted the provisions from don't recognize or refuse to acknowledge that their programs are flawed. The team also invents untried provisions based on theory, personal belief, or the demands of the bill sponsor. If pragmatic in their outlook, the drafting committee will have to compromise the integrity of the planning scheme in anticipation of political realities. The kind of strident regulatory scheme that is most likely to work in a technical context is now far outside the bounds of political reality in nearly every state.

The second common format for drafting land-use legislation is a state-assigned taskforce or study commission. This process creates its own dynamics. Commissions are normally established because of political impasse and intractable problems in existing statutes. The commission or taskforce will be a political animal, representing current power relationships in the legislature. The terms collaboration and consensus will repeatedly be expressed in statements to the press, but the reality is a competitive negotiation process among constantly shifting sub-coalitions. Commissions will be served by endless technical subcommittees, which include groups attempting to influence bill content at every level of consideration. Those interests that have the political power to truly influence the content and outcome of the bill will dominate, often in subtle ways that secondary taskforce members won't perceive.

The process, even with the most sincere members committed to developing a working compromise, will still be just that, a process of compromise among core interests. Local governments, development interests, environmental groups, and organized landowner constituencies will nearly always dominate the final outcome. Each group will protect its foundation interests and central biases. The final product will likely push each empowered interest group to the near limit of its constituency support but not beyond, based on the power dynamic at that moment in legislative history. The eventual bill will be a conglomerate of delicately worded compromises, some that are intentionally vague, subject to multiple interpretations. It will feel like a bold achievement to the participants after spending two years fighting with each other.

The reality is far more likely to be procedural modifications in the status quo – minor improvements from each actor's perspective and a soothing of troubled waters instead of an effective permanent solution.

What are the odds that either of these two bill drafting processes, the taskforce or internal working group, will result in a technically sound bill? For purposes of the probability analysis that follows, let's assume a 50-percent chance, although the reality is more likely less than one in five.

Bill Passage and Gubernatorial Support

The second link in the kinetic chain of statewide planning performance is bill passage and gubernatorial support. The typical state legislature meets for 60 to 120 days and will entertain 2,000 to 3,500 bill introductions. State legislative processes are rigorous, intentionally designed to prevent passage of the vast majority of introductions. Based on my research, the average passage rate in state legislatures ranges from a high of 45 percent to a far more typical 7 to 9 percent of all bills introduced. The vast majority of bills that pass are relatively minor housekeeping amendments to existing statutes. High profile bills that constitute major change or new policy initiatives are nearly always controversial, and have far lower passage rates than those cited above. Serious growth-management initiatives certainly fit into this category.

The typical bill following an ideal path, which is rare, has between nine and eleven gatekeepers to negotiate in the legislative process. They include committee chairpersons, standing committees, rules committees, two substantive chamber votes in both the Senate and House, and the governor. At each juncture the bill can be blocked or dramatically amended into an ineffectual mush. In addition, each bill faces at least four major cut-off-dates by which a bill must clear a committee or chamber. Cut-off dates alone kill a high percentage of introductions because of intent, lobbyist incompetence, or just plain bad luck. Hundreds of bills are competing for attention as cut-off dates approach, and only one bill may be considered at a time. Budgetary implications in many planning-related bills also kill legislation. Commonly, a bill is passed only to have it underfunded or to receive no implementation funding at all, effectively destroying legislative intent.

Competent lobbyists have scores of opportunities to kill legislation outright, even against what would appear to be surefire coalitions for passage. Amending bills into ineffectiveness is even easier. Growth-management bills, particularly those that rely on a command-and-control strategy, are particularly easy targets that attract the attention of powerful interests.

Dozens of legislative tactics can kill a bill. One can attach a killer amendment so distasteful to bill sponsors that they withdraw their own legislation. One can flood the bill with ever-changing objections and amendments, causing time delays throughout the process. Committee chairpersons can delay scheduling a bill for hearing or executive session until it is too late. Floor leadership can keep moving the bill to the bottom of the agenda so that a bill that makes it out of committee dies in the chamber of origin in the logjam of cut-off dates. Bills can be ruled out of scope and object, referred to unfriendly committees, converted to a study commission, or simply tabled at too many points along the process.

The ability to kill or fundamentally change the intent of a bill through amendment is only limited by the imagination of the lobbyist or hostile legislator. The ability to pass substantive planning legislation, particularly stringent mandates not riddled with subtle and not-so-subtle loopholes, is something entirely different. Growth-management legislation as a class of bills has a number of handicaps. Besides the inevitable controversy that surrounds them, they tend to be long, complicated bills that are inherently difficult to explain and easy to attack. Task-force bills carry the extra burden of containing delicate compromises that can't be breeched if internal coalition support and trust is to be maintained. Legislators hate to be told that the commission package in front of them for deliberation is a no-amendment proposition.

Finally, there are always the necessary political concessions to small-scale development, agriculture, forestry, and the rural sector. These inevitable provisions, which are required for the political survival of the bill, are the predominant, or at least a significant minority, of development activity in many jurisdictions. From 20-acre thresholds and family exemptions, to minor subdivisions and occasional sale provisions, development follows the path of least resistance. Rolf Pendall, in his study of Maine's growth-management history, documented these implications in both Maine and Washington state (Pendall, 2001). They constitute obvious political concessions and major loopholes in every state where I have been a practicing planner or legislative lobbyist over the last 30 years: Virginia, North Carolina, Oregon, Washington, and Montana.

What are the probabilities today of passing a truly stringent, command–and-control, growth-management statute with matching administrative rules, something with at least the fortitude of the Oregon law? In solidly progressive states, it's probably no better than the low single digits. In swing and conservative states, that probability drops to something only slightly higher than zero. What is the probability if such legislation were in place that it would not be amended by either referendum or future legislative amendment? Absolutely zero.

State and Local Government

The next links in the chain of growth-management performance are state and local governments. While both can have an impact, the competency, resources, and – of particular importance – commitment of local jurisdictions, are the critical factors in effecting government performance. Research has shown that specific mandatory planning requirements at the state level do improve the quality of local plans if enforced by state certification, sanctions, or financial assistance. But does plan quality equate into local government commitment and compliance?

The political viability of any state growth-management approach faces two tests, one at the state legislative level and the second in local politics. The local dimension has two facets. The first is local government resistance to conceding land-use policy and enforcement prerogatives back to the state. Stringent growth-management programs that shift local discretion to state agencies and regional boards is routinely resisted by local governments. The League of Oregon Cities opposed adoption of the Oregon growth-management program, and the Association of Oregon Counties supported repeal of the law in 1982 (DeGrove, 1984). In Washington state, the Association of Counties and Association of Washington Cities have routinely been sensitive to issues of local land-use prerogative, acting to curtail hearing-board powers and restricting state oversight in the initial growth-management act. Local government defense of land-use discretion is routine behavior in statehouses across the nation. When that discretion has been curtailed in statute, it has not been enthusiastically endorsed at the local level.

In one study, Dalton and Burby analyzed hazard area plans in 176 communities in the states of Florida, North Carolina, Texas, California, and Washington to measure quality and compliance against the state mandate (Dalton & Burby, 1994). The study found that local government commitment and implementation did not vary with the strength of the planning mandate and was highly variable between jurisdictions. Local factors tied to the political climate of public support within the jurisdiction were more influential.

In a second study on local commitment to state-mandated planning in coastal North Carolina, it was concluded that local governments were complying minimally with protection rules (Norton, 2005). Fierce resistance to state involvement on local land-use policy was cited as the critical factor. Other studies have concluded similarly. State mandates can improve the quality of plans if the statutory mandate is specific enough, but local commitment to plan implementation is highly variable (Burby & May, 1997; Deyle & Smith, 1998).

The second facet at the local level is the latitude of planners and elected officials within the political culture of their local setting. The test of local government political viability in state growth management is implementation and enforcement on the ground. Without research analysis that truly measures on-ground effects, people have a tendency to accept program passage and implementation as proof of effectiveness, ignoring the not-so-obvious loopholes and breaches in administration. The Florida and Hawaii growth-management programs are two examples out of many. The Hawaii program is generally considered to be one of the top two state programs in the nation (Callies, 1992; Kelly, 2004). Part of that assessment comes from the analysis of land-use data for lands classified as agricultural by the state. It shows 95 percent of the original designations are still in place. Since 1976, Hawaiian law has permitted only farm dwellings on agricultural designations. However, it has been accepted practice to issue approvals for resort developments on agricultural designations based on the premise that providing, "a splash of green, such as decorative avocado trees or an ornamental coffee plantation," meets the spirit of the Act's provisions (WSJ, 2005). There was a

$1 billion, 1,550-acre development on the Big Island underway in 2005 with state permits precisely under that rationale, one of many in the pipeline or previously developed. Countless administrative and private sector practices fly below data detection in the majority of growth-management programs, undermining assumed program effectiveness and reducing political pressure for overt weakening of statutory provisions.

What are the probabilities in the chain of performance that stringent state mandates will be fully enforced at both the state agency and local government level? A guess is that in swing and conservative states we might expect enforcement in the spirit of the law 70 percent of the time or less. Over time, these breaches in implementation lead to cumulative program failure.

Community and Market Response

The final links in the growth-management performance chain are community and market response. Both have connections to the tests of social validity and political acceptance. A fundamental weakness of command-and-control planning statutes in the American culture is the inherent clash that they provoke in a society accustomed to the unrestricted exercise of personal freedom. While organized business and government interests dominate statutory debate in the legislature, community sentiment impacts growth-management implementation much further down the chain. At the local level, abrogation of socially invalid growth-management approaches can take a number of creative forms, some that manifest themselves in market response, as has been previously discussed, and others that are expressed in community political response.

A classic example of how entire neighborhoods can be mobilized in creative resistance is the community response in King County, Washington, to the 1990 State Growth Management Act. William Fischel has documented in research that between 1990 and 1999, ten new cities were incorporated in King County (Fischel, 2001). The legislation stimulated unincorporated suburbs within the designated growth boundary of the Seattle metropolitan area to organize and incorporate. The primary motivation was to maintain community control over lower density zoning so that growth-management strategies that required upzoning within the growth boundary would be blocked. It had long been privately predicted by taskforce members on the 1994 State Regulatory Reform Commission that Seattle's neighborhoods would strongly resist, and ultimately succeed in, preventing the required upzoning to implement the strategy. What was not anticipated was the creativeness of the communities. In previous years, virtually all of these areas had resisted or shown no interest in either incorporation or annexation.

A second display of how communities can resist is the recent typology of growth-management urban-containment programs developed by Nelson and Dawkins (2005). In their study they analyzed 131 urban containment programs, classifying them into one of four categories based on the strength of the urban boundary and willingness to accommodate growth within the boundary. The four models were weak-restrictive (force growth out to the periphery), strong-restrictive (force growth further out into the region or across jurisdictional lines), weak-accommodating (does nothing or provides mild incentive), and strong-accommodating (Portland model of incentivizing). Sixty-two percent of the programs were in categories that suggest little beneficial effect, thus indicating program political dilution, or in categories that suggest elite community exclusionary practices. The remaining programs were heavily concentrated in states with existing strong growth-management mandates unlikely to be politically acceptable in most states.

This section started with the statement that for any state growth-management program to be truly effective, a chain of requirements has to be meet. Each requirement in that chain has a probability of success, but it is the accumulated probability in a complex system that matters. While completely speculative, a probability analysis that all these requirements can be sequentially met to a reasonable standard makes an important point. Political limitations of the current command-and-control growth-management model nearly always ensure ineffectiveness in the American culture.

Assuming for analysis purposes that each component is an independent event, here is one highly conservative probability summary, but again, it is purely based on personal legislative experiences and a handful of suggestive research studies. The optimistic odds that the bill draft is structurally sound and effective if appropriately implemented is no better than 75 percent. The ridiculously optimistic chance that the bill draft will pass in a swing state without substantial weakening amendments is less than 10 percent. The odds that a strong program will not be amended or rescinded over time to render it largely ineffectual, is less than 30 percent. What are the chances that state government will have the resources and commitment to fulfill their obligations under the Act? It's possibly 80 percent. The probability that local governments will have the resources and political will to fulfill their obligations on a sustained basis, regardless of political power swings within their jurisdiction, is judged less than 40 percent. And finally, what is the probability that the market response can be controlled to align with program objectives and that communities will not subvert the statute's intent? In an act of euphoric optimism, let's assume 40 percent. Taking these sequential requirements into account, the combined probability of success that a stringent command-and-control statewide growth-management program can be developed, adopted, implemented, and maintained is only three-tenths of 1 percent.

Interestingly, due to the large number of events that have to occur for a growth-management regime to work, adjusting the individual probabilities to a more optimistic outlook that is debatably within the range of reason does not render an appreciably better chance of success. Without a planning implementation model that is designed to achieve a higher standard of social and political validity, the odds of success do not improve materially.

Current Political Prospects

When one reviews the history of state growth-management programs and substantive environmental statutes, a pattern emerges. The rigorous programs were established early in the environmental movement in the 1970s, prior to the development of sophisticated opposition and other political dynamics. The Washington State Shorelines Management Program and Environmental Policy Act was established in 1971. Oregon's Land Conservation and Development Act dates to 1973. The California Coastal Zone Act was adopted in 1976, and Hawaii's state plan in 1978. All of the core federal environmental statutes were adopted in the 1960s and 1970s: the Clean Air Act (1963), the Water Quality Act (1965), the Endangered Species Act (1966), NEPA (1969) and RCRA (1976).

Further evidence of this political trend can be found in the total number of comprehensive growth-management programs in America today, weak or strong. There are approximately 6,000 municipalities with a population of over 2,500, as well as a total of 3,100 counties in the nation. Among state governments we only have six to eight comprehensive programs, depending on your definition, two of which are generally deemed to work – Oregon's, which has recently been disemboweled by initiative, and Hawaii's. In addition, an estimated several hundred local government programs exist, primarily centered in the growth-management program states (Kelly, 1993, 2004; Nelson & Dawkins, 2005).

The growth-management movement is hardly young. If regulatory-based regional growth-management programs had broad political support today, one has to suspect that there would be far more programs in existence, and new programs would be substantive, not weak. The only arenas in which we see new regulatory programs of substance being established are exclusionary growth-deflection formats undertaken by individual jurisdictions with elite socio-economic characteristics – not a healthy development in that such programs simply deflect growth into outlying jurisdictions and impact housing affordability. As an innovation, the current generation of growth-management programs is mature and has likely reached its maximum maturation.

Today, none of the existing substantive state or federal statutes, if they were to face enactment, would likely survive in its original form, if at all. Much has changed since the golden era of bipartisan environmentalism. Nearly all of the original rigorous programs from the 1970s have been weakened by amendment, revision, and faltering commitment to implementation. State growth-management programs adopted since this early era have been progressively weakened in a regulatory context. This includes the Georgia, Maryland, and Washington programs, and the new Maine program that is voluntary in nature.

In the case of the early statutes, legislators had limited understanding of what they were voting into law. In the mid 1980s I conducted a series of informal interviews with the original Washington state Republican leadership that shepherded the creation of the state's Environmental Policy Act, Shorelines Management Act, and the creation of the Washington Department of Ecology in the 1971 legislative session.

They expressed that they and their colleagues had no real conception of what they were creating. The initial statutory language tended to be vague, and legislators did not fully comprehend the regulatory implications that would follow. Further, land-use and environmental laws were viewed as progressive needs by both parties during that time frame. More than a decade later, they expressed that they would never have created the programs, given the resulting experience. Frank Popper reported similar conclusions in a political analysis of early programs in Vermont and Florida (Popper, 1981).

In addition, today other factors retard the likelihood of seeing the enactment of any new rigorous command-and-control as state growth-management programs. Organized opposition to these types of programs is far more sophisticated and vigilant than in the past, both among local governments and private sector interests. A decided polarization has occurred in many state legislatures and trade associations over the last two decades. State legislatures have always been combative environments, the democratic battleground where ideas and interests clash. And as American society has drifted toward a greater orientation of self-interested behavior with its associated harder edge, state legislative climates have reflected the change.

Sophisticated redistricting has created more safe seats, which has in turn empowered the conservative and liberal wings of both parties. Moderate country club Republicans have been integrated with elements of activist conservatives like the Religious Right, while Blue Dog Democrats that will cross party lines have been marginalized by liberal party loyalists. What defines a political moderate is the willingness to seek consensus and compromise along with distaste for ideological zealotry. As a broad generalization, moderates will attempt to avoid confrontation, while ideologues on both the left and the right, are driven by political passion. It is rare to find a feisty, fighting moderate by definition. This has empowered the more ideologically-driven in key trade association positions and legislative leadership.

The private property rights culture has been strengthened as narcissism has increasingly replaced communitarianism in the culture. Consider that in a 2006 nationwide poll taken by the Center for Economic and Civic Opinion at the University of Massachusetts showed that 81 percent of Americans opposed the taking of private property by eminent domain for any purpose. The American Planning Association in its Growing Smart initiative has periodically been tracking the activities of its campaign to modernize state planning statutes and promote smart growth programs (APA, 2002). Without question, the Association's grassroots efforts by local chapters are sincere, but I would offer an alternative interpretation of the results so far. What has been reported as an increase in activity reflects a combination of routine amendatory activities normally surrounding planning statutes, and efforts at incremental reform, which have largely been unsuccessful.

In analyzing legislative activities since 2000, no comprehensive state growth-management programs of true substance have been adopted into law. A number of legislative taskforces have been created, and gubernatorial proposals floated, but as described earlier, that in no way constitutes advancement in the current political climate. A number of states have added or strengthened the requirement that local governments plan (for growth management), a strategy that has already been shown to be of marginal value unless linked to a number of other critical components in state law and down the chain of program implementation. In review, the picture is primarily one of political gridlock of the contentious or failed strategies than the comprehensive reform that will lead the profession out of the current morass of ineffectiveness. Strategic thinking in all things political requires a pragmatic assessment of those fights that you likely can't win and those that you may succeed in when given the resources and tactical capabilities at your command. The current political climate for growth management in America suggests the following conclusions:

- The model of highly rigorous regulatory-based growth management works technically, particularly when practiced at the regional scale, but it is not politically sustainable in American culture, nor is it politically achievable in a widespread capacity in the vast majority of states. In a limited number of states, possibly as many as 20, planning advocates may be capable of passing largely cosmetic programs given the nuances of political compromise, but not regulatory programs with the type of rigor required for true effectiveness.
- As a society we have rejected the feasibility and desirability of enforced regional growth targets whereby caps are established in

metropolitan areas with subsequent growth diversion to other regions or jurisdictions through a variety of existing planning techniques. Ultimately, without such a commitment, we do not have the ability as a profession to maintain distinct jurisdictional edges except in the extremely rare case where large-scale greenbelts have been established that ring an urban area as in the modest example of Boulder, Colorado. Without such ability, growth management gets reduced to the staple of comprehensive planning, that is, the continuous accommodation of growth pressure with a focus on public service delivery, timing, and community design.

- Stand-alone, local government growth-management programs can be effective from the jurisdiction's perspective in diverting growth, but they are fundamentally flawed from a regional perspective. We will continue to see elite socio-economic communities establishing rigorous growth diversion programs that will be politically sustainable at the local level, but that will impact housing affordability and contribute to sprawl growth patterns.

Assuming the above conclusions are accurate, it makes more strategic sense to focus growth-management research in two areas. The first is the design of growth-management regimes that have social validity and political acceptance in the culture at a coordinated state level. Political sustainability and on-ground effectiveness are more likely to be found in approaches that cater to American cultural traits, including freedom of choice, market inducements, and behavioral incentives.

The second strategic focus should be the rural sector – areas located beyond the bounds of current metropolitan growth pressure or landowner exurban expectations. Creative design still offers some hope of effectiveness there. Planning research has largely ignored this sector, and rural planners are in desperate need of research support catered to their needs and the culture in which they operate. The potential exists to affect a far larger physical land base than the suburban or urban sector for future generations of Americans, a land base that is highly sensitive to certain low-density development practices that can quickly destroy key attributes of rural character. The window of opportunity to establish workable growth-management regimes within rural areas is narrow. Potentially, with creative design, these areas could eventually serve as growth limit boundaries, or greenbelts, between expanding metropolitan complexes without the need for large-scale land acquisition or heavy-handed regulatory regimes.

Frank Popper noted, in his 1981 treatise on the politics of land-use reform, that programs based on centralized regulation in America "virtually always confront a powerful, well-financed, entrenched conservative opposition that can often block, weaken, subvert, pervert, or ignore them, but whose help will nonetheless be needed to carry them out" (Popper, 1981). If anything, that conclusion is even more salient today. It is no longer just conservative forces but mainstream American culture that opposes and ignores traditional planning formats if judged by action, not word. At its core, the current model has failed because it lacks social resonance and political acceptance within the society, and because interest-group politics enable multiple points of influence. If true land-use reform is to be achieved it must come from some other experimental path.

Behavior-Based Land Planning

SECTION Two

The Model and Techniques of CBIP

CHAPTER Three

Culture-Based Incentive Planning

CBIP is a techniques model specifically concerned with regulatory reform in land planning and growth-management practice. It has strong theoretical connections with other central organizing theories in political culture, economics, behaviorism, and planning. At a basic level, it is helpful to think about CBIP as operating on two planes - strategic and tactical. The model attempts to improve planning implementation by incorporating sensitivity to cultural factors and the tendencies of human behavior into strategic thinking. To improve implementation results, it is argued that this strategic orientation must be extended to considerations of implementation, and also to planning objectives and institutional design. Objectives, process, and implementation are approached as a coterminous design exercise, each influencing the other in the matrix of cultural and behavioral factors.

At the tactical level, concerns for cultural validity and behavioral response are captured through the construction of various incentive techniques and the application of tools of influence in communication and marketing. These four components of CBIP – culture, behavior, incentives, and influence – are all closely aligned in a myriad of relationships in both theory and practice.

This chapter provides a number of fundamental building blocks associated with regulatory theory and reform that underpin CBIP. It then introduces the CBIP model, providing a general explanation and diagram of its components and their relationship with existing planning practice. This chapter concludes with a discussion of CBIP's relationship with existing planning theory and questions of ethical application. The individual components and techniques associated with CBIP - cultural analysis, applied behavioral analysis, and incentives construction - are each then explored in substantial detail in the following three chapters.

Regulatory Reform

Today there is a movement by governments across the globe for regulatory reform driven by a general dissatisfaction with the effectiveness and efficiency (cost) of regulatory regimes. These concerns range from how to manage natural monopolies and predatory pricing, to how to provide public goods in a way that promotes maximum utility through market-determining mechanisms. Nearly all the government members of the Organization for Economic Cooperation and Development have ongoing regulatory reform efforts that involve both policy research and experimentation (OECD, 1997).

American theory and research in this area are widely acknowledged as being in the vanguard, the first and most developed, but representing the distinct cultural outlook of the United States with theories centered on markets and self-interested behavior as the principal paradigm in how societies most effectively organize themselves (Baldwin & Cave, 1999; Blundell & Robinson, 2000; OECD, 1997). European contributions on the topic are growing rapidly, and they are beginning to rival American efforts with an expanded view of relevant considerations. The majority of this work, particularly American, draws substantially from corollary contributions in property rights theory, incentives theory, and market efficiency models that, in turn, have parallel principles in behavioral psychology and increasingly, behavioral economics. They all have something to offer planning practice when transcribed to field application. The CBIP model integrates these considerations with an extension into cultural sensitivity and behavior management.

Governments undertake regulation under a variety of rationales. They include concerns over anti-competitive behavior, information inadequacies such as automobile safety ratings and food labeling, and unequal bargaining power in such areas as workplace safety and discrimination. They also engage in regulation for institution-building, or what economists commonly refer to as the "rules of the game," to allow markets to function such as the protection of property rights and contract law. They also engage in regulation for institution-building, to allow markets to function such as the protection of property rights and contract law. This is what economists commonly refer to as the "rules of the game." Each regulatory challenge presents a variety of management options, ranging from public command-and-control formats to engineered private-market mechanisms to achieve the desired public objective.

Land planners are most occupied with four regulatory rationales for government intervention: externalities, public goods, social justice, and the enhancement or protection of property values. The individual attributes of each of these four areas have specific implications related to human behavioral response and incentives associated with them. Those implications provide clues for the design of more effective regulatory or quasi-regulatory management schemes. A classic example is the issue of public goods in planning policy.

The land planning objectives and associated regulatory regimes of the American planning system are to a significant extent concerned with market failures in the provision of public goods. They are attempts in public policy to compensate for the inevitable imperfections that exist in market institutions. Some commodities such as security, clean air, and efficient transportation networks hold high value for society, but are inefficiently provided through traditional private-market mechanisms. The central policy debate in regulatory reform is not whether to drive toward a libertarian regulatory void, but instead centers around questions of how best to design for efficiency and price feedback in areas where traditional market mechanisms are less than ideal in producing and allocating certain high value public resources. It is widely acknowledged that markets fail for pure public goods and in many situations involving externalities, forcing some form of public intervention (Dolsak & Ostrom, 2003; Laffont & Martimort, 2002; Olson, 1965).

The question is how best to create the control mechanisms necessary, depending upon the attributes of the situation.

Pure public goods have a unique characteristic. The goods or services must be available to everyone if available to anyone, for instance, water quality, rural character, and national defense. The transaction costs of attempting to convert or allocate public goods into private goods with associated private property rights is too high to be practical, or it carries with it serious issues of social equity such as in public education or medical care.

In the emerging theory of private property rights, it is hypothesized that property rights will be combined into a public domain, "if the co-ordinating resources via organization and planning is less than the costs of coordination via market transactions," and a resource will stay in the public domain, "if the costs of assigning property rights over it exceeds the value created" (Webster & Wai-Chung, 2003). Under the Webster and Wai-Chung analysis, public goods will always exist since there will always be circumstances where the transaction costs of converting a pubic good to a private good exceed the benefits.

Further, new technologies and forms of organization create new public goods or common pool characteristics, for instance, the Internet and the business model of free-access software. Elinor Ostrom, a scholar of common-pool resource management, argues that the modern public corporation, which has become the most competitive organizational form in capitalism, has itself strong common-pool characteristics – a large number of shareholders, managers, employees, and customers who all hold identifiable rights in the corporation but no single individual or individuals hold all the rights (Dolsak & Ostrom, 2003). In considering the design of planning institutions under the CBIP model, it is helpful to think of public and private goods as being potentially transitory, migrating from one sector to the other as technology or organizational conventions either increase or decrease transaction costs. An example is the growing ability to create artificial markets for development rights or for air pollutants rights as the most efficient manner to achieve certain public policy objectives.

A second consideration in any behavioral-based approach to planning is that public goods, by nature, produce what economists classify as a "free-rider problem." Since it is difficult to prescribe property rights to public goods, non-payers can't be excluded from their benefit. While it is in the interest of the individual to have public goods provided to their level of maximum utility, there is an incentive for the rational, self-interested individual not to contribute and to free-ride off of the contribution of others. As Mancur Olson noted in his classic work on collective action, despite the high-value nature of certain public goods and services to the individual, "no appeal to patriotism, national ideology, or bond of common culture allows any government to support itself through voluntary contributions"(Olson, 1965). Compulsory payments or extractions through taxes, fees, and regulations are always necessary.

Olson and others postulate that individual members of large groups will not act to collectively produce public goods at the optimum level. Behavior in small-group settings, however, is more conducive to public-spirited support when anonymity is reduced, a finding that is supported in a substantial body of recent behavioral economics experiments. CBIP, as will be explored later, is concerned with designing behavioral-based planning interventions that capture and exploit these types of findings to enhance the production of public goods and the management of externalities.

Since normal market mechanisms don't operate to send price and production signals in public goods, public managers such as planners struggle to establish the ideal amount of public goods and services based on the public's true valuations and willingness to pay. Under the perspective of the Gibbard-Satterthwaite theorem and Social Choice theory, people will underestimate their preference for public goods if they think they have to pay for them (Sager, 1999). If they believe they don't have to pay for some public goods, they will overestimate their preference for the goods. The free-rider problem means that there is a strong tendency for public goods and services to be both underproduced and overutilized – the "tragedy of the commons." A classic example confronting governments today is how best to manage and ration the expensive prospect of health care and transportation. When individuals perceive, for example, that health service is free through either universal national coverage or by employer provided health insurance, the tendency is to overuse limited resources and demand marginally effective treatments.

The distortions that occur when pricing signals become vague is one reason why economists have been so interested in the question of how to accurately measure a person's true willingness to pay for public goods, for example, in the use of contingent valuation survey techniques. To achieve the most efficient provision of public goods through public policy, such as regulations and taxation, requires an accurate measure of their market value. In short, market mechanisms that are effective in determining the value, and hence production level, of private goods, break down for public goods.

Externalities, like public goods, are also central to many land planning interventions undertaken in the name of market failures. Under CBIP, the issue of externalities is approached from a behavioral management perspective. That is, regulatory reform is considered in the context of how to align underlying behavioral factors to overcome market failures. The traditional view of an externality has been a circumstance in which the price of a product or service does not truly reflect either the cost or benefit to society. The result is either excessive consumption in the case of a negative externality, or underproduction in the circumstance of a positive externality. For example, when a forestry corporation and its shareholders purchase and expend large sums of capital to manage millions of acres for timber production, the general public reaps significant unpaid benefits in open space, rural character, wildlife habitat, buffered watershed yields, and in many cases, free recreational access. If those positive externalities could be captured in market mechanisms, it is likely that there would be greater economic incentive to expand and retain corporate forestland ownership, and to modify management practices for the production of more public goods. The same issues of uncompensated positive externalities apply to the farming community.

Aldo Leopold, the father of modern-day game management, captured the basic nexus between economic behavior, market incentives, and externalities when he wrote in 1933, "If it pays, it stays" (Leopold, 1933). The principles driving today's initiatives in ecotourism are often a clever adaptation of the same relationships applied in one evolving branch of regulatory reform. But planners often face a more complex management environment that has extended the traditional definitions of externalities beyond pure economic values into new territory. A planner's circumstances require a more adaptive model for regulatory reform beyond just the traditional prescriptions of capturing and internalizing markets through economic institutions.

Consider the following issue of densification of urban areas. Pro-density groups, including planners, that advocate against exclusionary zoning and promote policies for urban densification to encourage housing affordability and discourage sprawl, receive a small personal benefit at a high social cost in terms of public controversy and other organizing costs. Anti-growth groups that defend restricted access in the form of exclusionary zoning or anti-development sentiment, reap large personal benefits in terms of increased property values and exclusivity, while imposing the costs on the broader society. In many instances they don't perceive the costs, both lifestyle and economic, that they are imposing on others and themselves because the costs are less obvious. Behaviorally they are less sensitive to them since they are extended into the future. To capture and correct for the externalities in this illustration requires an expanded perspective on behavioral incentives beyond just economic models that form the core of today's regulatory reform movement in America.

Markets are largely driven by self-interested behavior as people seek, in a general way, to maximize their personal utility, but that utility is often not economic in character, tinged by cultural conditioning and social convention. In a similar context, most human behavior can be explained by the consequences associated with our actions. We seek to maximize rewards and minimize penalties and punishments, however we might define them. The power of consequences to influence and even fully control human behavior provides a basis for the construction of incentive-based strategies that include, but extend beyond, economic considerations.

CBIP as a model of regulatory reform stresses the roles that behavioral psychology and incentives play in planning outcomes. It is concerned, in particular, with how to more effectively capture and channel individual self-interest for the accomplishment of community-oriented objectives. CBIP is a methods model concerned with what Mancur Olson characterizes as the "collective action problem," that is, how to overcome the behavioral tendencies and economic incentives for people to act in a self-interested way in the area of public goods when they would be better off individually if they worked with a collective mentality.

Regulation Strategies

Property rights theory argues that societies essentially have two basic strategies in how to engage in material advancement. The first is top-down, hierarchical planning and the second is a bottom-up approach that relies upon spontaneous, mutually beneficial exchange through such mechanisms as negotiation, markets, and contracts (Webster & Wai-Chung, 2003). The market oriented school of regulatory reform, which is dominated by but not exclusively restricted to scholars from the discipline of economics, argues that private land-use governance models will always be substantially more efficient as maximizers of collective societal wealth than centralized planning schemes. The primary reason is the limitation of information for central planning purposes.

To comprehend and manage highly complex systems like metropolitan land markets for peak economic utility requires omnipotent knowledge and management integration. Social desires, economic dynamics, behavioral response, and considerations in the natural and man-made physical environment all have to be reasonably understood and collectively integrated. In addition, central management functions have to anticipate accurately future technologies and changes in local, regional, and global circumstances, requiring planners to be practically clairvoyant. The alternative paradigm is for millions of individuals and institutions to be engaged in a Darwinian evolutionary process of self-interested decision-making through marketplace mechanisms. The paradox is that the more complex the system and the greater the need for co-ordination, the more spontaneous order through markets will outperform central planning in matters of economic efficiency.

To be fair, advocates of market-based solutions in planning do not dismiss the issues of public goods, externalities, and the need for central planning interventions in areas such as core public services. Instead, many make a distinction between attempts to guide metropolitan form and growth, or what has been described as the "municipal socialism experiment of the last century," from what they see as the task of managing public domain problems, externalities and service provision. Norton E. Long's comment that long-range comprehensive plans were, "Civic New Year resolutions," partially captures the distinction. The concern of advocates for market-based planning is in attempts of central planning to produce utopian visions. Their argument is that planning should focus on reducing public domain and externality problems, and on innovation to reduce the costs of market transactions (Altshuler & Behn, 1997; Altshuler, 1965; Blundell & Robinson, 2000; Webster & Wai-Chung, 2003).

Others have focused their market perspective on the distortions that common regulatory planning interventions are causing in juxtaposition to planning objectives such as the reduction of sprawl. Jonathan Levine in his recent book, *Zoned Out*, documents in a number of empirically supported arguments that sprawl is largely a planning failure, not a market failure (Levine, 2006). There is strong evidence that significant elements of the market desire and will embrace higher density residential options, but those options have been intentionally restricted by exclusionary zoning practices that have now become ubiquitous in America. It is also evident that such practices are restricting the ability of urban areas to transform themselves, over time by market forces, into more efficient configurations, a hallmark of city evolution in the past. Levine argues that planning policy should be market facilitating and not attempt to override market demands for a full range of densities and housing lifestyle options. Both Levine's work and that of others have concluded that the only solution to overcome the natural incentives for local jurisdictions to engage in exclusionary zoning is for local government authority to be restrained at the state level – a regulatory restraint placed on the regulators (Altshuler, Wolman, Morrill, Wolman, & Mitchell, 1999; Levine, 2006; Levine, 1999).

When searching for a model of improved effectiveness in planning implementation, the market-based regulatory reform outlooks, like those described above, harbor fundamental limitations for planners. It is not that regulatory reform models that advocate increased sensitivity to market theories are inaccurate; instead, they are incomplete for the public demands placed on planning. Clearly, improved planning performance can be achieved by both recognizing the limitations of hierarchical planning practice in dictating spatial order and urban form, and in being far more sensitive in the design of planning strategies to the use of market-based approaches. These are both considerations arguably that are not widely recognized in today's planning field practice.

But, there are at least two limitations to the current version of the market-based model of regulatory reform in planning. The first is fundamental in framing the discussion of regulatory reform in planning solely from the perspective of neoclassical economics, a value-laden belief system, like any other, that places priority on certain values over other considerations. Market-based outlooks focus on the issues of wealth maximization for society and the economic efficiency that leads to it. These are two laudable objectives in public policy, but they are not the only considerations. Standard-of-living is not an empirical replacement for quality-of-life, issues of social justice, moral obligations to current and future generations, or to considerations of environmental sustainability.

The problem with relying foremost or exclusively on a neoclassical economic paradigm in regulatory reform is it is an epistemological bungalow – no upper story. A planning implementation model concerned with regulatory reform requires greater scope, that is, market-based sensitivity combined with other elements. Deciding distributional issues on the basis of wealth maximization has a number of serious limitations. What if we can't accurately determine values as is the case in many public goods, or we have failures in the market distribution mechanism, as is the case in externalities? Further, questions of social justice cannot be answered in current economic models. Many may find it morally objectionable to transcribe basic human rights into a system of distributional private property for the purposes of economic efficiency, even if we can devise such institutions, for instance, in allocated rights between polluters and potential victims.

The second limitation is that while market-based schools recognize issues of public goods and externalities as legitimate arenas for public regulatory intervention, their prescription is largely restricted to market-based attempts to privatize public rights, or schemes to capture and assign free-floating costs and benefits. Both are useful concepts but provide too small a toolbox for the breadth of issues that planners face.

To improve planning performance, a modified public interest approach to regulatory reform is required that blends economic theories of regulation with other elements for a more adaptable and effective framework (a larger toolbox). This is the specific intent of CBIP. The act of that amalgamation broadens the definition of regulatory reform into a new realm of planning implementation that may best be described not so much as regulation, but more as a continuum of techniques based on control at one end of the spectrum to broad market encouragements, facilitation, and incentives at the other end, depending on the circumstantial need. In many situations under this model, command-and-control regulation gives way to decidedly non-regulatory approaches that rely on capturing human nature, cultural tendencies, and incentives for gentle interventions through market guidance. In other circumstances, the best course may be no form of market intervention whatsoever. Planning implementation in America is associated with command-and-control regulation, a most unfortunate image. CBIP is designed to provide an alternative reference point for planners when they confront issues of planning effectiveness and implementation. It partially does so by redefining regulatory reform into a broader universe of considerations that, in some cases, leads to non-regulatory approaches.

One way of viewing the potential tools of planning implementation is that it is a continuum extending from hierarchical regulatory control to purely market institutions (Illustration no. 1). The implementation universe for achieving public land-planning objectives, which can be defined as the specific legal, political, cultural, and market attributes in which we work, extends far beyond the conventional regulatory tools of mainline planning. Moreover, as the complexity of urban and land-use systems has increased, the distinction between public and private spheres of power and their respective concerns has become

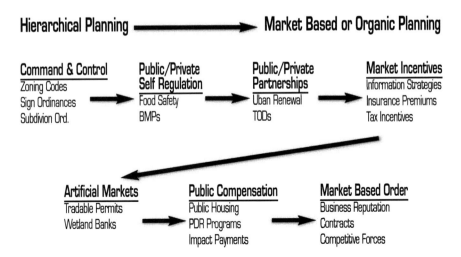

Illustration no. 1 – Continuum of Control Techniques

blurred for the planner. Public institutions are concerned with the health and internal operations of private business because of the larger ramifications to society. In turn, private interests, particularly large public corporations and trade associations, have assumed a large role in influencing and carrying out public or quasi-public functions from self-regulation, to defining and implementing policies of corporate citizenship.

As Leigh Hancher and Michael Moran have commented, American viewpoints on regulatory policy generally assume that the pubic interest is corrupted when private interests influence outcomes – an assumed illegitimate supplanting of the public interest by private interests (Hancher & Moran, 1989). The evolving European theory and practice on regulatory reform adopts a different perspective, the blending of interests where the complexity of management concerns blurs the distinction between public and private spheres. This latter outlook sets the implementation stage for collaborative approaches.

CBIP

The CBIP model that will be introduced momentarily is designed to provide an adaptable framework in terms of how to view and pursue effective implementation approaches. The framework is applicable to the full range of implementation strategies from command-and-control to purely market-based solutions. It recognizes the valuable contributions that market-based models can make in improving planning performance, including reducing undesirable market distortions in planning practice, but it extends beyond these current models. It does so by introducing a broader consideration of culture and behaviorism in how to conceptualize and design implementation approaches. The model is designed to improve implementation performance through the following broad design principles:

- Strive to design a cooperative rather than adversarial relationship between government and the regulated by recognizing issues of cultural sensitivity, market response, and behavioral motivations. Seek collaborative implementation strategies that rely on the provision of choice tied to tools of behavioral persuasion. Think in terms of generating a partnership with market forces in the supply of public goods and the constructive management of externalities.

- Introduce greater competition between implementation schemes as a means to drive improved performance. The over-reliance on standard command–and-control formats in planning implementation has both stifled innovation within the profession, and experimentation at the local government level. Theoretically, the large number of decentralized political units in America responsible for land-use policy should be conducive to injecting competition between implementation schemes since citizens have the power to exit jurisdictions that underperform in either results, or in the social desirability of the approach (Tiebout, 1956). Today, such competition and innovation largely does not exist due to the entrenched tradition of planning practice that is supported by incentives that work against improved performance. This needs to change if planning results are to improve, and it can be partially accomplished by changing the incentives of those charged with planning and regulation.
- Move towards forms of private governance and public-private partnerships in issues of public goods and externalities where such forms prove to be effective in achieving policy objectives. Excessive reliance on standard forms of government regulation in planning has crowded out other forms of implementation that may prove to be both more efficient and effective.
- In devising implementation strategies consider the full range of approaches that may be engineered from command–and-control and voluntary solutions to market guidance, and match the objective to the most appropriate, efficient, and effective approach, not necessarily the most expedient or traditional.
- Seek out implementation strategies that are more flexible, less prosecutorial, and more self-implementing by institutional design.
- Always consider the role that incentives play in the generation of outcomes. Individual behavior is driven by incentives (consequences) and that behavior directly influences the performance of institutions. Effective implementation of planning objectives is directly tied to the role that incentives play in human behavior. The construction of incentives schemes that support and don't undermine desired outcomes is the key to enhanced planning implementation.

- In the design of implementation strategies, focus on the pressure point(s) - product outputs, product inputs, institutional process, and intervention audience - that most efficiently accomplishes the stated objective given the five tests of performance outlined in Chapter One.
- It is impossible to advance planning practice without innovation, and innovation is impossible without mistakes. The incentive climate for public planners must be changed such that public policy-makers and the general public encourage experimentation for the purpose of innovation and advancement.

CBIP operationalizes a behavioral approach to planning through four integrated components – cultural sensitivity, behavior analysis, incentives construction, and principles in communications and influence. The term "behavioral" is used in both a generic context and in reference to the specific school of behaviorism in psychology. In general usage under CBIP the term is intended to imply the broad universe of human nature and behavior motivations that should be considered in planning program design. Included are considerations from social psychology, environmental psychology, applied behavior analysis, behavioral economics, and cultural values research. In using "behavioral" in this fashion, I have violated by necessity the specific meaning of the term in the social sciences, and in particular, psychology. Planning's vocabulary currently has no dedicated term that captures the broad concept of applied cultural and psychological considerations in practice, and hence, under CBIP the term takes on both a broad and narrow meaning.

Illustration no. 2 depicts the basic CBIP model. The four components that comprise the behavioral model are strongly interrelated as shown by the network of relationship lines on the diagram. Cultural considerations directly influence the construction of effective incentives and communication programs - considerations that can be location, audience, and issue-specific. In turn, applied behavior analysis provides guidance in the engineering of incentives that may range from framing effect techniques in command-and-control regulations, to the construction of market institutions to achieve public objectives. All four of CBIP's interrelated components form a behavioral matrix, influencing and being influenced by each other.

In combination, the four components of CBIP provide a quasi-linear process for the development of program implementation strategies in land planning. It is quasi-linear in that while one would normally start by thinking about cultural context first and then proceed incrementally with each of the other components, the sequential relationship is unlikely to be so direct, with feedback influence and modifications occurring throughout the planning process. It should be noted that the four components of the behavioral model directly influence the development of planning objectives and the design of planning institutions, as well as

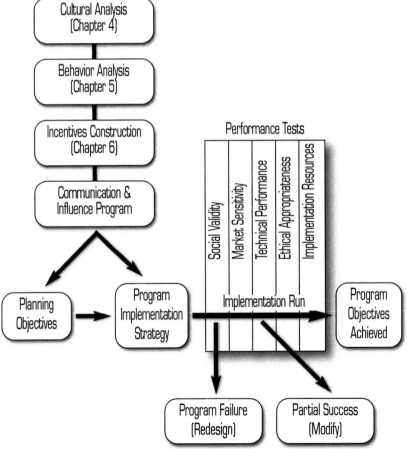

Illustration no. 2 – CBIP Methods Model

the program implementation strategy. Planning objectives and institutions are by nature a product of culture – political culture, professional planning culture, and socio-economic culture.

By definition under CBIP, an implementation strategy is only successful if it can navigate within an acceptable performance range through the five tests identified earlier – social and political validity, market sensitivity, technical performance, ethical appropriateness, and the availability of necessary implementation resources. As noted on the diagram, a CBIP-based implementation strategy once initiated, must run this gauntlet of performance tests, as would any other non-CBIP-based strategy. CBIP is a conceptual model with affiliated techniques that is designed to specifically navigate these performance tests that all planners face.

Once any planning implementation strategy is initiated (the implementation run), there are three possible outcomes as illustrated on the CBIP diagram. The strategy may completely fail one or more of the tests, as is so often the case under traditional command-and-control formats, requiring redesign if results are to be improved. It may partially achieve plan objectives, but significantly underperform in one or more areas, rendering the need for program refinement. In many cases, refinement options have their engineering limits in terms of the potential for improved performance. If within a chosen implementation strategy program objectives cannot be met within desired performance parameters, then a fundamentally different strategy must be considered. The final potential outcome, the one that is obviously desired, is that the strategy is successful in achieving sustainable results within all the desired parameters.

Cultural Context

The first of CBIP's four behavioral pillars is cultural analysis. The model attempts to correct for existing limitations in American practice by incorporating at the strategic level cultural sensitivity on a tiered framework. That requires planners to be intellectually aware of dominant and sub-dominant cultural traits and preferences within any given planning setting, and customizing the design of the planning program around those considerations to increase social validity.

Culture under CBIP can exist at multiple levels, a little like a three-dimensional chessboard. Planners must think geographically in the context of national, regional and local cultural traits. At the international level, American culture can be characterized by a number of attributes that make it unique from a planning perspective, a perspective that is explored at some length in the next chapter. At the regional level, the Southeast has a far different planning culture than the Northeast or Northwest. In local application, ranching communities, mining towns, and university jurisdictions could just as easily be in different universes from the perspective of a culturally aware planner.

But, accounting for culture requires more than just geographic stratification. Planners must also think in terms of socio-economic and demographic cultures, both in a traditional and non-traditional context. There are implications for the sexes, races, age groups and income classes. There are also cultural implications between traditional stakeholder groups. For instance, there are significant cultural differences between the building community and realtors, as well as differences between small rural builders and large national or regional building corporations. There are also distinct value classes within the planning profession itself.

CBIP as a model of practice calls on the planner to recognize and acknowledge political, lifestyle, social, and economic cultural traits and tendencies. The formulation of planning objectives should reflect a compatibility with that cultural matrix, and certainly should not ignore it, or assume that it can be bullied into submission under a pure command–and-control approach. However, the concept of cultural sensitivity should not be taken as a passive endorsement of current market tendencies. While resistant to rapid alteration, enlightened policies-and-planning approaches can, over time, spur cultural transformation resulting in modified landscape preferences, market behavior, and community response. Cultural tendencies can be accommodated without being viewed as unassailable, influenced to move incrementally in new directions that are still consistent with underlying social values when internal persuasion and political skill is employed (Harrison, 2007). All cultures and markets are to some extent artificially manufactured, managed and manipulated. What CBIP implies is cultural sensitivity, not fatalist capitulation. As such, it is an activist, advocacy-based model.

Behavior Analysis

The second pillar of CBIP is behavior analysis. As previously mentioned, CBIP is a behavioral-oriented planning practice in both a broad and more specific context. The specific context is that of applied behavior analysis (ABA). ABA, which is explored in a planning context in Chapter 5, is a particular school of techniques in psychology most closely associated with B.F. Skinner. ABA restricts its practice to the measurement and modification of observable behavior through a variety of applied techniques and is less concerned with cognitive explanations. ABA focuses on the consequences (incentives), both positive and negative, that influence people's actions, and modifies these consequences (incentives) to obtain the desired behaviors.

One note on nomenclature is that ABA psychologists consistently employ the term "consequences" in essentially the same fashion as economists use the term "incentives." The two terms mean the same thing within the respective disciplines, loosely defined as the total family of outcomes with the power to motivate that occur as a result of an earlier behavior. They may be specifically engineered, as in the case of legal penalties, or they may be undirected outcomes, such as the implications of putting your hand on a hot burner. For an outcome to be a behavioral consequence in ABA or an incentive in economics, the implication is that the individual must be able to make the connection between the action and the outcome. As an example, consider the relationship between smoking and lung cancer. Prior to any suspicions in the healthcare community or general public of the connection between smoking and a variety of health impacts, there existed no health consequence or health-related incentive for the individual not to smoke. The consequence from a behavioral perspective was only activated when the potential implications were perceived.

Under CBIP, an analysis of cultural factors aids to frame the role that certain incentives play in planning outcomes. Existing behavior incentives are identified that both support and undermine planning program objectives through the tool of behavior analysis. Implementation of the planning program largely rests on attempting to eliminate or modify incentives that are encouraging counterproductive behavior to planning objectives, and engineering new incentives that stimulate desired behaviors. The tactical core of CBIP is the three-term contingency model of applied behavior analysis whereby human behavior, which is triggered by antecedents, is largely controlled by the consequences that follow.

The three-term contingency model of ABA is clearly in play in land planning practice across a spectrum of players from developers, landowners, and planners to housing consumers and elected officials. CBIP, when employed in a comprehensive fashion, addresses the role of these behavior incentives for all the key actor groups in the land-use equation, including planners themselves.

Incentives and Their Construction

Designing effective incentives to encourage certain behavior responses is the third pillar of the model. CBIP relies on the enhancement of quality-of-life as both a normative objective in planning and as an encouragement to change the behavior of consumers and other actors in the land-use equation. Implicit in the model is an aggressive form of advocacy planning utilizing tools of behavioral persuasion and influence, social marketing, and incentives. It is a set of techniques that alter behavior while preserving freedom of choice.

Incentive design techniques under CBIP are aimed at the individual, but have larger system implications in the performance and design of planning institutions. Those institutions can include market rules to manage public goods and externalities, organization structure, and process design. As explored in Chapter Six, CBIP integrates the contributions of incentive theory and the principal/agent model, along with specific findings in behavioral economics and ABA, to provide guidance in how to better design effective incentive-oriented programs in planning.

In a free-market oriented culture like America there is a tendency to think of incentives as being primarily economic in nature. Economic incentives can be powerful motivators if you get the structural parameters correct, which is rarely done in current planning applications. But beyond economic incentives, lies a treasure trove of other incentive categories that hold great promise for the profession. Incentives can be engineered around human behavioral tendencies such as risk aversion, time discounting, and reciprocation to name just a few. Process, lifestyle, social, and technical assistance consequences can be strong motivators over and above economic inducements for all the actors in the land-use equation.

New findings in economic behaviorism that maintain an individual's freedom of choice are beginning to find their way into various management schemes. One area is the application of certain human decision-making tendencies in voluntary pension programs to encourage personal savings. Public health campaigns in smoking and obesity are another. Behavioral economists have labeled such approaches "libertarian paternalism" or "soft paternalism"(Glaeser, 2006; Sunstein & Thaler, 2003). It is an approach that replaces rule-governed behavior, or what some have characterized as hard paternalism, with a more subtle and socially accepted approach. Rather than trying to dictate planning outcomes by regulatory fiat, psychological incentives provide a behavioral nudge in the right direction, but still provide freedom of choice, reducing political resistance. Chapter Six specifically looks at a number of these emerging behavioral incentive principles and applies them to planning practice.

Communications Science and the Principles of Influence

The concept of CBIP, however, is more than cultural sensitivity combined with the application of a number of behavioral techniques to influence people's decisions in an environment of freedom of choice. In the best of American traditions it calls on planners to compete in the marketplace by creating and marketing a superior product for society. Currently, American land planners rarely influence market preferences or use the tools of persuasion in voluntary choice. We don't view ourselves in a marketing role since our professional image is not that of designers and manufacturers of products or services in competition with other lifestyle visions. Instead, it is assumed that participatory process and the public interest, as we inevitably define it within our own moral reference system, should suffice to carry the day under command–and–control regulatory formats.

The fourth and final pillar of CBIP's behavioral model is the power of communications science and the techniques of influence. Incentive-based persuasion is a form of social influence that depends largely on symbols, images and language in behavioral interventions. The CBIP concept suggests using the power of the marketplace and cultural tendencies for program self-implementation, that is, to harness these forces to achieve the desired objectives. The types of behavioral interventions prescribed under CBIP cannot be accomplished without some level of sophistication in communications practice, and in particular, the application of social marketing.

CBIP implies aggressively marketing an expanded concept of quality-of-life, life satisfaction, and subjective well-being through planning policy and implementation practice. Lowdon Wingo defines quality-of-life in a planning context as the "quality of the social and physical (both human-made and natural) environment in which people pursue the gratification of their wants and needs"(Wingo, 1973). Now consider the emerging definition for the marketing sciences, "the science of positive social change," a definition which planners could equally claim as their own (Sirgy, 2001).

Interestingly, a quality-of-life construct is now beginning to permeate the marketing sciences in a redefinition of both role and approach that far exceeds the sophistication of planning theory in the same context. It also is a construct of quality-of-life which extends to a variety of levels: the individual, community, and larger societal and global obligations (Sirgy, 2001). Marketing as an applied organizational science increasingly views its mission to assist profit, non-profit, and governmental organizations in effectively marketing goods, services, and programs that enhance the well-being of their clients.

These marketers must focus their behavioral science on customer satisfaction, competitors, and long-term profitability (Berkman, 1996). We planners have precisely the same task when you translate our vocabulary to theirs. A culture-sensitive construct for American land planning could just as easily replace the indefinable notion of public interest with a product/service orientation aimed at customer quality-of-life. Long-term profitability is interchangeable with notions of sustainability. Such an outlook requires land planners to abandon the implicit notion of the intellectual and moral superiority of our public interest value system, and instead treat alternative ideologies within the American culture as competitors. It also requires recognition in public practice that local government has its own self-interested agenda. That agenda tends to narrowly define the public interest in terms of the interests of the government institution, not broader issues of life satisfaction.

CBIP assumes planners must adapt to underlying values and norms in any given culture to be relevant. In America, that partly means application of democratic ideals through organized competition. Planners cannot expect to be successful in the American culture unless they engage directly in that competitive game. The heart of that game is market competition between ideas, policies, and products. It is not enough to have a superior product, which at this point, planning is not producing. It also requires the aggressive application of the tools of modern competition: an effective communicative message, the techniques of influence, marketing, lobbying, and tactical thinking. None of these dynamics is currently captured in existing planning theory or public practice. Only in private practice are planners operating in a market competition mode, often constrained by their public colleagues.

The concept of social marketing is one example of a CBIP application, although there are a significant number of other behavioral tools embodied in the model. Fox and Kotler argue that the goal of social marketing, like economic marketing, is to create change in people's behavior (Fox 1980). Kotler and Zaltman define social marketing as "the design, implementation, and control of programs calculated to influence the acceptability of social ideas, and involving considerations of product planning, pricing, communications, distribution, and marketing research" (Kotler and Zaltman 1971).

Social marketing under CBIP embodies the concept of capturing in combination the construct of quality-of-life, cultural sensitivity and a behaviorist approach under the banner of advocacy planning. Behavioral models such as Maslow's hierarchy of needs provide an operational basis for marketers to study and trigger consumer motives, as does the Rokeach personal values scale, psychographics (lifestyle patterns), and semiotics (the study of symbols and icons in human behavioral response) (Berkman, 1996). With the development of planning-related value and lifestyle typologies linking personality traits to behavior, it is possible for the land-use planner to design value-sensitive tools of public influence. We currently make little effort to match our planning product to the individual's, community's, or culture's self-image. Nor do we expend any research or practitioner energy in identifying media, communication, or other influence strategies linked to inducing the desired responses in a land-use context.

Habits can be strengthened, weakened, or changed by marketplace stimuli. Need recognition, such as the many lifestyle benefits of planning, can be induced and amplified. We do virtually none of it as practicing planners in a society awash with its application. As the fourth pillar of CBIP, communications science and the techniques of influence are directly tied to cultural context, behavioral analysis and the employment of a broad range of incentive techniques.

It is beyond the scope of this book to attempt even a cursory overview of the contributions of communications science that are applicable to incentive-based planning practice. Entire curriculums and hundreds of volumes exist in the areas of influence, public relations, marketing psychology, and political communications. For those who desire some basic exposure to the discipline, a small number of the many fine texts with an orientation toward applied planning practice are referenced (Cialdini,1993; Coney, 2003; Seitel, 2006; Trent and Friedenburg, 2000; Woodward, 2000).

CBIP and Planning Theory

The basic model of CBIP just described raises a number of fundamental questions regarding its place in planning theory and its ethics in application. Those questions are best addressed now before delving into the actual techniques of CBIP described in subsequent chapters. In addition, one way to better comprehend the larger framework of CBIP is to compare it against other theories of practice.

Planning students during the course of their academic training almost all receive exposure to formalized planning theory. It can be a heady and disorienting experience that leaves people grasping for a handhold. Most often that handhold turns out to be rational comprehensive theory, also known as synoptic theory. The rationality of it all appeals to planners' minds, particularly land-use and environmental planners with conditioning in the natural sciences and the scientific method. Students interested in physical planning are inherently self-selecting with personalities that admire and expect rational decision-making. Rational comprehensiveness is the theoretical backbone of how we have taught and practiced physical land planning forever. I confess to sharing that preference, not because it is effective in the American culture but because it is so wonderfully logical if you discount results.

Land planning students can comprehend rationalism at that stage of their professional development, but they struggle with John

Friedmann's transactive planning model. They comprehend even less the messages of John Forester's communicative planning, and are completely baffled by postmodernism (Forester, 1989; Friedmann, 1987; Sandercock, 1998). Without the benefit of substantial professional experience, most planning theory makes little sense to the student with the exception of rational-comprehensive theory and advocacy. One contention is that in the early years of a physical planner's development, the rational-comprehensive model often has a significant impact on personal practice. Here is a case where theory drives practice, or at least the outlook of the practitioner. But then things begin to change for the average practitioner, which in a sense mirrors the evolution seen in planning theory with the additions of transactive, communicative, collaborative, and radical planning theory.

As American practitioners mature, they often unknowingly modify their rational-comprehensive model of practice, literally evolving into new approaches born of necessity. It is not inaccurate to describe this professional development as literally making it up as you go, while simultaneously observing other planners in various stages of evolutionary development and experimentation. Young planners often hold in contempt the political maneuvers of their older colleagues as wholly inappropriate, only to find themselves in agreement years later and using the same tactics.

This process of professional evolution in the individual normally occurs in a vacuum from the trends occurring in academic planning theory, but it is not entirely immune from it. It is this partial disconnect that Donald Schon addresses when he states, "there is a tendency for research and practice to follow divergent paths, live in different worlds, pursue different enterprises and have little to say to one another" (Schon, 1983). The practitioner's personal evolution is best explained in the pragmatism concepts of Charles Peirce, William James, and John Dewey, but it would be inaccurate not to recognize the influence and contributions of scholarly theory in the philosophy of field professionals and vice versa. Unlike the origins of synoptic theory, Friedmann's transactive theory, Lindblom's incrementalism and particularly Forester's communicative theory, all draw heavily in an inductive sense from the observations of practice (Forester, 1989; Friedmann, 1987; Healey, 1997; Lindblom, 1959). The same can be said for the various branches of advocacy, which holds its roots not so much in planning practice, but political empowerment and mobilization tactics that extend back into history (Davidoff, 1965; Sandercock, 1998).

These later contributions also represent a trend in the incrementalization of planning theory. As planning theories have multiplied, they have narrowed in scope. In truth, they reflect a partial collection of the tools practitioners continue to develop and apply independently. As such, most planning theory could be characterized from the practitioner's perspective as inductive, reflecting the myriad of approaches that are drawn upon, depending on circumstance and judgment.

Another interesting trend in planning theory would seem to be a preoccupation with means, social process, and a new moral order as opposed to an ends or a results-oriented spatial outlook that is the principal concern of the physical planner. It is a movement that some might characterize as neo-Marxist in perspective or at least anti-market. Many of today's planning theorists look more toward social process with an emphasis on various communicative, collaborative, and communitarian philosophies. Their interest centers on establishing a moral-based practice on communitarianism, social justice, and democratization. It is the language of egalitarians, a minority political culture in America that is the chief rival to competitive individualism.

To illustrate this point, a typology of planning theory from the land-use practitioner's perspective might be devised along two axes (Illustration no. 3). The first axis would have an end–means continuum. At one end of this continuum, substantive results and a normative focus would be emphasized with an orientation toward spatial order and economy of resources. At the other end is a procedural or means focus where paramount importance is placed not so much on what is produced, but how it is produced or social processes.

The second axis of this typology represents the type of power recognized at the core of practice. At one end of this continuum is directive planning with a top-down orientation to practice and republicanism in governance. At the other end of this continuum is a diffuse model of power in practice with emphasis on individualism, market mechanisms as the principle organizing force in society, fragmentation, full-fledged participatory democracy, and the right of community self-determination regardless of outcome. What is suggested in the placement of existing

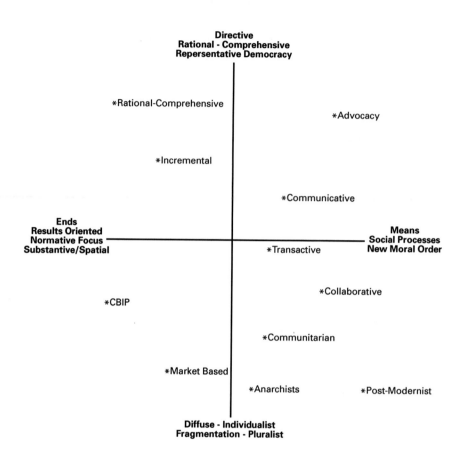

Illustration no. 3 – Planning Theory Typology

planning theories in this typology is that since the early 1970s there has been a decided trend toward means, social process, and models of diffusion of power. Transactive, collaborative, communitarian, and post-modernist models are all clustered in the lower right quadrant of the schematic, indicating an orientation toward means and diffuse institutions for social organization. CBIP and market-based planning theory represent the newest entrants, and they are the only models located in the lower left quadrant, indicating a fundamental departure from the other models as will be explored momentarily.

The earliest contributions to planning theory, rational-comprehensive and Lindblom's incrementalism, have strong overtones towards an 'ends' orientation and the planner as expert in the directive role (Lindblom, 1959). As such, both theories of practice are located in the upper left quadrant of the typology schematic (Illustration no. 3). For the planner the rational-comprehensive model in its purest form represents a professional short cut of sorts. It assumes a privileged relationship to power that American planners rarely have. Rather than having to fight it out in the participatory democratic trenches and marketplace like every other interest in the political economy, the initial model implicitly assumed that the sheer professional authority and righteousness of professional status demanded societal acknowledgement. Many have criticized this assumption from a variety of perspectives. Alan Altshuler, the current Dean of the Harvard Graduate Design Program, wrote at length as early as 1965 challenging the professional status of planning and its results by posing a variety of tests by which professional status can be claimed and implying that planning at the time, could not affirmatively meet any of those basic standards (Altshuler, 1965). Jane Jacobs and Leonie Sandercock have similarly attacked the rational-comprehensive model on the inappropriateness of assuming a top-down status (Jacobs, 1961; Sandercock, 1998).

Incrementalism was a partial acknowledgment that planners do not hold such a privileged position to power. This is not to suggest that rationalism has no place in physical planning, it clearly does, but it does so under a variety of constraints.

Next came Davidoff's movement of advocacy planning which began a trend toward means orientation, but still placed the planner in a directive role as the advocate, organizer, and spokesman for the disempowered (Davidoff, 1965). As many later critics of the advocacy model noted, including former advocacy planners, the approach was effective in blocking undesirable proposals from the community perspective, but completely ineffectual in formulating and advancing the implementation of alternatives (Goodman, 1971; Marris, 1994; Peattie, 1994). That may have been due, not so much to a flaw in the philosophy, but in the sophistication and resources required for effective application in the American culture.

Advocacy planning marked the beginning of a trend toward a social-sciences driven 'means' as opposed to 'ends' orientation, drifting from the design and hard sciences orientation that had dominated planning through the 1960s. It also centered on a concern with social justice and often the inner city, although it also had applications in the Great

Society program and issues of the rural poor. There are elements of advocacy that still hold real value for the land-use practitioner, but unfortunately, we tend to think of the theory only in terms of social justice issues.

With the continuing evolution of planning theory from the land-use practitioner's perspective, we continued to see a further drift away from an ends/directive orientation toward social processes and fragmentation. Transactive theory was an attempt to equally balance and combine directive and diffuse approaches to power in a strategic retreat from the criticisms of the synoptic models applied in the 1960s. John Forester's communicative theory has a similar orientation, continuing the trend toward means and social processes, but like John Friedmann, he continues to have some concern for results or end products (Forester, 1989). Communitarianism likewise retains some concern for results, but takes a hard movement away from directive approaches toward fragmentation (Etzioni, 1988). However, it was a fragmentation orientation to power that was decidedly anti-market, or at least not oriented toward current market theories that place the individual at the heart of decentralized power as an organizational force. Finally, post-modernism moves so far toward both the social processes and fragmentation axis as to represent the antithesis of ends-oriented directive planning.

These trends in planning theory leave the land-use practitioner both conflicted and adrift. In the search for models or techniques of practice that render results, the physical planner confronts a number of contradictions. How does one reconcile the need for regional coordination to make current command-and-control planning approaches work without being directive and overbearing at the community level? Why should you strive to empower community activism and social preferences when the outcome is exclusionary zoning and the rejection of your professional commitment to spatial order, efficiency, and conservation? How do you convert and apply theory that is principally concerned with social justice and issues of equity when your professional focus is physical development and the natural environment? How do you define or interpret the public interest without imposing your own values, thus compromising principles of self-determination and communitarianism?

Market-based planning models suggest answers to these questions by offering a different perspective. In the end-means, directive-diffuse typology that has been suggested, market-based planning models find themselves located in the lower left quadrant of the schematic. These are models that suggest a strong commitment to diffuse power through individual actions in the marketplace. They categorically reject top-down applications of planning except in the circumstances of public goods and externalities, and even in those circumstances forms of private regulation are to be preferred over public interventions. Urban form and land-use are to be organized by individual preference through market institutions. These models are essentially neutral in the question of ends or means orientation. Whatever ends are generated by market mechanisms, given the institutional rules of the game to deal with public goods and externalities, are the desired ends. It is a self-fulfilling prophecy. The concern for social process, or means, is accomplished through free markets and individualism. It is an outlook that matches closely with the dominant subculture of America – competitive individualism, not egalitarianism.

CBIP also finds itself in that lower left quadrant of the typology, but it has some distinct differences with market-based models. It has a strong ends orientation with a normative focus. It is a model that says physical results count – they count in life satisfaction, social justice, and in environmental sustainability for current and future generations. It is an outlook that suggests that the orientation of planners should be far more than the designated land-use conscience of a society, concerned only with public goods and externalities. Instead, it suggests that planners have a role to play as the designers and potential manufacturers of a social and physical product, but that product and the planners that produce it in whatever configuration, must compete in the political and economic marketplace just like any other interest. While there is no position of professional privilege, there is correspondingly every right to compete within the bounds of ethical behavior and market institutions.

CBIP also differs from market-based models in its orientation to directive or diffuse approaches to power and implementation. Unlike market-based proposals for planning practice that prescribe a diffuse approach to power through market institutions, CBIP is more techniques-neutral, recognizing the role that culture and human behavior should play in guiding the design of implementation mechanisms. The model of CBIP supports using any configuration of directive or diffuse strategies so long as they are efficient and effective, simultaneously satisfying five tests of performance. In the American culture, that implies behavioral incentives, market sensitivity, and the application of libertarian paternalism more than command–and–control mechanisms based on hierarchism.

A Question of Ethics and the Public Interest

The concept of CBIP clearly draws upon the heritage of existing planning theory and the theoretical contributions of a number of other disciplines. Like John Friedmann's social learning typology in planning, its origins lie with the American pragmatism of John Dewey in learning by doing (Friedmann, 1997). It has strong connections to the communicative planning practice model of John Forester and his proposition that "to be rational, be political" (Forester, 1989). But unlike Forester's model, it advocates communicative action not so much at the interpersonal level, but in the context of modern American culture, with tactical tools of influence aimed at various public sub-markets. Like the shifts we have seen in lobbying practice in the last decade, it is a model that not only supports the direct application of influence aimed at the seat of power, but also indirectly, by influencing the public opinions that drive policy formulation.

In addition, CBIP is clearly an advocacy-based model with elements from the social mobilization school. CBIP represents a general trend away from the notion of neutral objectivity (Hudson, 1979). And like the advocacy school, it could be criticized for continuing to place the planner in the role as expert, except that CBIP makes no such claim as will be explored in the question of ethics. It is a model of empowerment, political advocacy, and policy competition within democratic institutions. Returning to the typology of planning theories suggested previously, CBIP is placed with a strong orientation to *ends* as opposed to a *means* focus, similar to synoptic theory. But unlike both advocacy and synoptic theory, CBIP is placed in the middle of the directive/fragmentation axis. The reason for this placement is the nature of the tools and approach that CBIP represents. CBIP relies on tools of influence and behaviorism in a competitive political-policy and market environment. It blends both concepts of directive and diffuse practice.

CBIP draws upon many different heritages and it shares with these heritages the fundamental questions that plague each model when applied in practice. John Friedmann has effectively distilled these issues down to a number of key questions that face each of his four identified schools of planning: policy analysis, social reform, social learning, and social mobilization (Friedmann, 1987). The questions that Friedmann and every practicing planner confront are in the end, ones of professional and personal ethics. The following discussion addresses these questions in the potential application of CBIP as a model.

What is the Nature of the Public Interest?

In explaining the political basis of regulation and planning interventions, three general schools have emerged — public interest, interest group, and private interest theories. Under public interest theory, those seeking to institute or develop regulations are acting in pursuit of public rather than private interests. Planners theoretically are disinterested while serving in an expert role in the context of neither substituting their own personal values that may be biased, nor being motivated by political or other personal considerations. Moreover, since planners only act, by and large, in an advisory capacity in America, public interest theories of regulation imply that elected policy-makers also act in a disinterested fashion concerned only with public interests. The assumptions of disinterested action, among others, have come under substantial criticism.

In contrast, interest group theories postulate that the conventional divisions between public and private spheres of power have lost a substantial amount of their distinction in modern political and regulatory institutions. Large institutions, whether corporations, labor, government agencies or interests organized under non-profit associations, all have an integrated relationship in public policy and regulation that muddles the distinction between public and private spheres (Hancher & Moran, 1989; Mitnick, 1980). Under interest group theories, regulators, such as planners, implement and administer systems that represent negotiated settlements between organized interests and government institutions. Private interest theories, notably public choice theory and the Chicago school of economic interest, go one step further in challenging the public interest model of regulatory behavior. Under private interest theories it is assumed that all parties in regulation are motivated to maximize personal utility whether the politician, planner, or landowner (Peltzman,

1976; G. Stigler, 1971). Both interest group and private interest theories of regulation imply a problem where the regulator can be "captured" by private interests and cease to serve in the public interest even if not engaged in their own self-interested behavior.

When a profession stakes its entire ethical standard of practice on serving the public interest as Friedmann intimates, "just what characteristics of the good society, the social ideal are to be realized in practice, now or in the future?" (Friedmann, 1997). The flagship of the American Planning Association's ethical standards upon which most of professional practice supposedly depends, is "to serve the public interest" (APA 2002). It is also the foundation of contemporary planning theory. The standard assumes that the contents of the term have some universality and definability. It also assumes that planning is primarily a public enterprise and that planners are capable of serving without personal biases or latent self-interested behavior.

APA attempts to bracket the concept with six elements: long-range outlook, interrelatedness, full information, citizen participation (not citizen control), expanded choice, and protection of the natural environment. In contrast, consider the position of many political theorists that the public interest is an illusory concept unless the phrase means, "only an accumulation of individual wants, the merits of which others have no public right to judge" (Lucy, 1996).

Intellectually conscious practitioners quickly become aware that there is no reasonable way to define the concept of public interest under current planning theories without imposing their own moral judgments. It is done repeatedly under the veil of social processes and public involvement. In so doing, we commit a serious breach of ethics that is most often ignored, that of intentionally or unintentionally misrepresenting personal politics and positions as public mandate and the moral high ground. The only ethical solution for this dilemma is full disclosure. For the planner, public or private, that means abandoning any pretense of neutral objectivity in the definition of public interest. The public interest in Western contemporary society can only be defined through open participatory democratic processes and countervailing systems of judicial oversight to protect minority rights. That raises the next linked question that both practitioners and planning theorists face – the relation of planning to politics.

What is the Proper Relation of Planning to Politics and Power?

The CBIP concept makes a fundamental break with current planning theories and APA's conception of ethical practice. As has been contended here, it is impossible for the land planner to intellectually and ethically reconcile the position of communitarianism, citizen participation, and participatory democracy, with the notion of defining the public interest as neutral intermediaries. To pretend objectivity behind a smoke screen of artificially constructed citizen participation processes is simply disingenuous.

Planners are and should be wary of the common defects in citizen participation. Our standard participation tools are subject to manipulation and are not representative samples of the population or deliberative sentiment. Moreover, we are dealing with issues of great complexity in which the average citizen has neither the time nor the inclination to become fully conversant. As a profession, we lack internal agreement and substantive answers ourselves. Why should we expect faulty citizen participation processes to provide clarity where we cannot as a profession?

The CBIP model reconciles the planner's dilemma by advocating an overt and personal political advocacy position of practice. It replaces the epistemological roots of practice with a foundation of personal ethical beliefs. The profession can only resolve the logical incompatibility and ethical breech of assuming to act as the interpreters of the public interest by coming out from behind the veil of neutral objectivity. By encouraging the planner to compete using the recognized tools of influence, new product development and marketing, we likely improve performance and resolve an ethical dilemma.

The only way for the public planner to maintain moral legitimacy in a participatory democracy is by having a direct relationship with the society's recognized mechanisms for political action and power establishment. As Lucy points out, "while elections have many faults – including being too unfocused on planning issues to provide clear guidance – they do offer the widest forum for participation" (Lucy, 1996). Within the American culture a model of competition and approved mechanisms of influence is the format under which different policy agendas vie for adoption and implementation. If we choose to abstain from playing in the game according to the rules as established within the culture itself, then we should not expect to be effective in advancing personal ideals of practice. Different planning ideologies, as represented by the various views of practitioners, should expect to compete in the electoral process. It makes far more sense to elect your planner and her or his associated ideology than it does to elect the local sheriff. To do so will automatically raise planning issues higher in the public consciousness and stimulate the necessary societal debates. It will also morally empower the victors with some type of public mandate, as flawed as the process may be.

Effective planning theory for the practitioner must be an integrated system whereby ethical means is the natural choice for effective goal attainment. This implies that for practitioners to be effective while simultaneously being true to their personalized sense of ethics, full political practice is required with all the tools of influence customarily employed in American culture linked to complete professional disclosure.

CBIP is ethical as a model of practice, arguably more ethical than current models, but only under the following principles. It must be undertaken in such a way as to ensure the right to accurate information and informed decisions. The planner must practice full disclosure of personal positions rather than assuming the posture of representative of an objective standard of public interest. In addition, ethical practice in a pluralistic democracy implies the right of society to choose and to have redress. Authoritarian approaches, regionalism, and heavy reliance on command-and-control tools can only be legitimized when overtly explained and selected by the general public in the realm of public policy debate. For the public planning director and major planning initiatives that means being subjected to the electoral process. Explicitly competing in the policy marketplace with other points of view, utilizing widely accepted tools of political and market influence, may be the only ethical and effective model of land planning practice in the American culture.

Chapter Four

Culture and Planning

One way to comprehend the American land-use planning experience is to consider American culture and its interplay with the nation's land base and development heritage. Land-use patterns and development preferences reflect cultural traits. Cultural conventions, including the values underlying personal and collective behaviors, influence landscapes, planning regimes, and the public response to those regimes. The public perception of density, neighborhood design, and architecture is impacted by cultural norms and values. As Joan Iverson Nassauer reports in her work on landscape ecology, "Landscapes are a concrete, public statement of culture" and "cultural conventions and customs directly affect what people notice, find interesting, and prefer about the landscape" (Nassauer, 1992; Nassauer, 1995).

Implicit in this argument is that the development patterns of American society are not a product of centralized government planning and policy gone awry or an engineered result cleverly conceived by business interests and sold to an unwitting general public, although both of these factors are present. More accurately, they are a publicly-driven, bottom-up creation - the embodiment of a set of values with imagery and symbolism that is manifested in administrative and judicial land-use policy, as well as landowner and consumer behavior.

If culture provides at least a partial explanation for how planning programs evolve and how publics react to them, then program design will benefit from a closer nexus with cultural traits. By better understanding cultural values, planners are capable of making more reasoned adjustments in practice that will enhance social validity and political acceptance.

The concept of culture has defied a uniform definition in the social sciences. Anthropologists tend to assign to the term a broad and inclusive definition, encompassing social relations and a way of life, while sociologists and political scientists focus on values, symbols, attitudes and norms (Benedict, 1934; Thompson, Ellis, & Wildavsky, 1990). Social conventions and cultural variations can exist in multiple dimensions – geographic, political, socio-economic, demographic and professional.

There are management implications for planning in all these dimensions, often where they have to be considered simultaneously in program design. This chapter addresses a number of specific cultural considerations in American planning by looking at several of these dimensions.

Grid-Group Typology and Cultural Theory

It is important to introduce a concept that will find direct application throughout the remainder of this book. That theoretical construct is cultural theory. It finds its early roots in sociology and the later work of Mary Douglas, a cultural anthropologist (Douglas, 1978, 1982, 1996). Most recently it has been advanced in work related to applied political science (Ellis, 1993; Lockhart, 1999; Thompson et al., 1990; Wildavsky, 1994). Grid-Group typology and cultural theory is relatively young by the standard of major theories, having been first created in its modern state about 30 years ago. Heretofore, it has not been extended as a tool in land planning and is relatively unknown in the profession.

For planners applying a culturally-sensitive approach, the grid-group typology provides a utilitarian framework or systems outlook to organize behavioral-based land-use strategies. The format provides an effective way to understand and characterize the various elements of American culture, and in particular, it helps to identify the likely behavioral response of each of four major cultural groups to various planning interventions, their preferences and perceptions.

The grid-group typology, first created by Douglas, recognizes four major and distinct political cultures: Competitive Individualism, Egalitarianism, Hierarchicalism, and Fatalism (Douglas, 1978). The focal point of the typology is an explanation of the modes of social control in a society and how individuals align themselves into various cultural camps based on that consideration. In providing a framework on regulatory cultures, the theory goes to the heart of political preferences and outlook. Under the construct of the theory, these four categories capture the range of human preferences and justifications that constitute cultural outlook in the area of social control.

Advocates of the theory maintain that every society in the world can be characterized by these four cultural subsets, and while a given society can be dominated by any one of them, societies have all four groups present. In fact, a case can be made that no healthy society can thrive without the unique contributions that three out of the four groups have to offer. The expansive free market benefits of competitive individualism cannot function without the regulatory oversight, market rules and legal systems of hierarchy and the bureaucracies that it spawns. The egalitarian preference and contribution of non-hierarchical social support networks cannot sustain a society without the structure of top-down management or dynamism of market forces. Without the coalition of egalitarian support for small group self-management and competitive individualism's disdain for hierarchical control, participatory democracy is at risk. Three of the four individual political cultures provide contributions that the others cannot produce. As Lockhart notes, "In this sense, societies tend to be multi-cultural"(Lockhart, 1999).

The four culture types are derived from a typology based on two social dimensions or patterns of social relations. The first is the degree that an individual subscribes to and respects externally imposed prescriptions in the form of institutional controls, regulations, and hierarchical relationships (grid). The more one subscribes to grid-based controls on behavior, the more one concedes individual autonomy by adhering to their assumed station in life and supporting a regulatory-based society.

The second dimension is the extent that an individual desires to be socially affiliated with others or incorporated into bounded units (group). Social control through group affiliation is a form of social-psychology power whereby group members can manipulate behavior in the creation and application of strong group boundaries. The stronger the desire for social group affiliation by an individual, the more one submits to social group norms and the less to individual autonomy.

Both social dimensions, grid and group, create boundaries and restrict individual autonomy to the extent that the individual endorses one or both, but each does so in a different way that results in different political cultures. The two dimensions, grid and group, when combined, generate only four distinct social-relation outlooks, although variations can be identified in each of the major groups (see Illustration no. 4).

Competitive Individualists

Competitive individualism is the dominant culture in America, reinforced by social norms, institutions, and government policy. As a political culture, competitive individualism cuts across political parties, religious and nonsectarian affiliations, races, regions, and the bipolar characterizations of conservatives and liberals. American LIVES, Inc., a market research and opinion polling firm, estimated in more than a decade of extensive profile surveys, that competitive individualism, roughly translated by the firm as "moderns," constituted 48 percent of the adult population in 1999 (Ray & Anderson, 2000). American LIVES recognizes four sub-groups within the classification: business conservatives (8 percent of public), conventional moderns (12 percent of public), striving center (13 percent of public) and alienated moderns (15 percent of public).

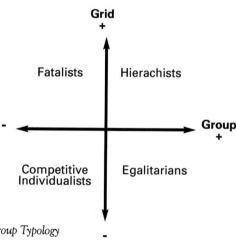

Illustration no. 4 – Grid/Group Typology

Competitive individualists harbor weak feelings for group membership and its accompanying sense of social obligation to the collective (group), and they are suspicious or rebellious against institutional authority or external prescription (grid). They prefer a society that functions largely under self-regulation by private social contract and market enforced discipline. They do not like externally-imposed limits. Community intervention, either governmental or nongovernmental, is endorsed only as a necessary limitation to allow markets to function and societies to maintain basic order. As Thompson and others have noted, in the individualistic subculture, "all boundaries are provisional and subject to negotiation" (Ellis, 1993; Thompson et al., 1990).

Competitive individualists, practicing a form of economic conservatism, believe that society should be organized around competitive principles, free market enterprise, and the invisible hand of Adam Smith, principles that they believe also apply to the practice of democracy. Self-interested behavior is the expected and desired norm, elevated to the principle of social welfare maximization under neoclassical economics. As such, competition and wealth accumulation is embraced as a cultural objective in the name of societal material progress. Consumption is a continuous source of personal fulfillment, a viewpoint so committed to by competitive individualists, that they have a difficult time conceiving of an alternative perspective. In the realm of competitive individualism, the natural environment is a bountiful resource to be employed for human enrichment, not conserved for future generations or other outlooks.

Competitive individualism in America has strong roots that have been supported by historic events that span the very creation of the nation to the present day. Early settlers rejected the hierarchical culture of Europe and feared the power and restraints of centralized institutions. Wilderness settlement patterns that extended for 200 years through the westward expansion required and reinforced self-reliance and independence, and a national self-image of rugged individualism. The nation's founding principles as embodied in the Constitution and Bill of Rights were Lockonian in philosophy, representing an anti-authority consensus and strong embedment of the sanctity of private property and personal freedom. Those with a commitment to a hierarchical social culture were largely marginalized or migrated out of the country.

Successive emigrant waves over time have attracted those with the individualist sub-culture orientation in the pursuit of the American Dream, reinforcing and re-energizing the competitive individualist orientation.

As substantiated in polling profiles, the concepts of freedom and equality have specific meanings for the competitive individualists that vary from other subcultures (Ellis, 1993). Equality means equal access to compete, that is, equality of process under the law and opportunity to engage in economic pursuit, not equality of results. It is an attitude embodied in the American idiom, sink or swim. The definitional outlook has specific implications in areas such as affirmative action, income equality, tax policy, and local concerns such as exclusionary zoning and housing affordability. The equal opportunity to compete legitimizes the results of both those that win or lose in the game, and it also embodies equal justice and fairness before the law. Freedom is interpreted as the freedom to pursue self-interest, freedom of speech and freedom of religion.

The American LIVES polling results in the areas of values, attitudes and opinions for moderns strongly correlate with the predictions and observations of the grid-group typology for competitive individualists (Ray & Anderson, 2000). They found that among the political subcultures, moderns were the most likely to support financial materialism and give success a high priority in life, while they were the least altruistic, idealistic and relationship-oriented of the major groups. They do not support the Religious Right, are cynical about politics, and prefer to put their wealth on display in a conspicuous manner – big houses on big lots.

Competitive individualists perceive risk primarily as an enterprising opportunity and fear potential outcomes that could limit freedom of self-interest (Rippl, 2002). Personal security for the political subculture comes in self-reliance, independence, and not being beholden to others. The implications for land planning in America are many as the outlook translates into a strong desire for autonomy, mobility, and freedom of action with minimal government restraint.

The Egalitarians (Communitarians)

Egalitarianism is the principal rival to competitive individualism in America. Market analysis by American LIVES and Paul Ray has a closely-aligned values culture that they describe as the cultural creatives

(Ray & Anderson, 2000). They place the psychographics profile at 26 percent of the American adult public. Demographically, the core group of egalitarians has a disproportionately large percentage of women at 66 percent. Egalitarians tend to be educated professionals who hold strong views on intolerant behavior. Ray notes in their marketing research that among all political subcultures, they have the strongest desire to rebuild neighborhoods and create a sense of community with a response rate of 90 percent. They also hold pro-environment values, believe in voluntary simplicity, and more than other groups, tend to be activists.

The egalitarian social outlook prefers group affiliation and strong group boundaries. Egalitarians believe in voluntary small group affiliation where decision-making is by group consensus and collaboration, resulting in a hypothetical social solidarity. As such, participation, process, and a strong civil society are of pivotal importance to the political subculture. As Richard Ellis notes, "Egalitarians condemn individualism for isolating the individual from the community, dimming the sense of collective purpose, damming the springs of civic virtue, and creating unconscionable inequalities" (Ellis, 1993).

Like competitive individualists, egalitarians are resistant and suspicious of certain institutional controls (grid), particularly in America. With the competitive individualists, egalitarians have formed an anti-authority political culture coalition in America that dates to the debates between the Founding Fathers. Where individualists fear hierarchical control because of the risk to their freedom to engage in unencumbered self-interested behavior, egalitarians fear the imposition of social privilege, inequalities, and a stratified society enforced by hierarchical institutions. Their desired society is based on cooperation, not competition, and is also free of hierarchy and privilege.

One of the basic weaknesses in the construct, however, is its inability to claim legitimacy in leadership – a ship without a pilot and often more than one rudder. Without authority to exercise control over others, the construct of hierarchicalism, or the organizing principle of competitive markets in a collective free-for-all of self-interested behavior (individualism), egalitarianism faces a practical management dilemma in complex industrialized societies. Despite this limitation, egalitarianism has manifested itself in a form that successfully challenged the political culture of competitive individualism during several eras of

American history: Jacksonian populism; the cultural backlash to the Gilded Age – progressivism; the New Deal era; and the War on Poverty and the civil rights movement of the 1960s (Ellis, 1993).

Egalitarians perceive social progress not so much as wealth accumulation, but as social equity and solidarity. They would define equality in terms of not only access, but also of results. The concept of freedom is largely the freedom to participate directly in the democratic process, not by proxy (Ellis, 1993). They are disenchanted with materialism, status, and self-interested behavior. They oppose risks that may heighten social stratification or constitute perceived dangers to large groups of people or future generations (Rippl, 2002). As such, they see nature as fragile, a resource to be protected and preserved, and adhere to the concept of sustainability.

From a planner's perspective, the following marketing research conclusions are particularly salient. Egalitarians prefer older, authentic architecture, established neighborhoods with ample trees, and significant privacy. They prefer walkable communities and open space, and believe that master planned communities can effectively recreate community. They do not like status display homes, prefer hidden residences, internal and external privacy in design, and eclectic decoration styles that reflect understatement but high quality (Ray & Anderson, 2000). With conspicuous consumption endorsed by many competitive individualists, conspicuous virtue is the hallmark of egalitarians. Toyota's Prius hybrid, for example, which is not cost-effective for the consumer, was intentionally designed to be a distinctive symbol of personal enlightenment.

The Hierarchical Subculture

The Hierarchical subculture, sometimes referred to as traditionalism, subscribes to a higher level of social control by both group process and institutional direction. In its purist form, it is a philosophy that sees societies rationally organized into vertical collectives based on expertise, talent, and collective contribution. In this fashion, social welfare is maximized through strong external prescription and collective sacrifice of individual freedom. It is a cultural outlook concerned with the creation and preservation of expertise and order, one that often sees a market-based process as too haphazard, chaotic, and in need of control (Lockhart, 1999). It is also the foundation of bureaucratic forms of governance in the belief of benevolent paternalism and the power of experts to provide needed guidance, and as such, it is the basis for many government interventions.

In America, the hierarchical subculture defies political and ideological stereotypes. American LIVES, in their psychographics surveys, have found that the group is just as likely to be liberal or centrist as culturally conservative on many issues. Their work indicates that traditionalists constituted 24 percent of the adult American public in 1999, down from nearly 50 percent around World War II. Only 8 percent of the population can be classified as both religious conservatives and business conservatives. As a group they cross political parties and are strongly pro-environment. They see the natural and social worlds as requiring careful management, deferring to the limits recommended by experts. As a group in America, they tend to be concentrated in small towns and rural areas and harbor a nostalgic desire for stable communities and a feeling of certainty (Ray & Anderson, 2000).

Because of American cultural sensitivities, the use of the terms hierarchical or traditional can evoke certain negative images that can be misleading when considering the political subculture. The dominant political cultures of Britain and Europe fall within the classification - highly secular, humanist societies with strong pro-environment values. The highly successful land planning systems of Britain and Western Europe are built and supported on their hierarchical subcultures.

In America, the classification has never represented a serious challenge to the predominant culture of competitive individualism supported by the anti-authority fears of egalitarians. As such, America has never had the strong hierarchical institutions and values of England, Europe or even Canada. It is not by random chance, for instance, that of the four societies, only America did not evolve a nationalized nonprofit health care system.

Fatalism

When people find themselves controlled by institutions and excluded from group civic engagement or membership, they are relegated to a fatalist political subculture. The fatalist has little individual autonomy and no ability to influence the decision-making mechanisms that control his or her life. The institutions of slavery, totalitarian states, and life within certain communist regimes would be examples of this political subculture. Today, it constitutes a small element in the American cultural scene, although certain disadvantaged elements of American society subject to the nation's more serious social injustices, could arguably be included in the classification.

Grid –Group Typology and Planning

American political core values are often described as liberty, equality, individualism, democracy, pragmatism, free market enterprise, the rule of law under the Constitution, and a concern for limited government (Devine, 1972; Huntington, 1981). Robin Williams in his seminal book, *American Society: A Sociological Interpretation*, approaches a characterization of American culture from a slightly different perspective, blending political and sociological observations into central traits that you would expect in a society dominated by competitive individualism (Williams, 1960).

> *"American culture is organized around the attempt to actively master rather than passively accept. This tendency reveals itself through a positive encouragement of our desires, a stress on the positive nature of power, an approval of egocentrism, and other characteristics through which we assert ourselves.*
>
> *"American culture is more concerned with the external world of things and events, with the palpable and immediate, than the inner experience of meaning and effect. The emphasis is more on manipulation than on contemplation.*
>
> *"American culture tends to be open rather than closed. It emphasizes change, flux, movement; its central personality types are adaptive, accessible, outgoing, and assimilative.*
>
> *"American culture values horizontal interpersonal relationships above vertical relationships: peer relations, not superior-subordinate relations; equality rather than hierarchy.*
>
> *"American culture emphasizes individual personality rather than group identity and responsibility (Williams, 1960)."*

American society, while hardly homogeneous, does harbor a set of commonly held cultural beliefs, values, and attitudes that dominate in public policy outcomes. For American planning, the dominance of competitive individualism and its coalition with egalitarianism in forming an anti-authority bias, have major implications in the design of effective planning implementation schemes. Those implications can be categorized under four headings: 1) American optimism and its implications in a sense of entitlement, 2) the American expression of security in land development patterns, 3) American mobility, and, 4) antagonism toward hierarchical power.

American Optimism and Sense of Entitlement

In comparison to other cultures, America is a particularly optimistic society. We believe in and perpetuate the legend of the American Dream, that with hard work and talent our society of unbounded equal access allows individuals to achieve whatever level of success they choose. Seventy-one percent of Americans believe that most people who don't get ahead should not blame the system, but themselves. In eight separate nationwide surveys conducted between 1987 and 1997, 60 to 68 percent of Americans disagreed with the statement that hard work offers little guarantee of success (Washington, Kaiser, & Harvard, 1998). In contrast only 40 percent of Europeans believe that the poor have a chance to escape poverty. A majority of Europeans, except in the United Kingdom, believe success is outside of their control. For example, this belief is held by 68 percent of adult Germans (Inglehart, 1990).

Success in American society has increasingly been defined as material accumulation, financial independence, and power – an assumed formula for happiness and fulfillment. Combined with the mythology of the American Dream, the definition of success has resulted in a number of behavioral aberrations. American optimism, fueled by popular media images of success that permeate nearly every venue of mass communication, has been transformed in the general public's mind from an achievable objective to a near birthright or sense of entitlement. In recent surveys, 68 percent of American teens assumed that one day they would be wealthy, while more than 60 percent of college students seriously expected to be millionaires (Washington, Kaiser, & Harvard, 2005).

As the sense of entitlement grows in American culture, it has specific ramifications for land planning. Political leaders, motivated by election prospects, are abhorrent to suggest conservation strategies, given previous public reactions to calls for personal sacrifice. Americans have never liked being told there are limits. American political campaigns are constructed around images of opportunity, personal advancement and optimism, not natural constraints or restrictions. Cheap gasoline and unfettered highways are considered to be, when they occur, not a pleasant result of current supply-and-demand circumstances, but a near fundamental right by major elements of the American public.

These same dynamics are at play for planners in an American society steeped in a sense of entitlement. When individuals perceive a sense of entitlement, for instance, the right to develop their property without restriction in the pursuit of the American Dream, they will interpret it as unfair that these activities may be restricted. Equally, existing neighborhoods will perceive it as unfair that open space is converted or roads become more congested due to growth because of their sense of entitlement. Given the cultural traits of optimism and entitlement, planning interventions in America need to be framed in terms of expanded opportunity or enhanced lifestyle, not appeals to self-sacrifice. In some circumstances, the design of planning tools, such as zoning and subdivision ordinances, should avoid the creation of a sense of entitlement. Just as many employers are now eliminating permanent salary increases, replacing them with the concept of potential annual bonuses based on performance, so too do planners have to explore how to more effectively manage the endowment effect and a growing sense of entitlement in land regulation.

American Expression of Security

In a culture with the dominant outlook of competitive individualism, personal security is found in self-reliance, or as Jeremy Rifkin notes, exclusivity, not community (Rifkin, 2005b). To obtain self-reliance implies a scramble for wealth, since one can't rely on the European model of communitarianism as an insurance policy. In the act of self-preservation to obtain wealth, individuals operate at a competitive advantage when given increased freedom of action and adaptive mobility, and they will feel threatened when opportunity is restricted. In America, making money and preserving assets has always been more than blind ambition, it has also been about self-preservation.

These cultural attitudes that have manifested themselves in various forms of governmental policy and land-use law, have ramifications in planning practice. America's self-interested culture is conflicted between an anti-authority bias that permits the unencumbered pursuit of personal wealth and the desire for governmental controls to protect or enhance that wealth once acquired. Land planners are often caught in the middle. Communities, on occasion, are now generating demands for governmental action that exceed their own cultural support for hierarchical controls.

These same security implications in a competitive individualist society often manifest themselves in a general disengagement from community. In European society, freedom and security are found in community, which is quite the opposite of American culture. If it is every man, woman, and child for themselves, the family becomes the principal, if not the only, unit of social support, and community engagement and responsibilities take a distant back seat. These feelings of disengagement, in turn, feed the taste for exclusivity and privacy in housing development patterns. Housing exclusivity becomes a symbol of independence and refuge from a hostile society, in which one is always in competition rather than being cradled in community embeddedness and social support.

American Mobility, Hyper-Activity and Lifestyle Complexity

Dr. Dean Ornish, a pioneer in heart disease research who has explored the role of community embeddedness and social support systems in human health, reports asking audiences as large as 3,000 people:
"*How many of you can say all four of these statements are true? (Ornish, 1997)*

- *You live in the same neighborhood in which you were born and raised and most of your old neighbors are still there.*
- *You've been going to the same church or synagogue for at least ten years and most of your fellow congregants from ten years ago are still there.*
- *You've been at the same job for at least ten years and most of your coworkers from ten years ago are still there.*
- *You have an extended family living nearby whom you see regularly.*"

He reports no more than three or four hands will go up in the audiences of several thousand people, including those held in rural communities. As he acknowledges, most of the hands would have gone up in the 1950s.

American society, which has always been marked by dynamism, has changed in the last half-century as hyperactivity and mobility have become the norm. Americans will on average move every six to seven years, with housing now conceived by most Americans as primarily an investment vehicle with little emotional attachment. It is a house, not a home. The average American worker spends far more time on the job than British or European counterparts; ten more weeks a year than the average German worker (Mishel & Bernstein, 2001).

Lifestyle complexity for the average American is reflected in high average daily trips per household with suburban residences generating six to ten trips per day. Dual career families with active households find it nearly impossible to coordinate housing location with daily activities without resorting to excessive use of the automobile. Even two income households with an established preference for pedestrian-oriented urban villages have been shown to have little reduction in weekday car usage (Jarvis, 2003).

The issue and solution are less ones of supportive urban design than the lifestyle preferences and learned behaviors of Americans. While enhanced design can contribute to the opportunity for neighborliness, a developed sense of community is strongly rooted in the enduring social relations and history that an individual has in the broader community outside of the immediate family. America's modern version of an individualist nomadic lifestyle linked to a frenetic pace, inherently impacts both planning process and planning outcome. The best designs can only provide an environment for sense of community - they cannot ensure it. That outcome lies more with the chosen lifestyles of residences.

European culture has a rich heritage of community connection and leisure time social outreach that is supported by an orientation toward quality of life more so than standard of living. American culture does not. Simply providing the physical environment, a retrofit task of unimaginable proportions, is not going to transform the current addiction of certain American subcultures to economic motion over social connection and deep play, especially that observed in the competitive individualist outlook.

The issue of mobility also impacts public outlook and debate on community improvements, impact fees, and thinly-veiled efforts at cost shifting. Who better to blame for community underfunding of infrastructure and who better to charge than the politically-absent future buyers of new homes? The building community concedes to impact fees, basically a tax on mobile Americans who make the mistake of buying a new home as opposed to an existing home, not because there is equity in the approach when examined closely, but because of political realities for the industry.

Self-interest and Antagonism toward Hierarchical Power

America's dominant political culture of competitive individualism has strongly embraced the paradigm of neoclassical economics, which in turn has enshrined self-interest as a near virtue, not a character flaw. Combined with a historical antagonism toward government institutions, the two themes have blended together with cultural implications in altruistic behavior, consumerism, and private property rights.

American society has a general resistance to government controls, unless it is perceived that such controls can be utilized to advance or protect one's own self-interests. Consider that in Gallup and Pew national surveys taken since 1987, 60 to 70 percent of Americans agree strongly or somewhat agree that government controls too much of their daily lives (Washington et al., 1998). In Gallup polls taken since 1965, six out of ten Americans believe that big government represents the largest threat to the nation, while only 25 percent believe that it is big business, and 11 percent believe that it is big labor (Washington et al., 1998). Only an average of 30 percent of the American public polled from 1966 through 1998 trusts the government to usually do the right thing, and in polls conducted since 1980, 59 to 65 percent of the American public agree with the statement that the government has gone too far in regulating businesses and interfering with the free enterprise system (Washington et al., 1998).

A fierce commitment to private property rights plays a particularly important role in American culture. A recent example is the public and political reaction to the 2005 Kelo v. New London U.S. Supreme Court decision on eminent domain. In July of 2005, polling indicated that 68 percent of the American public was opposed to the taking of private property by eminent domain for any purpose. By November of 2005 after the details of the decision had became more widely reported, 81 percent of the public opposed the use of eminent domain (Saint, 2006). Five states enacted legislation in 2005 curtailing the power of eminent domain by local governments in response to the Supreme Court decision. In 2006, 42 of the 43 states that had gone into session had bills introduced to curtail eminent domain powers and 12 states passed and enacted such laws (NCSL, 2006). The core of America's land-use, real estate, and corporate law, centers on the protection and judicature of real and intellectual property rights.

The implications to land-use planning in a culture immersed in an ethic of self-interested behavior and resistance to government controls are substantial. Command-and-control planning formats that are rigorous enough to be effective are typically resisted, both politically and by the open market reactions of the general public. Planning formats that offer a full range of options, in short, choice, linked to creative behavioral incentives and consequences are likely to be better received than attempts at complete restriction. But there are limits. Incentive-based regulatory approaches in the American culture will likely never be as efficient or as effective as the culturally accepted hierarchical approaches of Britain and Western Europe.

Grid-Group Typology and a Cross-Cultural Perspective of Planning

Since the grid-group typology is theoretically universal across all cultures and nations, it offers another application in planning. By comparing dominant national cultures against planning regimes, insight can be gained into what works where and why. One potential clue to improved performance in America is that in other developed economies, similar planning formats are employed, often with radically superior results. Why the different results, for instance, between American and Great Britain given our shared heritage of law and basic command-and-control orientation? The answer likely lies in the base culture and the sensitivity of any given planning strategy or intervention to that culture. Indeed, a significant number of technically appropriate solutions have proven unworkable in American practice because the cultural climate has either been missed entirely or is underappreciated.

Unlike American culture, the British and European societies have particular histories and dominant values that are hierarchical and egalitarian in nature. Where the American Dream implies equal opportunity to pursue individual financial success, European culture emphasizes community relationships and obligations, and a long-established respect for authority. Jeremy Rifkin describes European culture in contrast to American society as one that, "Emphasizes community relationships over individual autonomy, cultural diversity over assimilation, quality-of-life over the accumulation of wealth, sustainable development over unlimited material growth, deep play over unrelenting toil, universal human rights and the rights of nature over property rights, and global cooperation over the unilateral exercise of power"(Rifkin, 2005b).

The American interpretation of egalitarianism under the grid-group typology suggests not only an orientation toward community relationships, but also a suspicion of institutional controls. That interpretation may be colored by the unique history of egalitarianism in America and may be an overstatement of the true views on the government's role under the subculture in other nations. The purity and strength of views suggested under the grid-group typology is also more likely with political elites than the general citizenry, and likely intensifies in the individual as citizen activism increases (Coughlin & Lockhart, 1998). Regardless, egalitarianism in Great Britain and Europe has combined forces with hierarchical social and political systems to render a cultural consensus on the nature of governance. The subculture with the least amount of moral authority within European society is competitive individualism. Great Britain straddles this divide between America and Europe with a slightly stronger element of competitive individualism in the English culture, but it is still significantly constrained by American standards.

To fully appreciate the role that dominant political cultures play in planning outcomes, consider the contrast between American and Great Britain practice. Land planning practice in Great Britain consistently yields results that are unequaled almost anywhere in America if judged by physical outcome. England as a physical subset of Great Britain is somewhat smaller than Oregon with a population that is 25 percent greater than California. It is nine times more densely populated than America and triple the European average density. It is, in fact, one of the most densely populated nations in the world. Yet they have largely succeeded in maintaining rural character and bucolic landscapes between urban concentrations. Rural villages and mid-size towns across the nation tend to have compact form and distinct edges, far more physically noticeable than any urban growth boundary program in America. Their 11 National Parks and 40 designated Areas of Outstanding Natural Beauty constitute nearly one-fifth of England and Wales. Amazingly, the first of these designations did not begin until 1951, and all are in private ownership of 90 percent or more, managed through a combination of independent park authorities and local Council planning regimes at a level of regulatory stringency that is unimaginable in American society.

Urban development is compact and green belt separation between urban concentrations nearly sacred except in those areas where they specifically desire to accommodate growth. Metropolitan densities are three to four times that of America, while suburban densities are four times as dense (Newman & Kenworthy, 1989). Growth pressure is accommodated but specifically directed to desired jurisdictions and regions by national planning schemes coordinated through Council plans. New residential construction units are specially allocated at the national level to regional areas by hierarchical planning formats based on five-year projections. By national guidance, 60 percent of all new development is directed to urban renewal and brownfield sites, whereby the performance of local planners and Councils is closely monitored under a national reporting system to ensure that planning goals are met. National planning objectives based on the greater public interest routinely trump local resistance.

The English Heritage program has listed over 500,000 structures, nearly 1 in 40, in a non-voluntary secret process with secret criteria under which the building owner has no appeal after receiving one of three restrictive designations to protect the architectural heritage of the building. Listed properties average a 25 percent increase in market value as a result of receiving the designation (Burden, 2005). In addition, there are 10,000 areas of special archeological or historic interest designated with special planning protections, including some of substantial size such as the Yorkshire Dales Special Barn District.

England strongly promotes pedestrianism in both urban and rural environments. The nation maintains nearly 140,000 miles of trails, including 200 designated Long Distance Paths of national status. The

2002 Open Countryside Act opened most private moorlands above a certain elevation to public access. Nearly 25 percent of all journeys in Great Britain are made entirely on foot and 78 percent of journeys under one mile are walked (Ramblers, 2006). In 1998, 27 percent of the population found it unnecessary to own a car (National, 1997).

To achieve the effects described above, Great Britain relies heavily on a rigorous command-and-control planning format mixed with an integrated program of incentives, subsidies, and extensive use of public/private partnerships. The 1947 Town and Country Planning Act essentially nationalized development rights and the increased property values that the permitting of development entails. England has no "taking issue" since private development rights do not exist in most circumstances. There is also a broad acceptance that land development is a public issue, not a private matter.

As the Anglo-American planner, Barry Cullingworth, has noted in his comparative analysis of the planning atmospheres in the two countries, "American planning is largely a matter of anticipating trends, while in Britain there is a conscious effort to bend them in publicly desirable directions" (Cullingworth, 1993). He makes an interesting observation that goes to the heart of the two respective cultures. In hierarchical and egalitarian Britain, planning is clearly focused on advancing the broader public interest while in the competitive individualist society of America, the system is more often focused on preventing or resolving conflict between private interests through zoning separation and land-use law dispute resolution. America's system is far more legalistic than Great Britain's or Europe's with our appeal rights and extensive case law. In Great Britain, planners and elected officials control the land-use system. In America, that power is more likely directed to judicial process in the exercise of balancing private property rights with the public interest.

The British have a far greater respect for authority than Americans, placing trust and resources in the bureaucracy, matched by a demand for a high standard of professionalism and accountability. A rural English Council planning staff would typically have 20 to 40 planners specialized in their respective areas of responsibility, subject to periodic training at Council expense. Public deference is extended to the expertise of these planners with much of the decision-making authority lying directly with them. While in America, the same setting may have a staff of 2 to 5 people. In contrast to English planners, American planners are largely advisory, with administrative and judicial appeals present for even the most minor issues.

It is not being argued here that British and Western European planning formats need to be adopted in America to achieve results. Quite to the contrary, it is being suggested that at their foundation, they are not readily transferable between cultures. For the English to achieve the results that they do requires the imposition of regulatory regimes that would likely never be tolerated in American culture. They are generally successful in their planning programs, unlike American practice, because their strident hierarchical approaches coincide with dominant cultural values, contributing to a high level of social validity and political sustainability. That is, their planning systems are calibrated to dominant cultural traits to obtain results. Hierarchical social and political systems that are grounded in traditionalism and egalitarianism emphasize community responsibilities more than individual rights. As Barry Cullingworth notes about British practice, "Most planning applications, for example, are sub-judice until they have been decided. Thus neither the press nor the public are informed of them" (Cullingworth, 1993).

That is the antithesis of America's dominant political culture of competitive individualism. And yet at its core, American planning practice has attempted to impose the same fundamental approach as that employed in Great Britain and Western Europe.

Planning practice around the world tends to be hierarchical in nature, particularly at the implementation stage. Applied in America practice, planners have inherently been conflicted with the society's political culture of competitive individualism. Possibly more than any other factor, the failure as a profession to recognize this potential cultural divide has handicapped planning performance in the United States.

I suspect, without any quantitative evidence to support the position, that a majority of American land planners harbor a hierarchical cultural bias, but that the profession also contains a healthy subculture of egalitarians. Those of us that have chosen environmental and land development issues as our primary career interest, seem to place a particular emphasis on planning processes that render well-ordered, rational and comprehensive decisions. We have a desire for natural landscapes and urban form to be orderly, attractive, and managed on a sustainable basis, all in a society dominated by competitive individualism that conspires against hierarchical planning formats. The model that we can most strongly relate to and that has been readily developed in planning practice is a command-and-control hierarchical scheme based on comprehensive rationality. At its core, this is the British and European model. American planners attempt to reconcile and legitimize a top-down approach in an individualist culture through the application of egalitarian-oriented processes in public involvement, often disingenuously. In American culture, the approach has resulted in a train wreck of either weak and ineffectual regulatory schemes with market overrides, or programs characterized by low social validity and political instability. In some cases, both have been achieved simultaneously.

Conclusion

When planning interventions are conceived with sensitivity to cultural influences, they dramatically increase their power to persuade. When they are based solely on normative goals and lack grounding in cultural values and behavioral tendencies, their ability to influence preferences will be seriously handicapped. Cultural sensitivity under CBIP suggests the following principles:

- There exists certain latitude of change that is possible within cultural attitude zones. Program elements should be devised that avoid an obvious and identifiable confrontation with cultural tendencies. In some cases, that may mean clearly staying within current boundaries of cultural convention to maintain social validity. In others, diplomacy and calculation in technique are required when cultural evolution is the objective. The extent of change that can be engineered is expanded by the framing of the argument, effective issue management techniques in communications and public relations, demonstration projects, and by the redesign of planning institutions. On rare occasions, events can stimulate an entire paradigm shift.

- To achieve cultural sensitivity as a specific design criteria suggests that some American planning institutions need reconsideration.

Among those potential institutional changes, none may be more fundamental than a sector shift for the planning profession. It just may be that the only truly effective planning scheme in American culture is one that is fundamentally different from the models of other nations - private as opposed to public. In general, planners in the last four decades have chosen to define their profession as principally a public sector enterprise. Dispel that perspective and a new strategic approach emerges. There is nothing to prevent the American land planning profession from transforming itself into the nation's development profession using economics and the model of capitalism to influence public behavior. And there is nothing that says development can't be undertaken professionally as a non-profit or low margin exercise as, for instance, health care is practiced in other nations. The core of capitalist societies is market-based competition. Planners are more than capable of institutionally transforming development practices by offering a new model of competition into the land development marketplace – planners as the nation's premier and trend-setting developers. Such a change in outlook requires modifications in how we define the profession and how that new definition is institutionalized in planning education.

- Designing for the American culture implies a related set of institution changes that complement a stronger private sector role for the profession. Those institutional changes could be described as the engineering of a modified public interest model for planners as was suggested in the previous chapter. CBIP, in fact, has at its core one vision of that modified public interest model, replacing the current concept of a public planner as expert and facilitator in interventions for the public interest with an alternative role of open advocacy and market-based competition by the profession. This implies potentially making public planning director positions an elected office. It also suggests that in the American culture, the concept of zoning and other forms of land-use regulation should be framed as retained *public* property rights, managed in trust by government. By shifting the societal conception of the role of planning so that people internalize the concept of public goods as a private entitlement collectively retained, as opposed to planning as simply government regulation, the role of planning may become better calibrated to the American cultural outlook.

- By interpreting much of the conflict that occurs in American planning as cultural conflicts between competing ideologies, it may be possible to coordinate customized approaches for each of the individual political subcultures. For example, ordinance provisions and non-regulatory planning mechanisms can be customized to cater to cultural predispositions, whether of the dominant or co-dominant political cultural groups. By avoiding a monolithic characterization of national culture, recognizing the influence of other political subcultures, it is at least theoretically possible to design planning interventions that follow multiple pathways, each designed to appeal to a separate cultural audience if the circumstances warrant such an approach.

One example of this type of approach utilized in Virginia is provided in Chapter Seven. A rural planning regime, that includes zoning and subdivision ordinance provisions, is customized along two separate formats to appeal to politically and behaviorally different cultural elements in the community. This type of advanced cultural profiling is already applied in the private sector in community design considerations. There is recognition in psychographic profiling, for example, that egalitarians have fundamentally different housing and community preferences than either competitive individualists or hierarchists.

Ladera Ranch, a planned community in Orange County, California with 16,000 residents, is engaged in this type of subculture design and marketing format. Various villages within the larger project were customized specifically in terms of site design, architecture, and marketing format to appeal to the distinct political cultures recognized under the grid-group typology.

Terramor, one of the Ladera Ranch's village divisions, was specifically designed for the egalitarian subculture, emphasizing solitude, authenticity, and environmental values. It featured Craftsman-style architecture, with its propensity for private nooks and crannies, hidden entrances and a commitment to detail and high quality workmanship practiced in an understated fashion. Green building design was also emphasized in energy conservation and selection of materials. In contrast, other villages at Ladera Ranch were designed for hierarchicals and competitive individualists, featuring conservative colonial style architecture with large family rooms for the former group, and status-oriented display houses for the latter subculture. The intention was to socially engineer community at the village level by both cultural and physical design, maximizing long-term consumer satisfaction and, of course, market success. Anecdotal evidence indicates that the various political subcultures did, in fact, somewhat unwittingly separate themselves by village type in their purchasing decisions, and that stronger social networks and sense of community resulted, with less neighborhood friction and a higher level of resident satisfaction (McCrummen, 2006).

Some may take exception to the degree of social engineering involved in a project like Ladera Ranch, but to do so is to replace one value system with another. From the public's perspective, the quality of planning can be measured by the degree to which their life satisfaction is enhanced in the gratification of their wants and needs. The intellectual exercise for planners is to create a physical and social environment that the public desires, while simultaneously accomplishing any number of other planning objectives. The consideration and management of cultural preferences is a cardinal component of the equation.

One outstanding example of a land development innovation designed to advance planning objectives within the matrix of American cultural preferences was the invention of "cove" subdivision design formats (Harrison, 2008). Created by the site design specialist, Rick Harrison, cove development design was specifically created in recognition of the overwhelming space-seeking market preferences of American home buyers (80% of U.S. Market). It also reflects the market incentives that partially drive developer behavior. Cove developments are designed to reduce infrastructure cost and ultimately to increase housing affordability. It is also a format designed to advance environmental and urban design objectives. Coving does so by giving the housing consumer more of what they are seeking while maintaining project density. Infrastructure lengths, such as roads, are generally reduced +/- 20 percent, while average lot sizes and park areas increase +/- 15 percent. Streetscapes are also far more attractive along with other design benefits. Most importantly, it is done in a format that is part of the accepted landscape and housing vernacular of American culture – suburban development. Rather than trying to make the suburban environment look and function more like a displaced urban village, cove designs advance a variety of planning objectives through a format that offers broad market appeal.

Cultural conventions can and do change, particularly if people can make the connection between the values of their cultural orientation and the new lifestyle, landscape formula, or regulatory option being offered. Often the consumer decisions that people make are based on what product is available, whether as a result of community design or ordinance provision, and they do not necessarily reflect their true preference. It cannot be assumed that market preferences expressed in a survey reflect embedded preferences based on intransigent values or basic human nature. They may just as likely be a reflection of cultural conventions that can be moved by advanced product design and marketing that is consistent with underlying values.

CHAPTER Five

Applied Behavior Analysis and Planning

The second pillar of the CBIP model is the application of applied behavior analysis (ABA) in planning implementation. ABA is a field of psychology that focuses specifically on the techniques of behavior modification (Baer, Wolf, & Risley, 1968; Skinner, 1974, 1990, 2001). It has been applied in hundreds of diverse issue areas such as workplace safety, improvement in teaching, prevention of community crime, and the improvement of conservation-based behaviors such as recycling and water conservation. It is also widely practiced in a full range of clinical psychology areas, where it has its most widespread applications, such as the treatment of agoraphobia and substance abuse (Geller, 2001b). Heretofore, it has not been intentionally applied to land planning strategies.

Most behavior analysts don't dismiss potential cognitive explanations for behavior, but their primary concern is behavior change. They focus on the one thing that can be readily measured: did the given technique provoke an observable change, and was the change sufficient to meet the desired objective? In a sense, the techniques of ABA are applied to treat and eliminate undesirable behaviors (i.e. that is, the symptom), not to speculate on the psychological cause. ABA research has shown that convincing individuals to engage in certain desirable behaviors through engineered stimuli and consequences is far easier and more cost-effective than modifying behavior by changing the thinking of an individual, i.e. using appeals to logic (Glenwick & Jason, 1980; Glenwick & Jason, 1993; Goldstein & Krasner, 1983). Once the behavior changes, people often adopt and internalize the rationale later as an explanation for the behavior that they now engage in.

As an example, behavior analysts were heavily involved with the multi-decade campaign to get people to utilize seatbelts. They had to overcome ingrained habits and the negative consequences of mild restraint and discomfort along with having clothes wrinkled by the belts. Under a structured process of trial and error interventions, they experimented with a number of behavioral prompts and consequences that encouraged the desired behavior change in most people, incrementally increasing the percentage of Americans that used safety belts. First they employed a variety of public education campaigns to provoke the desired behavior change in the most receptive elements of the population, culminating in the effective crash dummies ad series. Then they experimented with technological prompts aimed at more resistive individuals. The old warning system sounded immediately after you started the car and would not stop unless you were buckled up. This was replaced in most automotive models with a system that has a ten-second delay and then is activated for 30 seconds. The delayed car warning buzzer system was designed for maximum behavioral irritation without prompting people to go to their local garage to have it disconnected. It is all based on observed behavioral response, not cognitive psychological explanations. Finally, rule-governed behavior techniques that employed legal penalties were implemented for the most resistant elements of the population.

ABA's three-term contingency model of antecedents, behavior, and consequences that will be described shortly, has an everyday presence in land planning. This chapter begins by discussing the discipline of applied behavior analysis and summarizes more than a half-century of applied research conclusions. It then applies these principles to various planning applications.

Applied Behavior Analysis

Many economists and applied behavior analysts argue that the consequences associated with our actions largely dictate and can virtually control human behavior. Scott Geller, a preeminent behavior analyst concerned primarily with community applications of ABA, makes the point that, "we do what we do because of the consequences we expect to get for doing it" (Geller, 2001a). Dale Carnegie captured the role of consequences in dictating behavior in 1936 based on the scholarship of B.F. Skinner when he famously wrote, "Every act you have ever performed since the day you were born was performed because you wanted something" (Carnegie, 1936). Under this outlook, one element to any effective planning intervention is to accurately observe which consequences are motivating or could motivate an individual's behavior in both a desirable and undesirable context, and then to engineer the appropriate adjustments.

While the conclusion that consequences largely control behavior is contested in certain quarters, and may be distasteful or even politically incorrect to humanists who believe in the sanctity of human self-determination, the current evidence is overwhelming. As much as we might hate to admit it, the average individual is largely controlled by the outcomes of his or her behaviors if the consequences are sizeable enough, timely, consistent enough, and relevant. For example, the belief that drinking a small glass of cyanide will result in the consequence of a certain, rapid, and horrible death dominates the vast majority of behavior in this matter; few people would knowingly raise the glass to their lips. The power of the consequence largely controls the behavioral response.

Consequences can be categorized as either economic, social, physical, or moral. In some cases, their power to influence human behavior originates from internal self-actualization, such as a sense of doing the right thing, or moral rectitude as conditioned by life influences. In far more circumstances, the power of consequences to control human behavior may be somewhat less noble, such as marketed lifestyles, immediate physical desires, social acceptance and recognition, or economic inducements.

Note that people's behaviors are often controlled by perceived consequences that are far from economically rational, which is the primary reason why energy conservation in building construction and household appliances was initially such a difficult sell. In the next chapter on the design of incentive programs, these common flaws in human logic and quirks in decision-making are explored. But for the time being, suffice it to say that consequences that motivate human decision-making often have little connection to the thinking of neoclassical economics. That is, people's behaviors are often not controlled by a desire to maximize economic utility in their lives. To be human is to often defy economic rationality in our weighing of potential consequences.

Beyond ABA there are other sub-disciplines in psychology with potential applications in land planning – environmental psychology, social psychology, and evolutionary psychology. But ABA provides the most direct applications for a behavioralist-oriented planning practice. Planners must deal with the reality of systems management and limited resources. One of the implications is that they must rely on cruder population-wide applications aimed at a collective, not interventions at the individual level. As an example, what consequences can be designed to encourage commuters to use mass transit or commute at non-peak hours?

Many of the successful applications of environmental psychology have been at the individual level. Cognitive and evolutionary psychology have contributions that a clever planner can incorporate, but from a systems management perspective, they tend to answer questions of what and why, not how. As Churchman notes, environmental psychology has focused its interdisciplinary discourse towards the architecture and landscape architecture communities in issues such as indoor crowding, personal space, privacy, and human preferences in landscapes (Churchman, 2002). These are specific design considerations most easily incorporated in architectural practice and landscape design, but they are not the foundation of broad-based behavioral interventions in communities or market economies – the realm of planners.

An example of how environmental psychology has contributed to questions of "what" are the findings related to landscape awareness and preferences in humans, both products of evolutionary and environmental psychology, and both valuable insights for the planner, but insights that must be incorporated into some other type of management framework for application. Gordon Orians' work on human preferences for open park-like settings with intermittent tree canopy cover, gives rise to his evolutionary psychology theory on savanna cover types (Orians, 1980, 1986). Human landscape preference studies and attitudes research from the disciplines of landscape architecture, forest management, and environmental psychology have similar findings that as a species we prefer intermittent tree stocking levels that create an open canopy effect with little bushy understory (Bradley, 1995; Kaplan, 1992; Kaplan & Kaplan, 1982). While planners have incorporated such findings into urban park design for a substantial period of time, this is a matter of "what" in design, not the implementation question of "how" in achieving comprehensive planning goals.

A review of the literature in environmental psychology yields a consistent pattern. When it comes time to address the question of implementation in a system-wide context, the concept and tools of ABA are the commonly recognized framework. As early as 1973, Platt's environmental psychology approach to the problem of the commons was to "re-arrange the positive and negative consequences of our behavior" (Platt, 1973). Paul Bell's analysis of psychology-based interventions in environmental issues is a direct description of antecedent and consequence strategies – nearly pure applied behavior analysis (Bell, Greene, Fisher, & Baum, 2001). Similar applied behavior analysis typologies of existing environmental interventions and prescriptions of practice are found among a large number of other authors (Bell et al., 2001; Geller, 1976; Kleindorfer, 2002; Lehman & Geller, 2004; Stern, 2000; Young, 1993).

Despite ABA's recognition by default as the implementation model of choice, questions remain as to its potential effectiveness in the problematic issues of American land planning. Only Churchman and Jones attempt to bridge the divide between planning's current models and environmental psychology. Jones does so specifically in the area of attitude research and the theory of Reasoned Action, not ABA (Jones, 1996). Churchman asserts in his work that planners "feel the lack of tools" to apply the knowledge originating from environmental psychology and that there is a complete lack of collaboration in the literature between the two disciplines in areas such as density research (Churchman, 2002).

ABA's previous environmental applications have been largely confined to the more pedestrian issues of litter control, recycling behavior, and residential energy use. As Lehman and Geller report, published research articles utilizing ABA in environmental issues peaked in the 1970s and 1980s with only 32 articles published since 1990, all in the three areas mentioned above (Lehman & Geller, 2004). So the question remains, can ABA be applied successfully to the dilemmas of American planning in an attempt to incorporate behaviorist considerations into a systems management strategy?

ABA, based on decades of success in a significant number of other unrelated applications, has the potential to serve as a potent management tool in plan implementation strategies. But expectations of improved performance in the field should be tempered until we gain further knowledge through trial and success experimentation. In almost all applications of ABA in other problem areas, such as workplace safety or the encouragement of seatbelt use, pragmatic experimentation has been required to discover what works best as consequence motivators. A modest and realistic application of the ABA model to planning's standard tools is certainly possible in the short term. For instance, the modification of a zoning code or subdivision ordinance to create positive consequences for desired landowner/developer behavior is an easy and effective exercise. But modifying housing preferences among American consumers is more problematic and would certainly require more radical applications of an ABA strategy over a longer time period. Planners are forced to think long-term, contending with complicated relationships between markets, politics, technology, and human preferences. ABA can play a particularly important role in making planning interventions both acceptable and effective because it offers an alternative to pure command-and-control approaches that have been problematic in the American culture. To unleash that potential, however, will require creativity and a willingness to experiment.

The ABC Model

Applied behavior analysis is based on the foundation of the ABC three-term contingency model of behavior. That model is simply a linear chain of events – before, during, and after:

Antecedents ⟶ *Behavior* ⟶ *Consequences*

Antecedents are activators or signals preceding behavior that tell the individual what to do to receive a given consequence, good or bad.

For instance, a traffic signal turning red is an antecedent that triggers the behavior of applying the brake to avoid the consequence of an accident. Antecedents can be written or verbal prompts such as signage or instructions. The legal penalties section of a subdivision ordinance would be considered an antecedent by applied behavior analysts. Antecedents can also take the form of information, education programs, modeling, demonstrations, commitment strategies, and various environmental design approaches, as will be discussed in a planning context shortly. Observational learning from the influences of television is another example. Anything that suggests to an individual what she or he should do to receive a given consequence is an antecedent.

The power of any given antecedent to induce a person to engage in a given behavior is directly related to the potency of the implied consequence for the individual. Tell a rural landowner who has never engaged in development before that public hearing requirements will be waived if she or he follows certain design requirements, and the power of the behavioral incentive (the consequence) may be small. Present the same antecedent to an experienced developer who just had a by-right project proposal rejected due to a stacked public hearing, and you can expect an immediate interest in the offered incentive.

The second element in the sequence is the induced behavior. A behavior is anything that can be observed and is generally a recordable statistic, including the lack of a response. A spoken sentiment by a neighborhood activist is a behavior, a public event, while an unrecordable thought, a private event, is not.

Consequences are the events that follow a given behavior, and every behavior has a consequence. The relationship between a response (a behavior) and its consequence is a contingency, hence the description of ABC as a three-term contingency. Consequences can either increase or decrease a given behavior. This relationship between behavior and consequence explains the motivation for most actions. Behavioral approaches in planning take advantage of this relationship through the intentional engineering of appropriate consequences.

Basic Conclusions in ABA Research

Thousands of ABA applied experiments and management applications have been undertaken over the last 50 years. This work is generally conducted under a strict regime that is the hallmark of ABA psychology. A problem behavior is identified for intervention. The frequency and intensity of the given behavior is observed and recorded, for instance, failure to wear safety goggles on a factory floor. Behavioral interventions are introduced one at a time, either in the form of an antecedent strategy or consequence strategy, and any changes in behavior are observed and recorded. The measure of success is any technique that can establish functional control over the target behavior.

To test the reliability and degree of potential control associated with a given intervention, one of two techniques are built into the research design. The first is the reversal technique in which the intervention, for instance, paycheck penalties for not wearing safety goggles, is removed to see if the behavior returns to baseline. The second approach is to establish a multiple baseline for observation – one factory shift is subject to paycheck penalties and another factory shift is not. As a result of the rigor associated with ABA applications and the sheer number of management applications over the years, certain reliable conclusions have emerged to help guide the design of any behavioral intervention. A summary of these conclusions most relevant to planning follows:

- The more consistent the consequence after a given behavior, the more reinforcing it is for the individual. In other words, the higher the probability of the consequence, the greater the impact.

For instance, our willingness to put a dollar in a vending machine for a soda is based on the consistency we have experienced in the past that the machine and similar machines will deliver the drink. If a given machine fails to yield a drink it is unlikely that we would put in another dollar on a second try. If enough machines were to cheat us on a regular basis, the general public would largely refuse to use vending machines anywhere.

When consequences become unpredictable, they lose much, if not all, of their power to influence behavior in many circumstances. Whether a child's behavior or the general public's adherence to speed limits, the consistency of consequences, good or bad, impacts behavior. European camera-driven speed limit enforcement results in a ticket in the mail if you speed, and it largely eliminates speeding where it is employed. Weak speed limit enforcement on the American Interstate system lowers the risk of an enforcement consequence to such an extent that speeding is ubiquitous.

There is a corollary to this effect. Once human trust is lost, it is extremely difficult to reestablish it. It also takes far greater time and effort to reestablish credibility than it did to establish it in the first place.

One of the fundamental benefits of planning for society is the predictability that it brings for neighborhoods, individuals considering a home purchase, businesses considering investments, and governments anticipating the delivery of services. The more predictable the outcome of daily plan and ordinance administration, the more empowered that planning process becomes.

When planning institutions allow subdivision review and approval to become highly politicized, consistency in the delivery of consequences is lost, conditioning the behavior of a full range of actors. The result can be that landowners/developers are encouraged to engage in speculative land acquisition and rezone requests, or to avoid any discretionary approval process, including processes associated with more desirable design objectives.

Similarly, lack of planning consistency can encourage neighborhoods to ignore guidance in codes and plans, conditioned to believe that with enough political pressure, projects that reflect adopted policy can still be rejected. When such a mindset gets established, as it is in most jurisdictions, it undermines the integrity of the planning process, encourages individuals not to participate in plan development processes, and causes loss of faith in the benefit of planning. Lack of consistency encourages all parties to further politicize the process, both in local elections and in ordinance administration. One example among many of how to use the consistency principle in planning practice is the establishment of quasi-judicial local land-use hearing examiner systems for project review and approval. By separating advanced planning functions (policy development), from daily plan and ordinance administration, consistency and predictability can be dramatically improved at the level where it is most needed.

- The sooner the consequence occurs after the behavior, the more reinforcing the effect. Consequences have their greatest impact when they are immediately delivered after the behavior, strengthening the association.

When your young Labrador Retriever shreds a sofa cushion in a fit of boredom and rebellion while you are at work all day, it is counterproductive to punish her when you walk in the door. She will associate your rant with your homecoming, not the cushion incident.

While the human animal with advanced reasoning capabilities is not quite so literal, the immediacy effect between behavior and consequence is still strong. Consider, for example, the response of most people when faced with the dilemma of a delicious bite of dessert if placed directly in front of them. The immediate reward, the taste sensation, tends to overwhelm the longer-term negative consequence of the extra calories. We rationalize, telling ourselves. "It's just one small piece, it won't have a real impact on our waistline." The immediacy of the reward tends to dominate behavior because the negative consequences are delayed.

The schedule of reinforcement is also important in this regard. The greater the regularity of the consequence, the quicker the behavior change. If an individual working significant overtime receives recognition for his or her diligence once every twelve months at an annual awards ceremony, the incentive will be nice but hardly will have the motivational power of a more immediate and routine benefit, such as being awarded several days off every time he or she completes a major project ahead of schedule. Regularity of consequences reinforces behavior.

In structuring and administering planning-related permits, the behavior incentive principle of immediacy should be applied to the extent that is practical. The implications will affect not only the behaviors of those immediately involved, but will influence others standing on the sidelines observing. Enforcement actions should be initiated quickly when a violation is observed. Land-use decisions should be made in prompt order, reinforcing the policy commitment to uphold both plan and ordinance provisions. This means that projects that are consistent with plans and ordinances should be approved quickly, and those that are not are just as quickly rejected.

- Between the two factors, consistency and timing, consistency tends to be of greater importance if the consequence is sizeable enough to overcome the immediacy factor. As Richard Malott has illustrated, if you tell an individual that if they take one puff from a cigarette they will absolutely die from cancer 10 years from now, and they believe it, the 10-year delay in the consequence is far less important than the magnitude and certainty of the consequence in influencing the behavioral response (Malott, 2000).

- The greater the magnitude of the consequence for the individual, the larger the effect on behavior.

In applications under CBIP, it is important that incentive strategies be sizeable enough to evoke the desired behavior change. In formulating density bonuses, for instance, an accurate pro-forma analysis should be conducted in establishing the magnitude of the bonus. That is what sophisticated builders and developers are going to do in making a decision. They are going to weigh the cost of providing the desired amenity or design feature against the economic benefit of the stated bonus density. If the incentive is not significantly greater than the cost, including considerations of added process times and permit risk, the consequence is going to be insufficient to motivate the desired behavior. Very few ordinances do this. The density bonus is simply pulled out of the air.

A second consideration in saliency is that what may motivate one person may be completely insignificant to another. Individuals' histories, particularly their learning histories, determine in part the reinforcing effectiveness of any consequence (Poling & Braatz, 2001). In the application of various incentive techniques it must be understood that individuals and distinct cultural groups will respond differently to different incentives. As a result, it is best to both assess the cultural traits of those that the intervention is aimed at, and to rely on multiple incentives within the design to influence as broad a population as possible. It is feasible to design incentive-based management systems along multiple paths to appeal to different sub-groups within a population: competitive individualists, egalitarians, and traditionalists; or homeowners and renters. Cafeteria-style benefit packages are one example of the technique. Sophisticated employers offer a range of performance incentives and benefit options, recognizing that what may be important to one individual, say more time off, is of little appeal to the workaholic who may place financial reward higher on the priority list. In the same context, planning strategies can be devised that hold different behavior incentives for different people. The use of language framing effects to appeal to different sub-groups within a larger audience is another example of the principle. Any technique that can be devised to segment and target specific intervention audiences will be more effective than the reliance on a single behavioral incentive strategy.

- Negative consequences (punishments) are as effective or are more effective than positive consequences (rewards) in directing behavior change, but positive consequences are better for developing a positive attitude in the individual – an important behavioral consideration in several respects.

Humans are risk adverse, finding greater emotional pain in a loss than pleasure in a comparable gain (Camerer & Loewenstein, 2004; Kahneman, Knetsch, & Thaler, 2004; Thaler, 2004). As a corollary in psychology, people concentrate more on not losing than they do on winning. Most people's motivation to succeed is far more driven by a desire to avoid failure than the prospect of success (Katz, 1964; Rettig & Pasamanick, 1964; Slovic & Lichtenstein, 1968). This is why penalty provisions have more behavioral power to motivate than bonuses. In addition, guilt, fear, and shame are more effective motivators than happiness, or what Richard Malott terms the "Jewish Mother Effect" (Malott, 2002). The power of social norms and public disapproval, combined with the human urge for group respect, impacts self-esteem in most individuals. This gives potency to the motivators of guilt and shame.

The advantages of using negative consequence strategies under the CBIP approach is that they work if you can determine how to engineer the application for the desired behavior change. Rule-governed behavior, for example, mandates within development codes backed by enforcement sanctions, work as low-cost, indirect contingencies as long as the consequence is sizeable enough and probable (Malott, 1992). Because rule-governed behavior formats are a cost-efficient way to theoretically control large populations, and they are perceived as being absolute in their effectiveness, it is often assumed that all that is needed is a new regulation. Punishment contingencies, particularly indirect rule-governed contingencies, are relatively easy to adopt but often difficult and costly to enforce.

While negative consequence strategies certainly have their role, a dominant role in most behavioral interventions because of their power, they have several significant drawbacks, particularly in the American culture. As a result, whenever effective positive incentives can be identified and applied, they should be employed in lieu of, or in tandem with, negative incentives as opposed to a purely negative consequence strategy.

Typically when negative consequence strategies are removed, individuals quickly return to the baseline behavior. They are only motivated by the potential negative consequence and do not internalize the behavior change as self-motivated. As Scott Geller summarizes in his research, when behavior is "other directed" by negative consequences, individuals become accountable. But when the behavior is perceived by the individuals as self-motivated, they become responsible (Geller, 2001a, 2001b, 2002). The more the outside control, the less the self-persuasion and the less individuals perceive the behavior as self-directed.

Moreover, in the American culture, people are accustomed to consumer choice and a great degree of personal freedom in land-use-related behaviors. In general, positive incentives have greater social validity than negative incentives, and they will be better received and are more politically stable in planning applications.

Behavioral incentives based on severe threats draw attention and fascination, often provoking counter-authority responses. Further, many of the planning-related behaviors in question are in areas in which rule-governed approaches are either a limited or non-existent option, such as commuter preferences or home buying patterns. For all of these reasons, positive incentives should be routinely considered, although they may be less potent in affecting behavior change than negative consequences.

- In devising an ABC strategy in a planning-related intervention, one question needs to be asked: Is the target behavior a recurring behavior such as the daily decision to drive or take mass transit to work, or is it a non-routine behavior such as deciding where to purchase a house or the selection of energy-efficient appliances?

Different approaches are potentially required based on the answer to this question. In general, emotional appeals have stronger force than logical arguments in human behavior, but the effect is short term. Eventually logic will trump emotion if the ingrained habit of the behavior can be overcome. To influence a home purchase decision, marketers appeal to powerful emotional images and motivators, as do election campaigns. But if the object is to change routine, ingrained behavior, such as commuting habits, a different approach is formulated.

- An indirect approach to behavior change is more likely to enhance a sense of self-persuasion in the individual and a stronger sense of personal control.

The reward or punishment schedule should be large enough to get the desired behavior change started, but not so large as to serve as the complete justification (Lehman & Geller, 2004). When the object is to establish a recurring, self-directed behavior – property maintenance, for instance – a subtle incentives approach should be considered. When incentives, both negative and positive, are large and obvious, less room exists for individuals to internalize the behavior change as their own idea. Remove the incentives and the behavior returns to the base level. In many cases, due to the nature of the behavior in question, the incentives will have to be permanent. The choice of incentive depends on the issue and the nature of the behavior in question.

- A second question that has to be asked is how complex or difficult is the behavioral choice facing the individual? As I will discuss in the next section, low complexity problems that align well between individual costs and benefits require one type of intervention. High complexity problems with poor alignment to individual benefits are problematic.

Antecedent Strategies

In the selection of any interdiction strategy, antecedent, or consequence, one must consider a number of factors. How reliable is the technique in generating the desired behavior change, and how durable is the change in behavior? Some techniques have proven to be highly effective for short-term change, but not in evoking permanent modifications in behavior. If the behavior under consideration occurs on a one-time or infrequent basis, such as a land development proposal by a novice developer, then the technique need not be durable. You are only concerned with influencing the decision at that one critical moment. Most of the attempts to change conservation behavior using antecedent strategies have only been reliable on a short-term basis and have not resulted in durable change (Young, 1993).

Other considerations are the speed of behavior change that the technique evokes and the generality of the technique. Will the technique, such as environmental education for water conservation, cause the individual to adopt other conservation behaviors, for instance, recycling or energy conservation?

Finally, we must be concerned with provoking a counter-authority response in some individuals. As an example, experience has shown that when using signage to encourage conservation-related behavior, a polite request avoids producing a counterproductive response. "Please pick up your litter," not "$500 fine for Littering." Moreover, any type of explanation associated with a behavioral request stimulates stronger compliance. In experiments even using the word "because" without any explanation for the reasoning is enough to increase compliance rates.

Education Programs

Within the antecedent formats, educational programs and social marketing have been utilized in an attempt to influence personal values and attitudes in the assumption that personal values would impact behavior. Several extensive literature reviews have been conducted to ascertain patterns of effectiveness among these techniques in limited environmental applications (Bell et al., 2001; Kleindorfer, 2002; Lehman & Geller, 2004; McKenzie-Mohr, 2000; Stern, 2000; Young, 1993). The conclusions of those reviews are largely consistent and discouraging. A weak linkage exists between values and behavior in environmental issues, hence information and educational approaches have yielded generally poor results.

As Stern notes, environmental behavior is strongly affected by context, "long causal chains involving a variety of personal and contextual factors" (Stern, 2000). Individuals commonly will profess strong environmental values, yet any number of consequences drives their behavior. This is the principal reason that new home shoppers will indicate in surveys a strong desire for advanced energy conservation features in a home, but in practice they allocate their consumer dollars into other house features. Behavioral economics research has shown that individual behavior often strays from economic self-interest due to the distortion of reference points, personal accounting, and various framing effects, as I will discuss in the next chapter (Camerer, Loewenstein, & Rabin, 2004; Genesove & Mayer, 2004; Kahneman, Knetsch et al., 2004; Thaler, 2004).

The research implications from both ABA and behavioral economics are that antecedent information strategies have serious limitations in intervention programs. It is hard to imagine, for instance, that a public education program emphasizing the lifestyle and economic advantages of owning a smaller house in a more central location would be effective in changing American preferences for McMansions on the back forty, when two-hour commutes to work have been slow to alter the behavior.

Despite all of the limitations of antecedent strategies based on education and information programs, they still obviously can play an important role. Expecting anyone to engage in certain unfamiliar behaviors is unreasonable, regardless of the positive consequences that may be engineered, if they do not have the technical knowledge of how to engage in the desired behavior. You can motivate planning students with the not-so-subtle consequence of grades, but if you want them to excel in advanced development techniques, consequences are not enough. The professor needs to give them the tools and training as an antecedent to do so.

Prompts and Demonstrations

Beyond education-based strategies, environmental antecedent strategies that employ prompts and demonstration approaches have a somewhat successful record (Geller, 1976, 1981, 1987; Lehman & Geller, 2004; Young, 1993). Modeling and demonstrations, television and movie images, or the provision of new urban design communities within a jurisdiction, all rely on observational learning. For instance, in English broadcasting, standard practice dictates showing individuals buckling their seatbelt when getting into a car. In a similar vein, a grade school class from Olympia, Washington, made a request in the 1980s that Mr. T buckle up in the TV action show. The networks and actor complied with the request, recognizing the social message that it sent to both kids and adults if the toughest character in the series always made the effort.

Demonstration strategies in planning are likely to offer far more promise than the use of prompts. The limitation of prompts is that their application is most practical in certain low-complexity classes of environmental behavior that would exclude land planning. Likewise they lose effectiveness as they lose novelty (Bell et al., 2001; Kleindorfer, 2002; Young, 1993). Signage and other forms of prompts need to be routinely changed to capture an individual's attention.

Unlike prompts, demonstration and modeling strategies offer a far more valuable tool in modifying planning-related behavior. Well-designed demonstration strategies have the power to persuade. That power originates from several psychological factors. Individuals are influenced by crowd behavior, particularly social sets that are perceived to share similar socio-economic characteristics, political views, and value systems. We like people who appear to be like us, and we extend more credibility to positions that seem to be endorsed by large groups of like-minded people (Allison, 1992; Cialdini, 1993). It is a consensus born of group conformity, and it is most effective when the individual is undecided about a prospect or dealing with an unfamiliar situation. Humans also respond to authority figures and symbols of authority in developing issue positions and behavioral patterns.

For all these reasons mass demonstrations, stacked public hearings, testimonials, and various applications of the mass media from advertising to public relations management, can be highly effective forms of modeling and demonstration in American society. Audiences are routinely targeted based on their media biases. Research has shown that electronic media-based people believe the TV more than any other source of information, including other people. They prefer low-involvement environments and don't want or need data. Instead they rely on visuals over words. TV continues to be the most effective advertising environment and the exclusive source of how the majority of Americans make voting decisions in presidential races.

In contrast, individuals who rely on print media for information are far more likely to use multiple sources of information and are far more likely to be concerned with issues. This latter group is estimated to comprise only 10 percent of the American public. Both groups are subject to the influence of modeling and demonstrations, but they rely on different media sources.

The role of demonstrations and models can be an important antecedent tool in planning, both intended and unintended. Consider the following examples. Most modern Americans have little experience with anything outside of the standard suburban lifestyle – a design format that encompasses two-thirds of all housing units in the nation. The market response to new urbanism design formats, and large-scale planned communities with a greater pedestrian orientation and central village core, has been extremely encouraging. Project designs of this type as they continue to spread are serving as valuable demonstration tools to provoke behavior change in the marketplace. Market preferences likely can be shifted further as the American public experiences more examples in the built environment. Only a handful of traditional neighborhood developments were undertaken from 1980 through the mid 1990s. Today, according to the *New Urban News*, an industry trade publication, there are more than 500 such developments with the projection that 20 to 30 percent of all new projects will qualify as neo-traditional development within a decade (Carlton, 2006).

This trend has not been driven by regulatory planning efforts; in fact, most current codes act in some capacity as a behavioral disincentive to such designs. Instead, the trend has been driven by demonstration projects that are providing a new model in the marketplace. These projects serve as a demonstration for both potential consumers who see their friends and neighbors buying into the designs, but also for government jurisdictions and community interests.

How a jurisdiction treats a high profile project, or any project by a well-known developer/builder, also serves as a powerful antecedent demonstration to others in the development sector. Builders/developers have a recognized professional core, normally organized through local homebuilder association affiliates of the National Association of Homebuilders (NAHB). NAHB has over 900 local associations in America, constituting the industry's civil society where information is exchanged, issues debated, and leadership reputations are established and recognized. The best builders/developers set a model for others in the industry that drives project quality. Moreover, their project proposals are closely watched by other development-related interests in terms of how they are received by regulatory bodies and neighborhoods. When good project proposals are treated shabbily in the review process, the demonstration effect serves as a powerful antecedent to others in the profession.

The inverse, of course, is also true. When builders/developers see quality design proposals that implement planning policy rewarded with quick processing, consistent approvals, and reasonable requirements, they quickly receive the behavioral message. Jurisdictions can reinforce this effect by generating positive publicity for the desired planning behaviors. This can be accomplished through annual award programs and the placement of appropriate media comments and stories, among other techniques.

When models become institutionalized, as they have in much of today's public planning practice, they can also serve to retard advancements. Surprisingly little experimentation in land planning strategies exists, given that well over 20,000 local government jurisdictions are present in America. So why has planning innovation at the local level been so muted? The answer likely lies in professional tradition coupled with limited funding that encourages "off-the-rack" standardization. The profession has become dependent on the influence of a handful of model code and statute approaches at the state and local levels, the vast majority of which continue to yield poor results in the American culture. The profession also relies heavily on a limited number of case examples from certain jurisdictions from around the nation. How many articles and studies can be written on Portland, Oregon; Boulder, Colorado; or Montgomery County, Maryland? Models can be powerful antecedents directing behavior, but they can be good or bad, effective or ineffective, and may have limited transferability based on the underlying circumstances.

One of the few structural advantages that land planning holds in the American culture over Western European cultures is the flexibility to experiment. Since planning in America is largely a local function and so many local governments are engaged in land planning from coast-to-coast, the ability to experiment is enhanced if it is taken advantage of. Despite the occasional grumbling over restrictive state statutes that hamper local government planning efforts, substantial freedom exists to experiment far beyond current approaches. State and federal grants to encourage local experimentation may offer one solution to promote the existing latent potential.

Commitment Strategies

A final area of antecedent tools is the use of commitment strategies. Research and experience have long confirmed that when individuals make a commitment, they will strive to uphold that commitment. The more public and active the commitment, the more power it has in conditioning behavior. A commitment made in a public forum or before a large audience has more power than a commitment made in private. Conversely, commitments made in writing, a handshake, or spoken directly, all have more power in relative order than a vague mental or verbal expression.

Commitments derive their influence as behavioral antecedent tools because of the human desire to appear consistent. We want to appear consistent to ourselves and to other people. Giving your word to someone is powerful; we translate it into a matter of personal integrity. The more public and active the commitment, the more personal pressure we feel to maintain our consistency.

Public commitment campaigns are employed in a number of ways. The Weight Watchers weekly weigh-in procedure is one example. Public advertising encouraging designated driver behavior through pre-drinking commitment models, is another. Public commitment techniques are used in teenage smoking abstinence, teenage sex abstinence (resulting in only a slight delay), substance abuse, and with various interest groups in the political arena – for instance, the signing of a "no new taxes pledge" by candidates.

Consequence Strategies

Beyond antecedent strategies, of greater value to the planner is the reasoned application of consequence strategies – tangible rewards, positive reinforcers, negative reinforcers and penalties. The approach relies on the power of operant conditioning in human psychology. Currently, planners rely heavily on what Richard Malott would describe as mechanisms of "rule-governed behavior," nearly always associated with punishment contingencies in the form of threats of legal action if established regulations are violated (Malott, 1992, 2002). But these threats of punishment are aimed at questions of process violation, not specific planning objectives (i.e., if you attempt to market a residential lot prior to formal subdivision approval, legal action may be initiated). Except for the occasional use of residential development density bonuses or the establishment of mechanisms like carpool lanes in transportation planning, few reinforcers are consciously incorporated into implementation strategies to encourage plan implementation.

Issues of saliency, consistency, timing, and the magnitude of consequences are not examined systematically for the various classes of behavior that impact planning outcomes. Moreover, the provisions of many American land-planning programs inadvertently create perverse behavior incentives juxtaposed to planning objectives. For instance, in a procedural and political context, obtaining planning approval for large-lot, exurban development is far easier than obtaining the same approval for inner-core suburban redevelopment. The end result is that the system encourages the undesirable developer behavior of leapfrog development when it needs to strongly encourage alternatives to overcome current market preferences.

Another example is that most subdivision ordinances make the approval of advanced planning design, which provides flexibility from standard requirements, far more onerous to obtain than the lower-quality options. Others have long observed that the development community is simply responding to the path of least resistance in ordinance construction and market response or, in other words, the three-term contingency model of ABA (Arendt, 1994; Duany et al., 2000; Jacobs, 1961).

The existing implementation tools of planning are readily adaptable through regulatory reform to a consequences-based behavior format. Both negative and positive consequences can be customized for various classes of behavior that reflect the underlying culture. Consequence-based strategies in planning can include monetary, process, legal, lifestyle, and technical assistance contingencies under a deliberative design approach. When one considers the variety of actors that impact planning outcomes, it becomes apparent that different incentive and disincentive packages are likely required in a system application. Consider the range of actors, both direct and indirect, involved in land-use-related behaviors that impact plan development and implementation.

DIRECT ACTORS

- Developers / Builders / Realtors
- Home Purchasers / New Businesses
- Planners / Lay Planning Commissioners
- Elected Officials – Town Councils / County Commissions
- Neighborhood Groups / Existing Area Homeowners or Businesses
- Local Government Officials – Engineers / Fire Chiefs / Building Officials

INDIRECT ACTORS

- Lenders – Primary and Secondary Market
- Adjacent Jurisdictions
- State Agencies
- Trade Associations
- NGOs and Environmental Interest Groups

Consequence Categories

Consequences come in four categories, two that reinforce or increase a given behavior and two that decrease a given behavior. Any consequence that gives you something you want is a *positive reinforcement*, and will tend to increase the behavior. An example is a bonus density in a subdivision ordinance. Any consequence that allows you to escape something that you don't want is a *negative reinforcement*. For instance, one example is the waving of a contentious public hearing requirement for private development interests, as has been employed in Portland, Oregon, for high-density urban infill projects. Both, when skillfully designed, will increase the desired behavior.

A consequence that gives you something you don't want is a *punishment* or *penalty*. A potential toll charge for entering the city by private automobile during peak traffic hours is one example. When you don't get what you expect after a given behavior, for example, neo-traditional project submittals are denied that are consistent with ordinance and plan guidance, it will eventually lead to *extinction* of the behavior. That is, developers will shun the option. Both punishment strategies and not being delivered anticipated consequences decrease a given behavior.

Of the four consequence categories, positive reinforcement is the only one that will optimize performance potential on the upside. Energy code requirements, for instance, are a negative reinforcement – build to the given code standard or be subject to an enforcement penalty. Negative reinforcements encourage individuals to perform up to a standard but do not encourage them to go beyond. In contrast, a well-designed positive reinforcement motivates people to achieve maximum reward. For instance, an alternative to energy code requirements is the establishment of a new home energy rating system that ranks all new construction for consumer comparison. The experience with such systems is that they stimulate energy conservation practices beyond code requirements. It is certainly possible to mix both negative reinforcement strategies with positive reinforcement incentives, as in the case of a code minimum with incentives to extend beyond the code.

When applying a behavioral approach to planning, people must think in terms of what motivates the other person or group, not what motivates themselves or the institution that they represent. Equally important is carefully thinking in terms of the various classes of consequences that you may be intentionally engineering or inadvertently creating. Remember that consequence in planning can be monetary, process, legal, lifestyle, and social in context, and that within each category you may be triggering positive reinforcement, negative reinforcement, punishments, or extinction. Consider the following two examples, one a positive reinforcer and the second a penalty in the establishment of desired planning behaviors.

Kalamazoo and the Application of Positive Reinforcement

The city of Kalamazoo, Michigan, has been struggling for years as an industrial city in decline. Many similar jurisdictions interested in promoting economic revitalization have relied on the use of property and sale tax incentives, industrial recruitment, urban renewal projects, new public spaces, and the creation of office and industrial parks in the hope that such incentives would attract new businesses and residents. The record for such programs has generally proven to be both expensive and relatively ineffectual in the older rustbelt manufacturing centers.

Kalamazoo, population 77,000, is pursuing a different positive reinforcement strategy based on education. The "Kalamazoo Promise" program funded by anonymous wealthy donors, guarantees to pay the college tuition cost of any graduate of the Kalamazoo public school system who is accepted into a Michigan community college or Michigan public university over the next 13 years. The amount of payment is prorated based on the number of years in the public school system. The estimated annual cost is $3.5 million in 2006, climbing to $12 million within the next four years.

Community and business response to the recently announced incentive indicates that a powerful positive reinforcement strategy has been devised outside of traditional venues. The program's underlying objectives of business and residential revitalization are being potentially achieved by a backdoor incentive that has overtones in lifestyle, quality of life, and social inducements beyond the obvious financial incentives involved. In the first year of operation, kindergarten enrollment rose from 193 to 277 students because suburbanites were attracted back to the city. Small business relocation inquiries and assistance quadrupled to between 20 and 25 calls a week. New home development and redevelopment were aggressively pursued after years of stagnation in the city. Currently, older students are now joyfully upgrading their career dreams and in-class motivation. While still unproven, the Promise is a compelling behavioral model for urban revitalization through positive reinforcement.

Stockholm and the Use of Penalties

During 2006 Stockholm tested one of the most sophisticated traffic management systems in the world in an experiment to reduce commute times and improve inner-city air quality. Unlike the London system that is a fixed-fee system, the Stockholm trial was based on dynamic pricing – a flexible punishment to change commuting behavior. Under the Stockholm trial, drivers would be charged a toll, automatically assessed and collected from bank accounts, based on the time of day they entered or left the city. The highest fees were charged during prime rush hour periods, falling off to zero, for instance, if you departed in the evening after 6:30.

Modest modifications in driver behavior can have dramatic impacts in traffic flow. The trial reduced traffic flows by 22 percent, traffic accidents by 10 percent, and exhaust emissions by 14 percent. The morning rush hour was reduced from triple the time of a non-peak trip to double the time. Public transportation ridership increased by 9 percent and bicycle usage both increased and became less stressful. This was all accomplished with an average toll of $8 for those who chose to arrive and depart during peak periods.

To increase political acceptability and a sense of personal control, the system was run on a trial basis and then offered as a permanent option in a ballot measure. The trial was stopped, allowing a return to previous poor driving conditions, serving as a behavioral punisher to remind the public of the consequences for voting no on the ballot. The measure was pending at the time of this writing.

Conclusion

The potential application of decades of ABA research to a behavior-based management approach in land planning is both fundamental and overwhelming in its possibilities. For land planning the intentional application of considerations of timing, saliency, magnitude, and consistency under the three-term contingency model is simply not part of current practice. American planning systems currently have a tendency to produce perverse consequence packages. We often reward destructive land-use behavior while penalizing desired behavior. Moreover, we fail to take advantage of the obvious and not-so-obvious possibilities of designing implementation strategies around behavioral motivators.

One of the central themes of ABA is the power of consistency in driving behavior, while one of the fundamental values of planning to society is the predictability that it offers all parties. The two considerations are complementary, consistency as a motivator in behavior and the role of predictable outcomes under planning institutions. The appearance of a conflict arises, however, between the power of consistency in driving behavior and the need for balance in planning between flexibility and predictability. This potential conflict must be addressed in a deliberative manner when designing planning institutions and their processes, but heretofore, they have generally escaped conscious consideration. The two considerations, the simultaneous need for consistency and flexibility, are not inherently irresolvable.

While the CBIP model of behavioral persuasion suggests that the design of planning institutions and their accompanying processes need to directly account for the role that consistency plays in human behavior, that should not imply that all planning processes should be designed to render maximum predictability. It suggests, instead, that the profession has to be far more engaged about where consistency is to be emphasized and where uncertainty is to be accommodated or even intentionally generated.

The consistency-flexibility design factor in planning operates in two dimensions. The first is in the area of certain critical or sensitive resource values. Negative circumstances result when certain resource values cannot be easily restored once lost, such as open space, rural character, and wilderness. Long-range planning likely needs to be structured in such a way as to be highly predictable, almost intractable, in such circumstances if the values are to be maintained on a sustainable basis. This is not to imply that there is only one way to protect such values, but it does suggest that the values themselves need to be approached with consistency in those circumstances in which they are deemed important. The contrast in the evolving land-use outcomes between England's most highly-regarded natural landscapes and those of Ireland, painfully illustrates the point that certain high-value natural resources can be lost in only a decade when the institutionalization of consistency is ignored. Then there are land-use considerations that clearly require an intentional element of flexibility, such as the conversion over time of man-made urban environments.

The second dimension of the consistency-flexibility question deals with process issues and behaviors to be encouraged or discouraged. Consistency is a key factor in administrative functions, particularly a system like planning that is so heavily reliant on rule-governed behavior (Baer et al., 1968; Daniels, 1989; Geller, 1976, 1987, 2001a; Malott, 1992; Malott, 2000; Poling & Braatz, 2001; Skinner, 1974, 2001). System designs that separate political policy functions, such as the development of plans, from the administrative review of specific development proposals that should be highly predictable and apolitical, but are not, could dramatically increase consistency in planning, as could hearing examiner systems or development-by-right formats.

Consistency and flexibility are best thought of as behavioral tools as well as process approaches that require deliberate engineering. Both offer tremendous behavioral power, but planning institutions have to recognize where each is desirable under different circumstances and design for the intended effect. The next chapter on the design of incentive programs addresses this issue in the context of specific planning techniques.

Chapter Six

The Design of Incentive Programs

Chester Barnard, one of the pioneers in incentive theory, noted that, "In all sorts of organizations providing adequate incentives is a central task of management"(Barnard, 1938). CBIP is a methods model that relies on behavioral reactions to incentive-based schemes, both regulatory and non-regulatory. It is a format that calls for the intentional design of behavioral-based incentives systems as a way to achieve planning objectives. Where possible, the model suggests using designs that emphasize the use of cooperation and an element of choice, as opposed to being purely focused on deterrent regulation and the punishment of violators.

In the previous chapter, the principles of applied behavior analysis were discussed as the tactical foundation of CBIP. This chapter adds further detail to that framework. It first suggests a role for incentive theory in intentionally designed management systems for planning. It then presents a typology of incentives under CBIP with general principles of design. The chapter concludes by exploring specific techniques in incentive strategies. In particular, a number of psychological elements in human decision making are applied to planning practice including mental accounting, time discounting, and framing effects.

It should again be emphasized that the CBIP model, in advocating a behavioral-based incentives approach, is not suggesting that command-and-control formats are to be avoided. In many cases, they may be the most appropriate choice among the options. It is important to be realistic about the levels of performance that can be anticipated from market-based planning approaches, command-and-control formats, and any other alternative that may be invented along that spectrum. All have their respective weaknesses, and each may not meet its full potential in a given application due to factors related to the setting or human performance. What the CBIP model does suggest is that implementation performance can improve dramatically if cultural considerations are integrated with behavioral incentives, regardless the intervention strategy ultimately selected. It also suggests that the tools available to implement planning objectives are far more extensive than current field practice would suggest. At the heart of those options is the employment of incentive-based strategies.

Incentive Theory

One of the central propositions of neoclassical economics is that people are motivated by what makes them better off, and that rational individuals always choose the best option among available choices. Behavioral economists edit those assumptions by pointing out that people make choices based on their perception of what makes them better off, not necessarily the reality of it. We are influenced by heuristic tendencies when we employ mental shortcuts, and by a loose definition of utility where we may find higher value in such things as social standing or revenge instead of economic gain. The fundamental assumption is that humans will trade, sell, or otherwise forego some benefit if they perceive enough enhanced value in another form. The role of intentionally designed incentives is to take advantage of this human decision-making dynamic. It is at the core of both applied behavior analysis and economics, and as such, substantial theoretical and applied research has been directed at the topic in both disciplines.

Incentive theory is affiliated with a variety of more specialized theoretical constructs that drive organizational and economic thought.

Organizational theory, for example, is concerned with how to structure management systems and institutions to capture cleaner incentive relationships to enhance performance (Jensen, 1998, 2000). It combines the interactions between human behavior and market functions to guide organizational design. Contract and compensation theory focuses on the construction of non-regulatory mechanisms to constrain and motivate through incentives (Bolton & Dewatripont, 2005). It is a model for how to develop contract arrangements under different circumstances, such as uncertainty or conflicting motivations, to produce desired outcomes. The theories associated with common-pool resources, public goods, and collective choice have as a central theme the clash of individual incentives with the production of optimum levels of communal benefits (Dolsak & Ostrom, 2003; Heckelman & Coates, 2003; Olson, 1965). Finally, public choice theory that blends economics with political science, concerns itself with the incentive relationships that motivate both individuals and institutions in public policy (Buchanan & Tullock, 1965; McNutt, 2002). As a general characterization, all of these contributions to a mosaic of a larger incentive theory have as part of their foundations the principal-agent relationship.

The central proposition of the principal-agent model is that in all complex enterprises, principals (who can be thought of as owners, investors, or the public in governance policy) must delegate tasks to agents (who could be characterized as employees, subcontractors, and elected officials). Tasks must be delegated because no principal is capable of doing all the work or possessing all the expertise or knowledge necessary. If both parties in the relationship are rational utility maximizers, it is unlikely that their interests will align. Take, for instance, the relationship between the CEO of a large corporation and its shareholders. The typical CEO is motivated to maximize her own compensation and level of control, not the profits to shareholders. Only by aligning the interests of the CEO, the agent, with the interests of the shareholders, the principals, can the shareholders hope to maximize their profits.

The principal-agent relationship creates control problems in all systems where self-interested behavior is not consistent with system objectives or those of the principal. It also has ramifications in how best to design institutions to capture clean relationships between principals and agents. The principal's objectives are to maximize economic profits or net utility from other perceived rewards, and to minimize the costs of producing those benefits. Agents are motivated by their own self-interests, which can be described as maximizing their own personal rewards at the least cost, for instance, by working fewer hours as an employee or getting re-elected as a public official. Agents can engage in hidden actions out of sight and understanding of the principal – the "moral hazard" problem. Or they may retain hidden information that the principal does not have – the problem of "adverse selection" that, for instance, empowers realtors in their relationship with clients. Incentive theory concerns itself with recognizing these inherent conflicts and devising incentives to align the interests of agents with those of the principal (Laffont & Martimort, 2002).

The cost of aligning those interests, known as agency costs, is essentially the cost of providing the necessary incentives for agents to perform in the best interest of the principals. It is in the best interest of principals to minimize these costs, but it is the cost of doing business if he or she wants to maximize institutional performance in the form of profits, output, or results.

Public planning institutions currently assume a stakeholder model, as opposed to a principal-agent model, whereby system management theoretically operates for the interest of all parties, not just identified principals. With this model, planning managers and other actors within planning institutions assume to define and operate in the public interest. The principal-agent model and incentives theory reject stakeholder models as fundamentally flawed since those at risk in the outcomes do not maintain control of the actions of agents (Jensen, 2000). Under public planning's current stakeholder model, the prescript for how to resolve conflicts between legitimate interests are vague at best, leaving agents accountable not to principals but to their own preferences.

To align the interests of principals and agents through incentive mechanisms requires that those bearing the residual risk of investment or public interest have the vested management control rights. In planning under current institutional designs, those control rights tend to be poorly defined – for instance, in the case of public goods and the free-rider problem – as do the objectives themselves. That allows perverse incentives among a broad array of actors to drive the outcome in many planning programs with little true management direction.

The complexity of principal-agent relationships in planning institutions is akin to that of publicly held corporations. Both hold similarities to common-pool resources where there are identifiable rights broadly dispersed, but no single person or persons can be identified as the principals who hold all the rights and power to control. Public planners are accountable to elected officials, not the scores of individual interests that collectively comprise an amalgamated public interest. Moreover, neither individual planners nor elected or appointed officials necessarily face incentive schemes that motivate them to act solely in the indefinable notion of the public interest.

Elected officials are often driven by the self-interest of political careers, not broader consideration of the public interest that may be unpopular with voters. Public planners are not rewarded to take risks or to deliver highly effective planning results. Their incentives are created largely through a combination of standardized salary schedules, conflict avoidance, and satisfying the political interests that are in control at any given moment. In that sense, they always run the risk of regulatory capture in their professional pursuits, such as the administration of exclusionary planning policies or the accommodation of ill-advised economic development.

The principal-agent model and the various branches of incentive theory are well developed in economics with a particular focus on wealth accumulation, markets for private goods, and business relationships in the form of management structures, contracts, and compensation. It is, however, undeveloped in the area of public goods, government functions, and in particular, planning. Principal-agent relationships clearly are at play in the realm of planning, but they tend to be more complex than those found in business applications, even corporation structures. Despite the potential complexity, the principal-agent construct, when combined with the techniques of applied behavior analysis, offers powerful guidance in the design of incentive-based strategies in planning.

Incentive Design Under CBIP

For lack of a better term, CBIP's incentive design approach could be termed a public-agent format (Illustration no. 5). In the private economy, principal-agent interests are easier to identify and align because at the base often lies profit motive. In the public sphere of planning, no such beacon provides an organizing light to guide management. The production of public goods, the management of externalities, and insuring social justice are not so easily organized around profit motive under the current stakeholder model of public planning. Modifications to current institutional approaches in planning are required to guide output and drive performance. Those modifications need to align behavioral incentives, including but not restricted to profit motives, with desired outcomes.

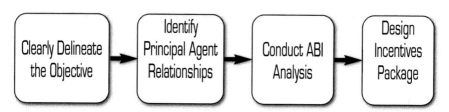

Illustration no. 5 – Public/Agent Format

Under the CBIP public-agent model there are four basic steps. The first is to clearly define management objectives. A prerequisite for the design of effective incentive-based systems is a clear vision of just what is desired. Performance in planning can only be measured against the yardstick of specific objectives. Moreover, it is an oxymoron to suggest regulatory or market-based planning schemes for improved outcomes unless objectives are specifically stated. What is the point to long-range planning and shorter-range implementation programs unless there are specific outcome targets?

Most local government comprehensive plans in America, as opposed to the example of English Area Plans, are vague to a fault. Goals and objectives tend to be so conflicted with each other and imprecise that they provide little meaningful guidance, and nearly unlimited latitude in interpretation. While it may be politically expedient, it undermines one of the principal benefits of planning – some level of predictability for all parties. It also makes it nearly impossible to focus planning management systems on definable results.

As has been previously mentioned, there is a natural tension between predictability in planning and the need for flexibility to accommodate shifting dynamics. Businesses and investors crave predictability to reduce risk and guide decision making. But they are also conflicted with the need for flexibility to drive innovation and adjust to changing circumstances. Homeowners, governments, landowners, and virtually every other sub-group that can be identified in the land-use equation have the same conflicted needs between predictability and flexibility.

The management challenge is in defining the ideal balance and designing planning institutions to allow that balance to be realized. Under CBIP's model of behavioral incentives, broad latitude is provided in how to achieve planning objectives, but the objectives themselves must be specific, whether driven by market institutions that help to define the level of public goods to be produced, or by more traditional hierarchical planning approaches that attempt to measure public preferences.

Institutional design that accommodates specific objectives and the provision of predictability, while simultaneously providing flexibility, is possible. Consider, for instance, how the objective of energy conservation in residential construction is promoted in building codes. Different prescriptive code paths are provided to achieve stated objectives, but the flexibility of an engineered code path is also provided.

The second step in the design of CBIP's incentive-based management strategy is the identification of existing principal-agent relationships. The exercise in the planning arena is to attempt to define with some clarity which constituencies have or should have vested control rights. Land planning is a management setting comprised of multiple principal-agent relationships, both individual and institutional. Consider that in consumer cooperatives the principal is the customer, while in corporations it is the stockholders. In traditional land planning applications you may have the following types of relationships:

Individual Principal to Agent
Elected official – Planner
Consumer – Developer
Spec. Builder – Realtor
Voter – Elected official

Institutional Principal to Agent
Lender – Builder
General public – Government
Commuter – Transportation Agency
Interest group constituency – Nonprofit

Control rights in appropriately designed planning institutions are vested with the parties who bear the primary financial risk, retain the underlying property right, hold the political majority, or hold a position of fundamental social justice or human rights widely recognized in society. In planning applications, which criteria determine control rights can obviously become complex, as can the distinctions between principal and agents. Under CBIP, for example, planners are encouraged to engage in institutional roles where they act more as principals than agents. The shift in role can occur when the planner's focus is that of a private sector entrepreneur, producing a lifestyle product in competition with other manufactured visions. In such a case, the planner serves as both a principal to certain interests and as agent to the general public who are the potential consumers of the product, not elected officials. While the determination of principal-agent roles in certain planning applications can be less than straightforward, in many circumstances they are easily defined. The exercise, complex or rudimentary, helps to clarify incentive design in later steps. It need not be an exhaustive analysis. Simply by thinking in terms of identifying the principals and agents allows for structure thinking in an incentives context.

The third step in CBIP's public-agent format is to conduct an ABI analysis (antecedent-behavior-incentives) to identify current incentive factors at both the individual and institutional levels that are impacting outcomes. This analysis should be conducted in the context of principals and agents in the incentive equation. The analysis results in an ABI grid (Illustration no. 2). The identification and classification of incentives that are driving current behavioral responses provides the blueprint for the final design of a directed incentives strategy. It also redefines planning issues and associated implementation strategies into behavioral terms, forcing the planner to identify incentives from the principal or agent's perspective, not his own. An ABI analysis has two phases. They are:

- Clearly identify and describe the problem behavior of interest, normally associated with an agent, and identify the desired behavior. Vague descriptions of the behaviors in question will lead to clouded analysis of little value. The current problem behaviors are normally identified by direct observation, although a number of other research methods can be reliable. Desired behaviors are

defined through standard management by objective analysis. That is, what is the specific goal as identified in the first step of the public-agent format, and what behaviors are necessary for the implementation of that goal?
- As accurately as possible, identify and classify the antecedent prompts and incentives that currently operate to both encourage the undesirable behavior and that may act to moderate it. A certain amount of speculation is always required initially at this stage, but some type of confirmation should be undertaken. It can be difficult to discover the true incentives that are the behavioral motivators. As such, it is important to list as many possible antecedents and incentives as you can reasonably suspect at this stage, and then confirm their potential role.

Basic research into antecedent and incentive motivators need not be expensive or time-consuming in most circumstances, and it is certainly within the realm of even the smallest planning offices. Observation and informal interviews will often suffice to tell you what you need to know. In more complex situations or where financial implications warrant, conducting a literature review in the search for similar efforts, focus groups, structured surveys, or more rigorous observation schemes may be required.

After the incentives have been identified, it is important to characterize each one as positive/negative, immediate/future and certain/uncertain. This analysis will provide insight into the power of certain motivators to provoke the desired behavior. The analysis should be undertaken from the perspective of the individual or institution engaged in the behavior, not from the perspective of desirable community outcomes or government objectives. Obviously, what may be considered a positive consequence from a planner's perspective can be a strong negative for a developer, landowner, or consumer. As has been previously described, any incentive that is positive, immediate, and certain from the actor's perspective has greater motivating force. It should be noted that the term positive should be construed as either a positive reward for the individual or the avoidance of a negative consequence.

A partial listing of parties to be considered in a planning-related ABI analysis might include: Incentive Analysis for

Individual Actors	**Institutional Behavior**
Consumer choice in housing	*Local government behavior*
Commuter choice in transportation	*Lender behavior*
Builder behavior	*Business Trade Association behavior*
Planner behavior	*Judicial institutions behavior*
Elected official behavior	*Corporate behavior*
Landowner behavior	*State Agency behavior*
Developer behavior	*Party Legislative behavior*
Neighbor behavior	

Notice that both individuals and institutions should be considered in the ABI analysis. As an example, it was recently noted in a series of government-conducted reviews of the English planning system that the property tax structure for local governments was distorting project review and approval dynamics across the country (Barker, 2006). In England, nearly all tax revenue is collected at the national level as a matter of social policy to reduce inequities, and once collected, it is then redistributed back to local governments. It has been noted that this has significantly weakened local support for development, and in particular, economic development that has benefits for the nation at large in the form of labor markets, product competition, and dispersal of growth outside of the greater London area. The costs of development are perceived to be local, immediate, and highly visible, while the benefits may be regional, long term, and less apparent. The proposed economic incentive is revenue sharing with local governments from locally approved economic development projects, and impact payments to local citizens. These changes are institutional in nature to allow for the alignment of individual incentives.

The following scenario demonstrates the ABI grid analysis technique. Imagine a situation where the goal is to promote clustering to preserve rural character, but the landowner/developer sector shows a strong preference for large-lot development. The county's PUD provisions are rarely employed with less than 2 percent of landowners/developers selecting the optional PUD contract rezone procedure.

An ABI grid analysis is constructed after interviews with elements of the development/landowner community. The findings are characterized in Table 1.

In this hypothetical analysis, the undesirable behavior is driven by a combination of positive/immediate/certain consequences that are only weakly counterbalanced by a single positive/future/uncertain consequence. When two sets of consequences operate concurrently, one that encourages and one that discourages a given behavior, the one with the more immediate and emotional outcome tends to control the individual (Malott, 1992). This is particularly true when the negative consequences or punishers tend to be too small and incrementally delivered over time. The cumulative impact of many small, negative consequences encountered over time, such as a long daily commute, may be strongly disliked by an individual, but their magnitude and delivery dilutes the effect.

Problem Behavior: Landowners/Developers refuse to use county's rural PUD provisions. More land is being converted to meet rural housing demand and rural character is being lost as a result.				
Antecedents	**Incentives**	**P/N***	**I/F****	**C/U*****
No one is doing it. My friend did a large-lot project and did fine.	Safety in numbers. No evidence in the market.	P	I	C
Ordinances make standard projects by-right and PUDs discretionary.	Standard development is less risky.	P	I	C
Standard projects have fewer review requirements.	PUDs cost more and take longer.	P	I	C
Surveyors advise landowners to just do a large-lot development.	I only have to hire a surveyor, not a planner.	P	I	C
Neighbors think PUDs will result in higher density and cheap housing.	I'm facing even more heated opposition in the public hearings if I do a PUD.	N	I	U
PUDs are sometimes provided more design flexibility.	I could do a more cost-effective project and a better design – maybe.	P	F	U

Note: * P/N (positive incentives/negative incentives), ** I/F (Immediate incentives/Future incentives), *** C/U (Certain incentives/Uncertain Incentives).

Table 1 – ABI Analysis of Problem Behavior

The final step in the public-agent sequence is to design an alternative incentives package to accomplish the stated objectives. That package may eliminate or modify existing incentives that are working at cross–purposes with desired outcomes, or it may create new incentives. It may also involve the modification of existing institutions or the creation of new institutions to better define principal-agent relationships and to align incentives for desired outcomes. The procedures for this stage of the ABI analysis are largely identical to those that preceded it, except that a greater level of speculation may be initially required. One is never sure what consequences will truly motivate people until they are attempted. Trial and error approaches are inevitably required if no former programs have been undertaken to provide guidance. As in the previous step, informal interviews can be helpful in identifying potential antecedent and incentive packages. Similarly, potential incentives to be considered should be characterized as positive/negative, immediate/future, and certain/uncertain.

Desired Behavior: Rural PUDs become the norm in development practice in the county, not the exception.				
Antecedents	**Incentives**	**P/N***	**I/F****	**C/U*****
PUDs are made by-right development in the ordinance.	My risk is significantly reduced.	P	I	C
Standard large-lot development is converted from by-right to discretionary.	My risk to do a large-lot, traditional development is higher.	N	I	U
County promotes the creation of a demonstration project.	I have evidence that the market will accept the development format.	P	I	U
The county streamlines ordinance requirements for PUDs.	My processing time and expense is reduced.	P	I	C
Free technical design assistance is provided to inexperienced developers for PUDs.	My design expense is reduced and I know that I will satisfy the county's desires reducing my risk.	P	I	C
County replaces planning commission review process with a hearing examiner system.	The approval process is depoliticized, increasing my assurance that if I follow plan directives and ordinance requirements I will be approved.	P	I	C

Table 2 – ABI Analysis for Desired Behavior

Normally, an ABI analysis will identify that the problem behavior lies in the disparity of incentives and disincentives – their certainty, size and immediacy. Undesirable behaviors are supported by one or more positive/immediate/certain consequences (PICs) that are not counterbalanced by negative/immediate/certain consequences (NICs) of greater influence. In turn, the desired behavior may be weak or completely unsupported by PICs and simultaneously burdened by NICs (Daniels, 1989). The intervention strategy is to reverse this order in a cost-effective and politically acceptable fashion, taking into account cultural traits and issues of social validity.

To return to the example of a planning intervention to encourage greater use of rural PUD provisions, consider the ABI analysis displayed in Table 2. The proposed behavioral intervention largely reverses the existing consequence package, replacing it with a series of positive/immediate/certain consequences that encourage the desired behavior coupled with negative/immediate/certain consequences that punish the undesirable behavior.

In the design of incentive mechanisms the following broad principles should be considered.

- Strive to design institutional mechanisms where there are clear relationships between principals and agents. Incentives should, as directly as possible, align the interests of the individual with the given planning objective, whether it involves the production of public goods, management of externalities, or advancement of social justice.

- Where possible, devise incentive institutions in planning that imitate market-based pricing systems to drive performance and efficiency. Such systems need not be solely based on economic inducements, but instead, can blend social and behavioral considerations into the market-based system.

- Those that determine actions should bear the cost and reward of their actions. Consequence free behavior provides no incentive for improved performance, but it does encourage free-riding in the area of public goods, and divorces responsibility in the case of externalities. The more each individual retains both the risk and residual reward of their individual actions, the stronger the incentive connection.

- Measure performance against specifically stated goals. Incentive systems should reward and punish individual performance in relationship to stated goals, but only to the extent that the individual has been directly empowered to achieve the stated goals.

- Only a separate and selective incentive that benefits an individual directly will motivate the person to work toward group interests, whether public goods or organizational goals (Olson, 1965). While most individuals will engage in some level of public spirited, altruistic behavior, that support will decline as the free-rider problem becomes apparent. In a systems management context, only individual incentives in the form of an excludable service, social reward, or punishment will support public goods.

- Do not think exclusively in terms of economic incentives. Social and behavioral incentives often have as much, if not more, influence in directing behavior.

- Incentives that are immediate as opposed to in the future, and concentrated as opposed to dispersed have more behavioral potency. Attempt to connect long-range planning objectives with more immediate incentives.

Types of Incentives

Incentives for planning-related applications can be subdivided into one of three general categories: economic, social, and behavioral. In a broad context all three are behavioral in that they can motivate behavior, but in this application, the term behavioral incentives refers to a category of decision-making heuristics. Proponents of purely economic-based incentive systems tend to assume that people are rational economic beings, and once offered an attractive proposition, will make a directed decision in accordance with economic logic. Social psychology and behavioral economics both clearly identify other factors that motivate.

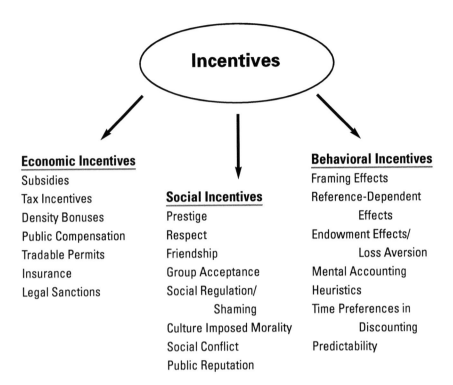

Figure 6 – Types of Incentives

Economic Incentives

The most common incentive techniques in planning today are economic in nature. Within the category most applications could be described as direct inducements that use financial payments, subsidies, discounts, or legal penalties. Tax incentives are employed, for instance, in housing policy, tax increment financing schemes, conservation easements, and for energy conservation. The threat of legal sanctions, litigation, and impact fees serve as financial deterrents. Direct subsidies exist in the form of conservation assistance programs, density bonuses, and transit.

This combined class of blunt-market interventions is well known and widely utilized in planning practice. While there is little question that positive economic incentives in the form of direct or indirect payments can be highly effective, they also have one overriding limitation.

They are heavily dependent on the availability of public funds. The demand for public goods and services will always exceed public resources except in those cases where market mechanisms can be engineered to find equilibrium between public demand and the public's willingness to pay. With limited financial resources, economic inducements in the form of indirect subsidies, direct payments, and tax breaks constitute limited tools for the vast majority of local planning jurisdictions and for most state governments.

There is, however, a second approach to providing economic incentives for behavior change. New economic institutions can be designed to capture and assign the costs and benefits associated with externalities, or to imitate market-based pricing systems for public goods. These alternative economic incentive schemes tend to be revenue positive or neutral for government. The following three examples are samples of creative institutional design for economic incentives. These institutional approaches attempt to align economic incentives with planning objectives.

Community Good Will Payments and Planning Gain Supplements

One provocative view of zoning is that it is not a form of command-and-control regulation to manage economic externalities, but instead, it is a collective property right retained by government as trustee for the community (Fischel, 1985; Levine, 2006). Zoning clearly does create a government sponsored private property right that creates value on the behalf of the landowner, a value that can be enhanced or diminished depending on market pressures and the provisions of the ordinance.

As a community owned property right, it is possible to establish market mechanisms between willing buyers and sellers to exchange the rights through community good will payments and planning gain supplements. Under such a system it is also possible to capture both negative costs and positive benefits associated with externalities. Both planning-gain supplement schemes and good will payments are institutional designs to align the interests of the individual with planning outcomes through economic incentives. Good will payments do so by providing market mechanisms to compensate those that suffer direct costs. In the case of good will payments, development interests – on a strictly voluntary basis – offer impact payments to adjacent neighbors to permit rezones and development proposals that would exceed baseline property rights as established in the existing zoning classification (i.e. by-right development granted under the code). The mechanism allows the sale of a regulatory property right under market pricing, and it permits the capture of externalities or negative spillover effects. Good will payments could theoretically be employed in reverse in the case of down-zoning proposals where rural landowners are providing uncompensated benefits of open space and greenbelts to adjacent neighborhoods.

Planning-gain supplement schemes transfer some of the monetary gains that private landowners receive when the public extends a grant of community property rights to them by up-zoning their property and permitting development at higher densities. Both formats are being employed in New Zealand and France, and are under consideration in England with pilot programs associated with wind farms in Scotland and the Langeled pipeline project.

A domestic example is the recent zoning change that the city of Seattle instituted for its downtown urban core. In 1989 a slow growth, citizens initiative put a cap on downtown density that limited office towers to 300 feet. Growth came anyway to the metropolitan area. Driven by a desire to reduce commuting times, and to lessen pressure for up-zoning for apartments in existing single-family neighborhoods contemplated under the state's growth management strategy, Seattle recently reversed course following the lead of such cities as San Francisco and Vancouver. Height limits have been raised to 500 feet or about 20 additional stories. The height liberalization, however, has a feature that allows the city to capture a planning gain supplement for public goods. The new code provisions require developers to pay the city for every square foot of space beyond the previous base, with the revenue going to a fund to build affordable housing downtown. The provisions will raise millions of dollars from any sizeable office tower approved.

The zoning change has quickly sparked landowner action that offers an urban transformation of monumental proportions. Clise Properties, a family owned business that has been acquiring prime properties since 1889, has announced that they will release for sale 13 contiguous acres for redevelopment, approximately seven city blocks that abut the current vibrant urban center. The land is currently in parking lots; low story, older warehouses; and several declining, low value motels. The sale will likely result in 13 million square feet of new development, rivaling London's Canary Wharf or the World Trade Center complex prior to the terrorist attacks. By getting the economic incentives right, the city will likely achieve both its housing and international market aspirations – all at little cost.

Government Land Bid Schemes

Land bid schemes are potential institutional designs where local authorities offer landowners the option of selling their land on a closed-bid basis to the jurisdiction. Under the closed bidding process the jurisdiction chooses to purchase, on a willing seller-willing buyer basis, the parcels that it desires. It then rezones them for development with a contractual site plan or concept plan, and places the parcels back on the market for resale to the development/construction community. If zoning is a community owned property right, essentially a public good, there is no reason why the community at large should not benefit from the enhancement and sale of that right. Moreover, it allows the jurisdiction to approach growth management, not from a regulatory basis, but as market makers.

To a major extent, local authorities and existing neighborhoods do not benefit financially from new development, particularly residential development. Land bid schemes represent one example of an institutional design that allows the alignment of incentives for the planning objectives of responsible and phased growth accommodation, housing affordability, and enhanced community design. In this case, the economic incentives are aimed directly at local government and the broader community that will benefit from the reinvestment of rezone profits into enhanced local public goods and more orderly development.

London Congestion Toll Program

London's congestion toll program, instituted in 2003, charges drivers special daily tolls based on the number of zones they cross within the city between 7:00 a.m. and 6:30 p.m. on weekdays. It is a scheme to change commuter behavior and to more efficiently manage a public good (transportation and parking capacity) through pricing mechanisms. For commuters outside the city who enter the central business district the current toll is the equivalent of $14 a day. A traffic camera system in the city records every car's movements, and drivers must pay their toll charge on a daily basis at special automated kiosks located throughout the city. The program has met with significant success, both in endorsement by the general public and in accomplishing the desired objectives. Traffic delays have dropped 30 percent, parking is now readily available in the central city, and mass transit capacity is being more fully utilized. The program maintains consumer choice: you can drive into the city if you want and experience less congestion and easier parking, but you are going to pay for the privilege.

Social Incentives

The second general class of incentives is associated with social norms and public acceptance. People have a strong need to belong through some defined sense of community. Social psychology has long established the power of social shaming and the desire for group acceptance to direct behavior. Marketers use this same desire in emotional branding by providing meaning for the individual through the artificially created sense of connection to a contrived community. Napoleon Bonaparte once commented to one of his generals that with a box of military medals he could command individuals to engage in the most amazing feats of bravery and self-sacrifice - enough to motivate men to die and for armies to conquer entire nations. The desire for prestige, respect, friendship, and group acceptance all serve as positive incentives. Various forms of social regulation, threats to public reputation, and culture-defined morality provide an even stronger set of negative consequences that control human behavior in most individuals.

Rarely has planning intentionally applied social incentives to achieve desired public outcomes. Planning institutions can be created whereby social incentives can be captured and applied for effect. Simple techniques of public recognition such as media-promoted award programs, is one avenue. There is no reason why public planning entities should not be engaged in juried awards programs of private developments that conclude with high profile media events and public recognition.

Comprehensive performance assessments of both public and private entities are another form of social incentive. As an example, all English local planning authorities are subject to annual "Best Value Reviews." Conducted at the national level, these ratings are established based on a number of standard measures of public performance including permit processing times, professional competency, and adherence to national and locally adopted planning objectives. These review scores are translated into star ratings that are made widely available to the community so that the general public can compare performance. These scores are highly influential in local politics, driving elected officials and staff planners to perform under public scrutiny. Jurisdictions with high scores promote those achievements, and bragging rights help to drive friendly competition between adjacent jurisdictions. The scores also have major implications for supplemental funding and grants that further motivate both the general public and government personnel. In short, it is a form of social and economic incentive that aligns the interests of the agents – local elected officials and planning personnel – with those of the principals – the general public and higher orders of government.

As another example, the economic value of a good reputation in business often far exceeds the behavioral power of other types of incentives. When people anticipate repeat dealing in the future, a certain social discipline exerts itself. In planning, that benefit tends to be informal and unstated, where the better development firms receive subtle deference in the review process. The incentive to perform to the highest standards of socially responsible conduct, however, could be formalized to drive planning outcomes. Company performance ratings could be established based on standardized criteria much akin to the parallel process that occurs in economic evaluations to establish municipal and corporate bond ratings. High performance ratings earned through repeat projects could garner certain privileges, for instance, expedited review, self-inspections, or the substitute of less onerous public review processes when certain procedures or standards are met. A violation or decline in performance would risk a lowered performance rating.

One particular area of interest in the development of social incentives is in the area of human reciprocity and the role that anonymity plays in behavior. Behavioral and experimental economists in the last 15 years have produced substantial research in the areas of reciprocity, altruism, and fairness that supplements findings in psychology. The results from this research should be of particular interest to planners because of the implications in areas such as public goods, and how to foster community oriented behavior. Clues as to how to design behavioral interventions for the "tragedy of the commons" scenarios so typical in planning practice are particularly relevant. The remainder of this section on social incentives focuses on these issues as an extended example of how social incentives can be utilized under the CBIP model to improve planning performance.

In behavioral economics, reciprocity is interpreted as the willingness of the individual to reward friendly actions and punish perceived unfair or hostile actions, even when they are materially worse off as a result. The term reciprocal altruism was coined in evolutionary biology to imply a net increase in utility for the individual as a result of cooperative exchange – the lobbyist's quid-pro-quo. The term altruism is used to describe the willingness of an individual to incur costs to benefit another, with no expectation of reciprocal gain – essentially unconditional kindness.

We often confuse pure altruism with reciprocal altruism or reciprocity. Doing something kind for your spouse, neighbor, or even an unknown driver while on the highway, is likely to be motivated by subtle and completely unconscious expectations of future positive consequences, such as social acceptance or acknowledgment. It is known, from applied behavior analysis research, for instance, that when pedestrians acknowledge courteous driving behavior by a quick wave of thank you to a driver, that same driver is far more likely to engage in additional courteous driving habits over the course of the next several hours. Creative research techniques have attempted to tease out these different motivations in people to distinguish true altruism from other forms of reciprocal behavior.

Research has shown that pure altruism does exist in human behavior, but the ugly truth seems to be that it is not common or particularly generous in most individuals. One measurement is the dictator game in which an individual is given an endowment, for instance $10, and allowed to share whatever amount they choose, if any, with another individual. When the individual is unknown but present in the same room, players tend to exhibit a small amount of altruism by allocating 10 percent to 20 percent of the endowment, most likely as a result of social pressure. When the game is played and the potential contributor is anonymous, and the potential recipient is placed in a separate room, the contributed endowment drops to near zero. In short, we know from numerous studies that the more anonymous a person can be in their actions, the more selfishly they will tend to act.

Another aspect of what we might call modified altruism, as characterized in work by James Andreoni and others is that, "People enjoy doing a good deed more than they enjoy not doing a bad deed" (Andreoni, 1995). Charitable giving tends to be stimulated more by the desire to feel good about ourselves for doing a positive act than if it is framed in the context of the negative outcomes that will occur if we don't contribute. As a result charitable requests, even requests to engage in environmentally friendly behavior, are likely to be more effective when framed in the positive context of personal self-esteem.

In contrast to pure altruism, strong evidence exists of reciprocity in human behavior as evidenced in hundreds of economic and psychology experiments under significantly different designs. Reciprocation can be thought of as a social obligation to make a concession or to repay a favor that someone else has made for us. It is strongly correlated to our sense of fairness. As a behavior, it is now being observed in primate experiments with monkeys, and likely has genetic roots for humans. Societies go to great lengths to condition members to the rule of reciprocation, and most people find the rule overpowering in their behavior (Cialdini, 1993).

Experimental economists have employed such research techniques as the ultimatum, trust, and public goods games in exploring various aspects of reciprocation and trust behavior (Camerer, 2003; Camerer et al., 2004; Davis & Holt, 1993; Kagel & Roth, 1995). In the various configurations of the ultimatum game, one individual is given an endowment of money and directed to offer whatever amount they so choose to a second individual. The second individual can either accept or reject the amount offered. If the offer is accepted the two participants divide the proceeds in accordance with the original offer. If the offer is rejected, then neither individual gets anything. No negotiations are permitted in the exchange.

While the economically rational behavior is for the first individual to offer the smallest amount possible, for instance, 1 cent in a $10 endowment, and for the second individual to accept – reciprocation behavior generates very different results. In typical trials an offer is made of 30 percent to 50 percent of the endowment. Offers of less than 20 percent tend to be rejected about 50 percent of the time (Camerer & Loewenstein, 2004). People who feel they were unfairly treated will reject the offer, essentially spending what in some games is a substantial amount of money, sometimes the equivalent of a month's wages, to punish the other individual.

The urge to engage in positive reciprocity has been shown to be weaker than the impulse to retaliate in negative reciprocity. In most people, the emotion to punish lack of trust is strong. In large, anonymous markets, such as the American stock market where a seller in Montana has no idea who the buyer is in Virginia, self-interest rules, since there is no inducement for altruism or reciprocity as recognized by market participants.

Consider the difference in behavior often observed between home buyers and sellers. When realtors are involved, price negotiations are one step removed from direct social contact, which encourages a hardening of negotiation tactics. In sale-by-owner transactions the dynamics change with social pressure to behave in a more restrained fashion. Individuals will exploit their bargaining power in anonymous, competitive markets, but normally will abstain in bilateral bargaining situations, particularly when conducted face-to-face (Fehr & Schmidt, 1999).

Given the opportunity without risk of social punishment in the form of public scorn or shame of some sort, approximately 30 percent of people will display purely self-interested behavior, and will never contribute to social goods (Camerer, 2003). Experimental techniques like the various applications of the Prisoner's Dilemma game and public goods games have been designed as models of economic externalities and tragedy-of-the-commons scenarios. In public goods games, players voluntarily contribute to a common community pot. Utility (payoff) is maximized for both the greater community and for each individual if each individual contributes as much as possible to the community pot. But individual players can free-ride on the contributions of other members in the game to maximize their own individual payoff at the expense of others. The game is generally played over multiple rounds, often as many as ten times in succession. What typically happens is that in the early rounds, people will contribute close to 50 percent of their endowment to the community pot. These voluntary contributions decline substantially over time in the subsequent rounds due to perceived issues of fairness and inequity aversion (i.e., it is unfair to give when others are not). By the final rounds, contributions to the community pot drops to nearly zero. If you are a contributor, the behavioral tendency is to reduce your contribution downward to the average contribution of the group, but non-contributors never adjust their behavior upward unless mechanisms for social punishment are present (Ashley, Ball, & Eckel, 2004; Bolton & Ockenfels, 2000; Camerer, 2003, 2004; Fehr & Schmidt, 1999).

The key to this downward spiral is the flow of information. If altruistic individuals (i.e., those willing to contribute to a public good) can perceive the behavior of self-interested free riders, the spiral effect will occur. Over extended time periods, 60 percent to 80 percent of people will contribute nothing, and the remaining individuals will contribute very little as a downward spiral is established to the level of the non-contributors (Camerer, 2003). The guilt of taking a bad action – engaging in purely self-interested behavior and not contributing to a collective welfare – is reduced the more you see others doing the same thing.

Social ostracism or enforcement of social norms is effective to prevent the decline caused by free riders in intimate market settings, such as church members at a benefit auction or the symbiotic relationship between lobbyists and legislators. But, for social norms to be effective, some mechanism for a punishment opportunity must exist (Fehr & Gachter, 2000).

A minority of purely selfish people can force the majority of fair-minded people to behave in a completely selfish manner in broad markets or in circumstances where there is no opportunity for enforcement of social mores. Inversely, a minority of fair-minded people can force a majority of selfish players to cooperate if punishment opportunities are constructed (Fehr & Schmidt, 2004). Social norms work because some individuals are so incensed they are willing to expend resources to punish non-cooperators.

Under the three-term contingency of applied behavior analysis, it is important to create some ability to enforce consequences related to free riders in public goods situations. Cooperation as a strategy consistently yields greater collective utility for all actors over self-interested behavior. This outcome has been substantiated in economic game theory experiments, and is obvious to any involved in the relationship between government, community, and business interests in planning policy. The trick is how to engineer against free riders and perverse short-term incentives that destroy trust, both of which lead to an arms race in self-interested behavior.

In broad terms, the winning strategy is to first cooperate if you are the initiator of action, in other words, the first mover. In subsequent reciprocation rounds, repeat the level of trust that others have shown. This means discriminating against those who have not reciprocated in good faith, and doing so quickly at provocation (Axelrod & Hamilton, 1981). The process must be structured so that cooperation may be resumed if self-interested players modify their behavior based on the consequences they experience. If individuals or interests believe that they will have to interact with you frequently in the future, they will have more incentive to engage in reciprocal cooperation. It also doesn't hurt to develop a reputation as a reliable reciprocator and one that does not insist on more than equity. It has been speculated that promoting reciprocity, in fact teaching it, makes others more cooperative and helps to isolate exploiters (Axelrod, 1984).

There are numerous social incentive implications for planning coming from the above referenced findings in reciprocity research. Direct and/or public negotiation will tend to provoke stronger reciprocity since it reduces anonymous behavior and increases the potential for enforcement of social norms. It is almost always advisable to establish some type of forum that is conducive to constructive face-to-face interchange, whether in advanced or current planning functions. Public hearings are the wrong kind of forum, unless the intent is to specifically engineer an environment for social ridicule and conflict. Task forces, study commissions, moderated discussion forums, design workshops, and participation in trade association and neighborhood council meetings all offer better environments.

Builders/developers are in a superior position to design constructive neighborhood work sessions for specific projects, and are better off to do so early in the proposal process as the initiator of reciprocity. Planners are also capable of using the dissemination of information and conditional project support as powerful reinforcers with development applicants, essentially delivering positive incentives to trigger reciprocal responses.

All parties who are routinely involved in issues of land planning, both public and private sector, should be educated in the role that self-serving bias plays in bargaining impasse. Numerous studies have shown a pronounced tendency in human behavior toward a self-serving bias (Babcock & Loewenstein, 2004; Baumhart, 1968; Svenson, 1981; Weinstein, 1980). Most people, for instance, rate themselves as far better drivers, better investors, and even more ethical than others. We can't all be better than average but that is what we think. This self-serving bias distorts what we believe to be fair in negotiations. Research has clearly shown that people will strongly resist any proposal that they consider unfair (Loewenstein, Thompson, & Bazerman, 1989). It has also been suggested that self-serving bias can easily lead to impasse since people are reluctant to collaborate in a position that they hold to be unfair (Babcock & Loewenstein, 2004).

The public goods research also reinforces the importance of planning for a strong sense of community. Neighborhood designs that emphasize everything from front porches and pedestrianism to village greens create a sense of collectivism and public connection. In so doing, anonymity is reduced and the power of social norms to enforce behaviors supportive of public values is increased. To increase the opportunities for social connection in rural cluster projects, I have gone so far in my own projects as to create community pubs, and large barn complexes where resident parking is integrated with art studios, workshops, and communal farm animal facilities. It is an exercise in social engineering to encourage routine contact. Public spiritedness is enhanced by project design that increases the sense of social oversight and reduces anonymity. The more public the oversight, the more power social incentives have on people.

Other planning applications in this topic area are appeals tied to reciprocal altruism. As has been previous mentioned, appeals that are designed to make us feel good about ourselves as contributors to civic improvement tend to be more potent than those that are framed in the negative to avoid being bad people (Andreoni, 1995). That is why various forms of positive public recognition should be fundamental tools of public planning. One obvious application of this principle exists in the development sector. The development industry is routinely demonized in the media, helping to establish and reinforce unfair stereotypes. The media is in the business of not just reporting the news, but of selling the news. What sells is controversy, and because of the nature of loss aversion and the endowment effect, which is addressed shortly, virtually all development proposals, outstanding or third-rate, produce controversy. More often than not, unfair recriminations are hurled against the "greedy" builders/developers, and just as often, against public planners caught in the crossfire of plan implementation.

The result can be a self-fulfilling prophecy. If builders are going to be consistently tarred and feathered publicly, why should they engage in acts of community-oriented altruism, for instance, in undertaking projects to provide affordable housing that increase project risk and reduce potential profit? In most communities there is never any public reciprocation - no "feel good" upside. To blame builders for growth is a little like blaming the obstetrician for an expanding population. Neither is responsible for creating the need, but they both provide an essential public service.

Public planning functions in America are missing a significant opportunity to recruit the development sector as a powerful ally in achieving community planning objectives. What is lacking is the intelligent design of public reciprocity systems, constrained largely by unproductive prejudice. From highly-publicized public award programs to reciprocal processing incentives, the collaborative possibilities are limited only by our own boldness and creativity.

Behavioral Incentives

The third general class of incentive is behavioral. Behavioral incentives under the CBIP model deal with the heuristic tendencies in human decision-making and patterns of faulty logic. It is the least utilized class of incentives in planning, largely unknown in field practice. But it holds great potential, in that many applications can be easily and immediately incorporated into current planning schemes. It is also a class of incentive techniques that hold broader implications for new institutional designs to improve planning outcomes. Behavioral incentives can be applied to both regulatory programs and purely voluntary strategies. In combination or applied separately, they represent an extension of the current toolbox of incentive techniques.

In the last fifteen years the two related but separate fields of experimental and behavioral economics have exploded on the scene, rocking the economics establishment as acknowledged in a string of Nobel prizes. The first modern article generally recognized in behavioral economics, "Toward a Theory of Consumer Choice" by Richard Thaler, did not appear until 1980 (Thaler, 1980). Since then the contributions flowing from behavioral and experimental economics research has accelerated at a blistering pace. Behavioral economics, with its strong roots in psychology and behavioral decision research, has heretofore been largely only of interest within the field of economics as a challenge to neoclassical economic theory and its predictive formulas. This is rapidly changing, but to date the field applications have largely been confined to areas of behavior finance such as investment, savings, and pension behavior. The subsections that follow introduce a variety of these key findings and suggest how to apply them in planning. The reservoir of transferable concepts with practical application is clearly extensive. The challenge is one of inter-disciplinary transfer and conversion to planning application. Because behavioral incentives are the least understood among the three general classes of incentives that can be utilized in planning, they are explored here in some detail.

Preferences Over Risky and Uncertain Prospects

Risk and uncertain prospects provoke a number of predictable patterns in human decision making. These behavioral traits constitute markers that need to be checked to ensure that in the construction of implementation tools, we have not inadvertently created undesirable behavioral incentives that are undermining planning objectives.

Humans clearly have an aversion to uncertainty in decision making. If the outcome of an action is uncertain, then people will tend to refrain from the decision. This creates an exaggerated preference for the status quo (Andreoni, 1995; Camerer, 2004; Samuelson & Zeckhauser, 1988). The status quo is some sort of reference point that we latch on to as an anchor, for instance, standard subdivision design over neo-traditional neighborhoods. As an everyday example in planning, consider the typical public reaction to any change in zoning. Rural communities that once fiercely fought against the imposition of any zoning, will years later be suspicious of any attempt to either up-zone or down-zone existing provisions – and don't even consider repealing the ordinance.

When a person faces a new situation where they have no status quo reference point, there is a decided preference in decision making for an established default choice. For instance, employers can intentionally bias new employee decision making by establishing a health insurance default option among numerous choices (Camerer, 2004; Johnson, Hershey, Meszaros, & Kunreuther, 1993). Recent experiments by David Laibson, a professor of economics at Harvard, consider systems to encourage retirement savings are indicative of the observed pattern. Laibson found that when the default option for new employees was enrollment in a 401(K), 60 percent enrolled in the program, but when the default option left the decision up to the employee, 90 percent did not enroll. In a second experiment if most of a worker's pay raise was channeled automatically into a 401(K) as a default option, they allowed it to stay in the account, even if the raise was only an inflation adjustment. At the same time, a control group indicated they could not afford to invest in the 401(K) program, or agreed that they would but then took no action to divert the funds (Economist, March 27, 2004).

Few people are willing to engage in behaviors that they consider risky. Most likely, many of the differences that we see in people's risk tolerance is in how they define or judge a risk. Perceived risk is both a matter of how we individually judge probabilities and how we respond to various risk categories. Probability judgment is commonly distorted by a number of heuristic tendencies. Humans suffer from order effects, imagine effects, and hindsight bias (Camerer et al., 2004; Hogarth & Einhorn, 1992). In order effects, recent information distorts probability judgment. In image effects we place a higher probability on those events that we can easily imagine or retrieve from memory. In fact, recent events in a person's life typically cause a person to overweight the probability of a similar event occurring. In hindsight bias those events that have actually happened in the past are easier for us to imagine, and we overestimate their likelihood to occur against other probabilities.

Recent gains, say in gambling, can distort our sense of probabilities and stimulate risk-seeking behavior. Recent losses will do just the opposite unless the proposition is seen as an opportunity to break even. People who recently made money in housing or land speculation are more prone to bet the farm the next time around regardless of underlying market conditions. The inverse is also true. Consider the likely response of a developer who recently had a well-designed TOD or neo-traditional design rejected based on neighborhood opposition. He or she is most likely to avoid developing TOD proposals in the future, even in other jurisdictions or other circumstances, opting instead for more standard development formats that may be by-right. Interestingly, attitudes that form from direct personal experience are more predictive of future behavior than attitudes that develop from say, public education campaigns or peer pressure.

In other quirks of human risk response, loss-averse people will take more risks if they are combined as opposed to broken down into sequential, one-at-a-time propositions. Evaluating risk prospects in combination make them appear less risky. Our judgments of risk and benefit are also negatively correlated. The greater the expected benefit the smaller the perceived risk in relative terms. The inverse relationship is also true (Fischhoff, Slovic, & Lichtenstein, 1978; Weber, Blais, & Betz, 2002). Further, the greater the sense of dread that we have about a risk, for instance, the feelings evoked about cancer verses heart disease, the more we are likely to overweight the probabilities (Slovic, Finucane, & Peters, 2006). In the "law of small numbers," small samples are thought to represent the probabilities in a larger population of possible outcomes (Tversky & Kahneman, 1971). That is why in a coin toss people will feel that the probability of a heads is higher if tails has come up 4 or 5 times in a row, even though the probability remains at 50 percent on every toss. It is just overdue: the gambler's fallacy.

Beyond how we make probability judgments, research has also indicated that a given individual is not consistently risk-averse or consistently risk-seeking in all aspects of their lives (Kachelmeir & Shehata, 1992; Weber et al., 2002). We vary in our response by domain – financial, health/safety, ethical, social, and recreational. In one research study it was found that no respondent was consistently risk-averse in all five areas, and only a very small minority were consistently risk seeking in all domains. The same study found that perceived risks reduced the likelihood of risk-seeking behavior the most in financial matters and the least in health/safety considerations (Weber et al., 2002).

Among all the potential behavioral factors considered in this chapter, risk response is likely one of the most potent for planning-related incentive applications. Nowhere are the applications more obvious than in the development sector, but risk management, creatively applied, is a potentially effective technique in others realms of planning. As an example, to encourage urban homesteading in blighted areas and to discourage out-migration in neighborhoods associated with property value anxieties, several pilot programs are underway where jurisdictions are providing what could essentially be called depreciation insurance. Homeowners/investors are having their existing property values insured again potential future neighborhood-related declines as a way to overcome risk response. Preliminary results indicate that such programs work, and in fact, offer very little financial risk to the insuring party. The same concepts could be employed to reduce risk anxiety in communities associated with the approval of neo-traditional neighborhoods and growth management related up-zones.

But, it is in the development sector where risk-related behavioral techniques offer the most obvious and immediate opportunity in mainstream planning tools. Developers, builders, and conversion-motivated landowners exert a dominant influence on where and in what configuration new development occurs (Baerwald, 1981; Hepner, 1983; Kenney, 1972; Leung, 1987). They maintain a priority position in the development process as those that set the agenda to which other players largely react, and with their ability to be mobile across jurisdictional lines, they hold an over-weighted influence in the land-use equation, particularly in fast growth regions where consumer preference exerts less market power. Among the big three players that determine residential land-use configurations (consumers, builders/developers, and government), housing consumers are at a decided disadvantage in exerting personal preferences. In most circumstances their mobility is restricted - they must find housing in a given market to match employment circumstances.

Often their time is limited. They need housing in an immediate time frame, and often choose not to wade through the substantial complications of finding a parcel and contracting for a custom home, a combined process that often takes several years if they are efficient. Finally, the consumer's market experience is limited. Few have any experience living in advanced land development designs that they might demand if they had the awareness.

The builder/developer or landowner sitting in the priority position as project initiator is risk averse, as you would expect anyone to be, given the characteristics of the proposition that they face. The magnitude of the investment at risk is substantial, increasing risk sensitivity. The nature of the risk is highly compartmentalized, not combined in a single proposition, which also increases behavioral sensitivity. Where a passive investor in a real estate REIT is accepting numerous risk factors, they are combined into a single proposition and hidden from psychic view, typically communicated as general market risk. By combining risks we know the behavioral effect is to underestimate probabilities of a serious outcome.

Builders and developers aren't so lucky. They are acutely aware of the individual risk factors since they are forced to make a series of decisions at each risk-laden juncture point – project design (market acceptance risk), land location (market risk and regulatory risk), land cost (business, regulatory, and market risk), parcel characteristics (environmental and potential design liabilities), timing (interest rate and business cycle risk), architecture and pricing (market risk), construction (weather, injury and timing risk) and financing (business risk).

Virtually all research into builder behavioral factors has indicated a high degree of risk aversion, particularly regulatory risk (Baerwald, 1981; Chamberland, 1972; Hepner, 1983; Leung, 1987; Mohamed, 2006a, 2006b). Research has also shown that regulatory risk for landowners and the developer/builder community speeds the pace of development of unregulated or lightly regulated properties effecting optimum structural densities (Turnbull, 2005). Because of the risk factor, land is converted earlier than it normally would be and at lower densities, contributing to low-density sprawl. During the course of my career, I, a dogmatic planner, was employed twice to serve over 14 years as the executive director of two large building industry trade associations representing over 2,400 industry firms. My appointment to these industry leadership positions was primarily about regulatory risk. They wanted a planner and experienced issue manager at the helm to deal with issues of regulation, not a builder.

Builders satisfice in their development decisions, that is, profit maximization does not typically drive decisions. Instead, development interests must work from a limited universe of available information and parcels in analyzing their options. No builder is aware of all potential parcels in a market since it would require an omnipotent view in an imperfect information environment. Nor would they be capable of accurately transcribing all the discretionary factors required even if they knew of all the parcels that landowners might be willing to sell at the right price. Developing a project pro forma, in conjunction with a preliminary land-use analysis and political assessment, is a major undertaking for any parcel. If the landowner is the developer then the decision-making analysis is restricted to a single parcel. For all these reasons, development options that may arrive at a builder's doorstep for consideration are largely incrementalized in decision making.

As Baerwald notes in his research on builder behavior, three questions must be satisfied in their analysis (Baerwald, 1981). Can financing be obtained? Can a profit within desirable parameters be turned given all the market, cost, and business cycle considerations? And what is the regulatory risk? The realistic objective, given the limits on information and project options before a builder/developer, is the selection of a project where costs and risks, to the extent possible, can be controlled to protect a reasonable return on equity. The management exercise is not to do an exhaustive search in the land market for the single best parcel for profit maximization. It is to avoid large losses while attempting to earn a reasonable profit.

One of the great uncertainties for builders/developers in this matrix of issues is regulatory approval. Will I receive it? How long is it likely to take and how costly is it likely to be? How many unanticipated conditions may be attached? Research has shown that builders/developers are particularly motivated by local government's attitudes and regulatory treatment (Hepner, 1983; Leung, 1987). They have a tendency to play it safe, adapting their business practices to conservative approaches that provide consistency and timely project completion.

Ordinance provisions and processes should undergo a behavioral audit to ensure that risk-oriented consequences are not influencing builder/developer behavior in an undesirable way. If advanced project design such as rural clustering, TODs, and neo-traditional formats constitute more risk for the applicant, say through the requirement to rezone or be subject to discretionary design review where standard development does not, the process is working at cross-purposes with desired outcomes. Implementation ordinances should be constructed so that the automatic default option among applicant choices is the preferred planning behavior. The planning community should construct desirable planning behaviors as high-certainty, low-risk outcomes, for instance, as expedited administrative processes that avoid the opportunity for political decision-making. This objective can be accomplished through a number of techniques.

Inversely, planners should increase outcome uncertainty and risk for undesirable planning behaviors by means of regulatory structure. Ordinance choices should be framed so this contrast is readily apparent to the applicant. If, for example, the objective is to reduce speculative rezoning activity or to encourage landowners/developers to put their best development proposals forward rather than to play negotiation games, ordinances can be drafted that restrict the number of times a parcel or development proposal may be submitted within a certain period.

Time Discounting and Time Preferences

A central issue in human behavior is how individuals trade off current costs and benefits against future costs and benefits. Economists attempt to capture the relationship in "discount rates" – a mathematical model that reflects the time value of money or other forms of human utility. Time discounting attempts to reflect human preferences between current and future consequences and it has ramifications in a broad range of market behaviors including such areas as interest rates.

Time preference relationships are also an important factor in applied behavior analysis in psychology. People disproportionately value current rewards and current penalties over delayed consequences. Humans are naturally impatient – we strongly prefer immediate gratification even when future consequences may be of greater utility to us, and we prefer to delay costs. When it is within our power to decide when to incur benefits and costs, human will is taxed if enjoyment is delayed and the cost is immediate.

Neoclassical economics assumes that people adopt consistent discount rates in decision making. That is, the rate that we discount future consequences remains the same over time. However, a plethora of behavioral economics experiments along with corroborating evidence from psychology indicates that this is not the case. Our preferences associated with immediate utility and costs over delayed utility and costs change at different rates. The implications are significant for any behavior-based model of planning practice. For a comprehensive survey of related work in the field of behavioral economics see Frederick, Loewenstein, & Odonoghue, 2004 and O'Donoghue & Rabin, 2004.

Human discount rates fall with time. Beyond immediate gratification we become increasingly indifferent to both punishment and rewards over time (Benartzi, Rapoport, & Yagil, 1989). In human discounting there is an "immediacy effect" in which people deeply discount delays in immediate gratification, but are less sensitive to delays between two future time periods (Poling & Braatz, 2001; Prelec & Loewenstein, 1991). Imagine a college student is forced to limit beer consumption during the semester to one of the following three options: tonight, in 21 days, or 24 days. The typical college student will find it particularly disconcerting to forego having a couple of brews now if it happens to be Friday night and he or she is standing at a bar with friends after a difficult week, but he or she will be far more indifferent in choosing between 21 or 24 days.

Not only does the rate of our time preferences change, but we discount gains over time more than losses. This latter effect is likely due to loss aversion – the tendency to feel the pain of a loss or cost more than a corresponding gain. The implication is that if you have to delay the delivery of a consequence in an incentive-based strategy, it will require a relatively larger positive incentive than negative incentive to motivate the desired behavior. In a corollary consideration, there is research evidence that under certain circumstances, certain people (such as those with a higher level of self-discipline) prefer to incur a loss or penalty immediately rather than have it delayed. This implies that humans overweigh future punishments in comparison to future gains (Benartzi et al., 1989; Frederick, Loewenstein, & Odonoghue, 2004; Redelmeier & Heller, 1993).

In a related effect, people dislike delays in consumption far more than they enjoy accelerating gains (Frederick et al., 2004). An individual would likely find it far more painful to delay a planned vacation on the verge of departure than they would find additional enjoyment in taking a vacation one month sooner than planned. Humans also prefer sequences that improve over time, rewards that increase rather than decrease, even if the total payout is the same or less over time as observed in workplace compensation systems (Frederick & Loewenstein, 2002; Loewenstein & Prelec, 1993). People prefer to have their pay start low and increase, as opposed to shrinking over time, even though from an investment perspective, they would be better off receiving more compensation earlier.

Time preferences have far-reaching implications for any planner interested in improved implementation. One of the key considerations as suggested by Camerer and Loewenstein is that people will make relatively farsighted decisions where all costs and benefits will occur in the future, but will make shortsighted decisions when some costs or benefits are immediate (Camerer & Loewenstein, 2004).

The very essence of land planning is the art and science of farsighted thinking. Many of the behavioral anomalies that undermine effective planning practice lie in the attraction of short-term expediency at the expense of long-term rationality. Local government policy-makers, consumers, and professional planners are routinely attracted by the siren song of immediate costs and benefits at the critical moment of decision. To do otherwise would be inhuman given behavioral time preferences. County commissions routinely yield to the immediate protests of residents or the pleadings of a longtime property owner. The short-term benefit of satisfying public opinion is far more alluring than the long-term benefits of supporting growth in pre-planned locations. The result is often that planning policy formulated in earlier times under a more deliberative climate is undermined.

Any planning-related process that encourages land-use deliberations to occur when the vast majority of costs and benefits extend into a distant time horizon, will likely result in more rational decision-making. It will also encourage a more civil discourse of the options. When planning decisions crowd the present, it is nearly guaranteed that some immediate costs and benefits will motivate current stakeholders, including local governments, and the outcome is far more likely to be shortsighted or unbalanced.

However, engaging in planning deliberations on an extended time horizon is not enough. Today we already theoretically extend comprehensive plans out to a 20 year time horizon. The difficulty is locking in these planning decisions at or near the time they are conducted. Many will argue that land planning needs to be adaptive, and that is certainly true. But land planning's value is in the predictability that it offers all parties, parties to which most people have both a joint and migrating membership during their lifetime: governments, neighborhoods, homeowners, those shopping for shelter, investors, landowners, and businesses.

There is a difference between reactionary planning, which is the predominant format of planning today, and adaptive planning. Reactionary planning jams behavioral response into real time with immediate costs and benefits that stimulate shortsighted decisions. Adaptive planning formats, on the other hand, place deliberations into a future time frame.

Consider the following example. This nation's single greatest land-use achievement and about the only thing that planning professionals from other developed nations admire about American planning practice, is the creation of our national forest and national park systems. They constitute a spectacular public resource with a value that is increasing exponentially for each new generation of Americans. As the nation's population doubles to 600 million and doubles again to 1.2 billion in subsequent centuries, their public value as open space, wilderness preserves, wildlife habitat and recreational resource, will be incalculable. The day may come when these massive federal land reserves are the only place where Americans can experience large expanses of undeveloped landscape.

The majority of their creation came during Theodore Roosevelt's administration 100 years ago, and not without significant controversy. But the establishment of the national forest system was done in a proactive time frame where deliberations over future benefits dominated the discussion over the relatively small current costs, given the magnitude of the proposal. It was essentially long-range planning at its very best with an implementation hook that locked in the decision. Today, these assets could never be created in their massive configuration. The value of the immediate costs and benefits would dominate the debate and result in shortsighted decision-making. It was only because of the timing of the land planning scheme where the true costs and benefits were far removed in the future, combined with bold leadership, that the two systems exist today.

There are two behavioral-based planning strategies to effectively manage the human tendency to overweight current costs and benefits. The first is to intentionally engineer self-control mechanisms that force us to honor long-range planning processes. Behavioral economists have labeled individuals as sophisticated when they are self-aware that their preferences are different depending on whether they are engaged in short-term or long-term thinking. Those that fail to recognize a distinction in their preferences have been labeled as naïve. People who are sufficiently sophisticated about their own self-control problems will often devise self-commitment devices to compensate. In one effective approach to encourage savings, employers are establishing automatic payroll deductions for future raises and bonuses. The employee is making the decision preemptively to save all or most of a future raise before it happens, and never feels the pain of the added savings rate because they never experience the added spending capacity in their paycheck.

Currently, most planning policy development is directly mingled with daily administration - a recipe for inconsistent and shortsighted decision making. Planning commissions and elected officials are charged with both the adoption of planning policy and its daily implementation in the form of project approvals and rezoning requests. The temptation to respond to immediate costs and benefits is simply too great and often undermines the farsighted thinking which should be the hallmark of advanced planning. Any self-discipline mechanism that can be devised that separates the legislative act of long-range planning policy development from the short-term time frame of daily administration will enhance the rationality and predictability of planning programs.

The legislative acts of plan development, code formulation, and the creation of non-regulatory incentive programs is essentially a political function where rationality is best served when deliberations are undertaken in a forward time frame. Daily administration should be largely procedural, not political, to enhance predictability and to guard against shortsighted response. Unfortunately, in American planning practice, particularly in the treatment of rezoning requests and site plan applications, we have not maintained this separation.

One technique of self-imposed discipline is to separate these functions through the use of a quasi-judicial land-use hearing examiner system. For current planning functions, such programs inject an element of commitment into the planning process, limiting future administrative choices to adopted policy. They isolate policy development and structurally manage the temptation of planning commissions and elected officials to tinker with policy change during actual administration.

A number of jurisdictions around the nation have gone to land-use hearing examiner systems. I was involved as a planner in the early system at Thurston County, Washington that included the cities of Olympia, Lacy, and Tumwater, and marveled at the improvement in project review decision-making that occurred. When properly administered, such systems largely de-politicized the process, adding consistency and credibility to ordinance administration. They do so partially by changing the communications dynamics of project review and hearings. Such systems force all parties to be more formal and direct.

A second strategy to manage the tendency to overweight current costs and benefits is to move both planning and implementation into the future time frame. As a teenager observing the construction of the Dulles International Airport in the 1960s, I can still remember the editorials questioning its placement in what was, at the time, the backcountry. In retrospect, it was a brilliant, farsighted planning strategy that locked in rationality through early implementation. One of the fundamental weaknesses of most advanced planning is that while it looks at the future, the associated implementation is placed in a near time frame. In so doing, the behavioral tripwires of near-term costs and benefits stimulate shortsighted preferences over farsighted decision making. Any strategy that can move both advanced planning and implementation to a future based time frame will encourage farsighted rationality.

In the next chapter, a case study of CBIP is presented that directly employs this strategy. An incentive-based approach to maintaining rural character is advocated that accommodates rural residential housing demand. It is designed for the conservative, private property rights cultures of counties that currently lie far beyond the bounds of the exurban fringe. The strategy is designed around early implementation that predates urban interface pressures by several decades. By locking in a socially valid development pattern that will generate its own political support for future maintenance, it is hoped that a modified greenbelt can be created around the metropolitan amalgamations of the future. It is a proactive planning strategy, as opposed to a reactive one, that counts on early implementation for success. If attempted in real time where near term costs and benefits are high, its political chances would be highly questionable, at best – essentially the environment that exurban counties find themselves in today that sit immediately on the metropolitan edge.

A second example might be the use of pre-planned, phased rezoning, or what might be called time-dated rezones, in the implementation of growth management strategies. Today, rezoning is exclusively undertaken in real time where near term costs and benefits drive emotionally charged, shortsighted preferences. Urban containment strategies nearly always require the up-zoning of urban and inner-suburban neighborhoods, a real-time action that is politically explosive. But what if we linked long-range planning with long-range implementation in certain highly predictive circumstances through the use of time-dated rezoning? Rezoning activities could be enacted in real time but not become effective for 10, 20 or even 30 years with contractual instruments to lock in the decision. Such a technique would clearly change planning practice in those circumstances where it was applied from reactionary to a predictive – directional model. More importantly, it would provoke a different behavioral response where the focus in public policy debates would be the merits of future costs and benefits, not the overweighing of current costs and benefits that tend to provoke shortsighted decision-making.

Beyond the broad planning implications of behavioral time preferences that have just been discussed, there are other more pedestrian applications to field practice. Regulatory incentives in ordinances such as expedited reviews should likely be framed in the negative since people have a greater sensitivity to time delay than acceleration of an expected benefit. For instance, in explaining options to a development applicant in a pre-submission conference the planner should emphasize that if they select format "A" (the less desirable choice from a public planning perspective), they should expect a review time of at least six months. On the other hand, the planner should convey that procedure "B" (the more desirable public choice) would take less than three months. It is speculated from existing research that this negative framing would be more effective in influencing behavior than stating the proposition as, "Option "B" offers a bonus of three months processing time.

Research also indicates that positive consequence strategies should focus on immediate, not delayed, rewards. Rewards can be disproportionately smaller due to the "immediacy effect" if designed for early delivery as opposed to later in the management regime. Since people dread future bad outcomes proportionately more than comparable future benefits, and in some circumstances, prefer to incur confirmed costs or losses immediately, the effectiveness of behavioral disincentives should increase by engineering the "dread factor." Planning processes that produce predictable results and that substitute public written comment periods for public hearings, should serve as a major behavioral incentive since they produce consequences of reduced business risk and reduced dread of future public controversy.

Mental Accounting and Decision Analysis

Humans use heuristic mechanisms, essentially mental rules of thumb and shortcut indicators, to draw judgments and make decisions (Chaiken, 1987; Kahneman, Slovic, & Tversky, 1982). We do so as a coping mechanism to deal with time constraints, information overload and living in extraordinarily complex societies. This use of heuristics often becomes so automatic that they become what Cialdini describes as "Click – Whirl" responses (Cialdini, 1993). Without thinking about it an antecedent trigger, the click, sets into motion a more or less automatic judgment on our part, the whirl. For example, when a man looking for a clothing gift for a woman is basically clueless, there is a tendency to equate quality with expense. Merchants have long observed that for certain market segments it is easier to move a piece of merchandise by pricing it higher since consumers interpret discount pricing as less desirable or a lower quality product. Branding is another heuristic technique in merchandizing where the consumer essentially links a name such as Lexus or Tiffany to an implied guarantee of quality.

People can't live in a modern society without heuristics – they would be frozen by indecision, consumed by the amount of time necessary to make hundreds of daily decisions. Good heuristics are fast and can be counted on to yield generally accurate measures for judgment. The issue, of course, is that heuristic patterns can lead to faulty judgments, and can be impacted by factors we are unaware of. They can also be manipulated by outside forces for either noble or self-interested applications. The only difference between social marketing and standard product marketing is the objective. The same psychological principles that influence human behavior are applied to encourage people not to smoke as are used to sell cigarettes.

So, what types of heuristics do we commonly rely on in our judgments and how is that knowledge employed by institutions and individuals to affect behaviors? When undecided we often rely on what researchers in influence describe as social proof, symbols of credibility and authority, and characteristics of similarity and liking. In social proof we take our clues from the crowd, particularly if we can relate to the crowd's identity. Large protests, public hearing crowds, and advertising testimonials all work in persuading the undecided and reinforcing the beliefs of those leaning in the crowd's direction. Presidential appearances, for instance, are often stage managed to only show a supportive and enthusiastic public response in the background. To project public support of presidential policies, negative venues are religiously avoided.

In planning, the extensive use of public hearings to provide for public comment invites abuse because of the all too predictable heuristic effect. Stacked public hearings have become the norm through the use of telephone trees, inflammatory mailings, and other community mobilization techniques. Because we feel a loss more acutely than a comparable gain, it is far easier to generate a hostile crowd than a supportive audience. People are motivated to action, say to attend a nightly public hearing, when they perceive that they have an endowment at risk – the existing value of their house. Planning policy and project proposals with implications for housing affordability rarely attract comment from prospective first time home buyers – a potential gain. How do you collect input from an affected class of stakeholders that either don't exist or don't recognize the implications to their future self-interest? The point of view goes largely without representation when the power of social proof is applied as a tool in defining public policy. Interestingly, even when we know or strongly suspect that public response has been generated by orchestrated effort, it still influences policy-makers because of its power, particularly when delivered in a public hearing.

As with all the human heuristic tendencies discussed in this section, social proof presents itself as a behavioral incentive opportunity. In the design of planning institutions, public hearings have taken on the role of a behavioral disincentive given the dynamics just mentioned. If the intention is to create a behavioral deterrent for certain development formats, then you may want to consider the use of public hearings as the primary mechanism to allow for public comment. However, if you want to design a given planning institution to serve as a positive behavioral incentive, diffusing the heuristic effect of social proof, other more effective mechanisms exist for the dissemination of information and collection of public comment. Written comment periods with staff-written response has been formalized in NEPA and SEPA related actions for decades. Community design workshops are a second alternative.

Probably the most studied variable in heuristic patterns in persuasion is the role of credibility and impression management. A high credibility source can evoke significant change, and the more extreme change that a high credibility source asks for the more likely they will get it. The variables that create credibility interact with each other in different ways, but these interactions are still not fully understood. We know that symbols of prestige and legitimatization do influence the perception of credibility. Clothing, mannerisms and vocabulary are all used as heuristic shortcuts in our evaluations. Academics, attorneys and those attempting to project the image of experts will stage television interviews with a backdrop of volume-filled bookcases as an example. People and professions will employ the technique of mystification in the use of words, symbols and jargon to project expertise and credibility.

Humans use similarity and liking in their judgment and decision-making. People are also attracted to and more easily influenced by physically attractive people, particularly individuals of the opposite sex. Advertisers select attractive people to pitch products and services for a reason. Height studies indicate a direct correlation between a man's size, salary, and likelihood of holding a management position. If we identify a person as similar to ourselves, for instance in socio-economic class, we are more likely to assume shared values and positions, which increases their ability to influence our decision making. The more a person is like us the more we tend to exaggerate the similarities in our minds and move toward their positions. The inverse is also true.

Sophisticated lobbying campaigns are careful to match the messenger to those being influenced. If you like someone and know him or her, they are far more likely to have influence. There are a host of techniques that those attempting to persuade can employ to take advantage of these behavioral tendencies, whether in speeches, issue campaigns, or marketing (Cialdini, 1993; Woodward & Denton, 2000).

Besides the manipulation of heuristic symbols just mentioned, there are a number of other common pitfalls that bedevil human decision analysis in economic and quasi-economic applications. A simple one is the "course of knowledge." People who know a great deal about a subject, say professional planners in the area of property law and development rights, find it difficult to imagine how little others may know. Our heuristic tendencies in economic analysis offer tripwires galore. Most individuals have problems with assessing costs that are incrementally encountered over extended time periods or that are not intuitively obvious.

Humans tend to ignore opportunity costs and search costs in their deliberations while incorporating sunk costs in our mental calculations. People will drive an extra 20 minutes across town to save two or three cents a gallon on gas. Their total savings may be ninety cents, but their costs in time and expense far exceed the savings. Sunk costs are always irrelevant to current decisions, but they have a strong pull on human behavior, affecting institutional decision making, as well as, personal deliberations. It doesn't matter that you have invested $500 billion in a war and may have tens of thousands of casualties. It is irrelevant to current policy deliberations about how to proceed, but human heuristic click-whirl responses, say something quite different emotionally.

Humans as a species have a problem with stubbornness and decisions. The earlier a decision has been taken and the more forceful it has been taken such as in a public statement or writings to a large audience, the harder it is for us to give it up. We want to look consistent to others and to ourselves, making mid-course adjustments particularly difficult for most people. The commitment and consistency principle is commonly utilized by professional issue managers to lock in policy-makers. Ease the individual into a soft commitment and allow these early seeds of a commitment to "grow legs," that is, for the individual to mentally rationalize proof for the growing opinion. When the time is right, encourage a more forceful commitment, for example, a public pronouncement in a speech. To maintain internal and external consistency at that point, the commitment is likely to be honored.

People struggle in accounting for basic probabilities in situations where they have little or no information. Do you buy an early bird nonrefundable $300 ticket to Prague for a planned holiday next summer that you might have to cancel, or wait until two weeks before departure and shell out $1,100? Most people wait since they don't want to be stuck with a completely useless ticket. The right answer when you have no basis to judge the probability of an event is to assume a chance of 50 percent. In this example the odds of cancellation would have to be greater than 73 percent not to be better off buying early.

In another heuristic quirk of human decision making, gain and loss functions display diminishing sensitivity as the dollar amount grows — the law of small numbers. The difference between $10 and $20 seems larger than between $1000 and $1010. In one experiment, people are asked if they would drive 20 minutes to save $5 on a $15 calculator. A second group is asked if they would drive the same distance to save $5 on a $125 coat. Most participants will go the extra distance to save $5 on the calculator but not the coat (Tversky & Kahneman, 1981).

One peculiar heuristic technique of humans is the tendency to create artificial mental accounts for expenditures, wealth, income and time. People compartmentalize their thinking instead of taking a more comprehensive outlook. These personal accounting practices result in decision making that is piecemeal and contextual in nature, missing broader picture interdependencies and trade-offs. Richard Thaler, one of the leaders in mental accounting research, has recently published a survey article in this important area (Thaler, 2004). What follows is a summary of key observations from that fascinating work with behavioral implications for the planner.

People often judge both gains and losses in reference to a narrowly focused artificial account that in a broader context makes little sense. To lose capital gains in a stock investment is less painful than to lose the initial principal. It is still money lost, but by creating artificial distinctions, in essence separate mental accounts, individuals fool themselves into a false reality. By creating compartmentalized reference points, transactions are often evaluated incrementally in a way that distorts decision-making. Most people are far more risk taking with gambling winnings than the original principal. Or a realized loss is more painful than a paper loss, which is why mental accounting favors selling winners and holding losers – typical investor behavior (Odean, 1998; Shefrin & Statman, 1988).

In mental accounting, prepayment separates the perceived cost of the activity from the benefit (Gourville & Dilip, 1998; Prelec & Loewenstein, 1998). This finding parallels ABA research on the timing effect in the delivery of consequences. Any device that decouples payment from the derived utility reduces the sense of cost to the individual, hence the power of credit cards to encourage spending. Paying cash on the spot feels more real than writing a check, which in turn feels more real than using a debit card. But nothing feels quite so disconnected as the use of a credit card, or even better, the delay of any payments on credit for six months.

Another example is the mental process involved in time-share vacation condos – the purchase is perceived as an investment but the time you spend in the condo is perceived as free. Or the mental process involved in new car leases where the true cost is cleverly camouflaged – you appear to acquire a new car but never get to the point of ownership with higher accumulated costs over time but delayed expenditures at the front end.

In devising decoupling strategies a judgment arises – do you construct a prepayment or post-payment approach? Which is more effective in motivating people to engage in the desired behavior? People tend not to like the feeling of what Thaler describes as "having the meter running" (Thaler, 2004). Telecommunications and cable companies have generally gone to flat rate billing to encourage consumers to enroll because of this trait. But, if you prepay vacation costs months in advance, the trip may feel more enjoyable from a financial perspective, but are you less likely to make the commitment than if using a post-payment decoupling? A related finding in applied behavioral analysis is that we strongly dislike having negative consequences hanging over our heads, but if you place the consequences far enough into the future they have a tendency to become less of a deterrent. The construction of a decoupling strategy must be approached on a case-by-case basis.

Planners should frame the marketing of an incentives program so that potential gains, monetary or otherwise, are broken into smaller incremental components, clustered for effect. People feel better if they win two lottery tickets, one for $50 and the other for $25 than if they win a single $75 ticket. In a planning-related example in the next chapter, an incentive-based approach is taken in model zoning and subdivision ordinance language using a variety of process and technical assistance incentives. To emphasize the incentives, they are broken into as many small increments as possible and listed in a variety of locations in an easy-to-compare table against the less desirable alternative.

Losses (i.e., undesirable costs to the actor) should be combined if planners want to de-emphasize them. Planners should avoid breaking out small losses since they have oversized psychological impact, combining them, if possible, into gains or benefit categories. In the business community it is extremely rare to have a corporation report a very small quarterly loss. Instead they rely on creative accounting to show some type of profit, no matter how small. Small costs in planning, in some circumstances, can be folded into positive incentive categories. In other circumstances, combining permitting costs into a single fee makes more sense than listing a half-dozen fees for the applicant.

If you are using costs as a behavioral disincentive such as monetary consequences or process disincentives (i.e., imposition of public hearing requirements or other less-than-desirable permit processes), planners should break them out into a large number of separate components to evoke a psychological overweighting of their significance. Again, they need to be clustered together in a visually explicit manner, for instance a comparative table, to obtain the maximum behavioral effect. It does little good to sprinkle disincentive costs throughout an ordinance where it is difficult to compare.

It cannot be emphasized enough that all of these techniques associated with emphasizing or de-emphasizing costs and benefits for behavioral effect are best done as explicitly as possible. Ordinance language for most people is an obscure and difficult medium in which to establish a behavioral incentive. The incentive message is better delivered in other formats, for instance, simple-to-interpret brochures where comparisons are easier for the individual. If you are proposing an advanced site design, say as a planned unit development, make the advantages explicit by comparing them to what would legitimately occur under a by-right, standard development submittal, and do so in an easy-to-compare format.

To reduce opposition to development impact fees, planners should decouple them from a sense of direct payment. The developer will simply pass along all imposed fees – market permitting – in the short run, and has no choice but to do so in the long run. Instead, officials should establish special tax assessments on the future property owners. While such an approach may be less economically efficient, it has a variety of benefits. It has less of a shock value on housing affordability, since like a mortgage, it spreads the cost over a longer time period and it tends to be more equitable for the future and subsequent owners of the homes.

Mental accounting research has also shown that people place an implicit value on time relative to financial context. For example when researchers asked subjects how much they were willing to spend to avoid waiting in a ticket line for 45 minutes they found that people would pay twice as much to avoid a wait for a $45 purchase as a $15 purchase (Leclerc, Schmidt, & Dube, 1995). It is possible that the purchase price of the ticket served as a heuristic in decision making, implying to the individual a greater reward (i.e., beneficial consequence based on price). One potential implication for planners is that expedited planning review and permitting procedures serve as both a powerful psychological, as well as, financial behavioral incentive. Given the psychological magnitude of the investment required for most development ventures, issues of time become highly sensitized.

Finally, in any incentive-based application that you may devise where the benefits carry unavoidable costs, attempt to decouple the rewards from the payments. In most circumstances you are better off to postpone payment until after the reward, not through prepayment.

Framing Effects

What is in the power of a middle name? If it is Rodham, it is strange indeed. In a 2006 CNN poll considering 2008 presidential contender match-ups, Senator John McCain had a 4 percent lead over Senator Hillary Clinton when her middle name, Rodam, was left out of the polling question. In the same poll when the match-up was presented with Senator Hillary Rodam Clinton, she took a 3 percent lead over Senator McCain. When she was matched-up against Governor Rudi Giuliani, the exact opposite effect was recorded. That is the power of the framing effect.

Research has repeatedly shown that how a decision choice is offered to an individual often has more influence than the content of the choices (Lichtenstein & Slovic, 2006; Loewenstein, 1988; Loewenstein & Prelec, 1993; Slovic, 1995; Thaler, 1980; Tversky & Kahneman, 1981; Tversky & Kahneman, 1986). This is because our preferences are often not well-defined or stable. Two equivalent outcomes can be offered to an individual, phrased in different ways, and a clear preference will be expressed for one choice over the other. For instance, in one marketing experiment labeling beef as 75 percent lean resulted in far more favorable consumer response, especially before tasting it, than labeling it as 25 percent fat (Levin & Gaeth, 1988).

What behavioral decision analysis has documented is that many, if not most, preferences are constructed by the individual at the time of decision evaluation (Camerer et al., 2004; Lichtenstein & Slovic, 2006; Payne, Bettman, & Johnson, 1992; Slovic, 1995). At the point of decision we are not revealing our preferences as much as we are constructing our preferences based on heuristic decision-making strategies and contextual factors that influence human information processing. This means that the way a choice is offered to a particular decision-maker, is rarely, if ever non-prejudicial. How options are framed, even when making every attempt not to manipulate the outcome, will determine the decision choice in many circumstances.

Another implication is obvious. Preferences can be intentionally directed by how options are framed, something that it is done continuously in marketing, public relations, and public policy. Contextual factors that affect human judgment can be accommodated in land planning interventions for increased performance essentially through behavioral preference construction. They can also act in numerous applications to undermine planning objectives. Whether these efforts are manipulative or socially responsible paternalism depends on your views and the application. Regardless, it is impossible to avoid causing the effect with even the most neutral of motivations. Framing effects must be taken into account in planning applications, if for no other reason than to at least understand how we might be influencing both policy decisions and implementation outcomes, intentional or not, by how propositions are presented. No matter how you present a decision choice, it is likely to influence the outcome.

Framing effects come in many forms, some that follow predictable patterns that are essentially heuristic misfires such as context effects, bracketing and agent metaphors that will be discussed momentarily (Rabin, 1998; Thaler, 2004). Other times, framing effects have a seemingly random quality about them, for instance, the weird preference reversals observed in the political poll example mentioned above. Communication and marketing specialists recognize that both unpredictable and established patterns may be at play in testing for framing effects. Focus groups and other forms of message testing are specifically employed to understand the meanings that people attribute to certain words.

When the National Association of Homebuilders formulated a recent public relations advertising campaign, they were careful to test the framing effect power of certain words. The theme, "Building Community, One Home at a Time," was selected because of the emotional influence of the word community, and the public preference of home over house in testing. It was also selected to allow positive visualization by the reader – one home – my home – my community, to offset characterizations of the evil builder and a growing suburbia. We know from framing research that when the benefit is perceived as high or the image is positive, there is a behavioral tendency to project a positive image by association, in this case, toward builders. Other recent examples of the intentional use of framing effects in public policy include: estate tax converted to death tax, tax relief not tax cut, and climate change not global warming. Phrases to avoid include cost/benefit, rollback, and cost-effective. Phrases to use include sound science, common sense and innovation.

We planners have no room to feel too self-righteous in this capacity. It is more than just current convention that the term village has become so popular in our ranks in advocating neo-traditional design and clustering. Collaboration, smart growth, stakeholders, green infrastructure, sprawl, and sustainability – we are as guilty as the next party in using emotionally charged words for framing effect. The only difference is that planners rarely have the money or the know-how to identify and target different demographic tribes for behavioral marketing. In fact, we can't even take credit for what may be our most successful framing attempt. The term "smart growth" was reportedly a carefully crafted public relations and political strategy developed by experienced communications professionals to sell the Maryland growth management program.

The framing effects permeate all aspects of the land-use arena, often without conscious notice. Behavioral economics research by Steve Levitt and Chad Syverson demonstrated that the incentive structure of real estate commissions encourages agents to strive for quick sales over maximizing sales price for the client (Levitt & Syverson, 2005). Since under the majority of real estate listing contracts it is the realtor's legal responsibility to represent the interests of the seller, subtle code words creep into ads, either knowingly or unknowingly, to suggest to potential buyers that the house can be purchased at less than the listing price. It is the psychological framing of a sales pitch for savvy shoppers. In the research it was found that ad terms like: fantastic, spacious, charming, well-maintained and great neighborhood all communicated likely weaknesses with the property and correlated to lower sales prices. Terms like granite, Corian, maple, state-of-art, and gourmet all correlated to higher sales prices.

Beyond the simple technique of using emotionally charged words to frame propositions, there are a number of other predictable framing effects that are less intuitive. Michael Morris, a professor of psychology at Columbia University, determined that agent metaphors are particularly powerful in investor behavior, implying that they may also have the same effect in other behaviors. Agent metaphors are words normally associated with living creatures applied to inanimate subjects. For instance, "The stock market leapt forward on Monday based on a healthy manufacturers report and docile inflation numbers." Morris's work indicates that when agent metaphors are employed, it implies to the human mind that the activity will persist. When object metaphors (inanimate) are employed, research subjects do not project a sense of momentum.

Framing a proposition in the positive or negative can dramatically impact selection preference due to human loss aversion. So can the use of numbers in contrast to percentages. In a classic illustration from the work of Tversky and Kahneman, subjects were presented with the following scenario and instructed to select from their respective choice sets (Tversky & Kahneman, 1981):

Imagine that the U.S. is preparing for the outbreak of an unusual Asian disease, which is expected to kill 600 people. Two alternative programs to combat the disease have been proposed. Assume that the exact scientific estimate of the consequences of the programs is as follows:

<u>Options Presented to Group I</u>

If program A is adopted, 200 people will be saved.

If program B is adopted, there is a 1/3 chance that 600 people will be saved, and 2/3 probability that no people will be saved.

<u>Options Presented to Group II</u>

If program C is adopted, 400 people will die.

If program D is adopted there is a 1/3 chance that nobody will die, and a 2/3 probability that 600 people will die.

The two pairs of options presented are equivalent, but the pair presented to Group I is framed in the positive (lives saved) while the pair presented to Group II is framed in the negative (lives lost). Subjects had a strong preference for program A in Group I (72 percent), and for program D in Group II (78 percent). In short, the framing of identical options caused a reversal of preference. The explanation likely lies in a combination of loss aversion and the vivid imagery that numbers bring to mind as opposed to percentages (Slovic et al., 2006). When choices are presented as 200 people living or 400 people dying, the prospects seem more real in the human mind. Framing that highlights losses will be more attractive with any technique that diminishes the sense of loss, say by the creative use of scales to create the illusion of smaller numbers (Rabin, 1998).

Additional phenomena in framing are context effects. Preferences can change depending on how a choice is paired with other options. Marketers have an interest in how consumers will respond to the introduction of new products when paired with existing competitors, including other products that they, themselves, may produce. The results from this work have implications to planning practice, both in the private and public sectors.

People are attracted to intermediate options that are bracketed on either side by more extreme choices, say, a far more expensive product at the high end and a low-quality product at the other end of the scale (Simonson & Tversky, 1992). They are also attracted to compromise alternatives – let's split the difference. Research has shown that sales of an existing option can be stimulated by introduction of a "decoy" that is designed to position the desired option in the middle of the choice set (Huber, Payne, & Puto, 1982). For instance, you are a retailer and you currently carry two women's coats, one for $75 and the second for $150. You want to stimulate the slow sales on the $150 coat. By introducing a third $250 coat to the line-up as a decoy there is evidence that sales will shift from the $75 coat to the $150 coat.

While framing effects are constantly in play in planning practice, to date they have rarely been intentionally analyzed or applied. More is the pity because such research doesn't have to be expensive or difficult to undertake, and is in the realm of possibility for talented Masters students. Despite the current lack of applied research for planning practice, we now know enough from other applications to be aware of the implications in our own work. All of the framing effects referenced in this section offer conceptually direct application in planning practice by creative practitioners willing to experiment. There are ramifications in public involvement, and in how alternatives and staff recommendations are prepared. There is also direct application in how we construct implementation ordinances to encourage the desired behavioral response. But the application of framing extends beyond just plan development and administration. It also has ramifications in planning-related consumer behavior. Project design concepts can push the landscape vernacular that housing consumers are accustomed to, but as noted in the next chapter, they have to stay within a range that provides some familiarity to past experiences and current expectations. Landscape vernaculars can be changed with the gradual introduction of comparative projects that offer increased utility to the consumer. Housing and lifestyle preferences are not stagnant and unmovable. They are created by historic and contextual factors and by deliberate intent. By intentionally framing project and lifestyle options for housing consumers, current decision patterns can be modified.

Endowment Effects and Loss Aversion

People's preferences in decision-making can be strongly influenced by artificial points of reference. These reference points may be monetary, such as the money you have already invested in a project still under construction, or a broad spectrum of non-monetary measures such as the open space next door that is farmer Brown's field. Reference-point-oriented behavior is common in many planning-related issues. In incentive-based strategies it offers both an opportunity to direct behavioral response and a cautionary note. Reference points can often lead to faulty logic. They also lie at the root of what has been coined the "endowment effect."

Consider how the asking price on a house becomes the anchor around which negotiations then revolve. In many situations it is extremely difficult for a housing consumer to judge accurately the true value of a house. The house may have unique features or may be particularly pleasing architecturally. Subtle considerations in the site, neighborhood, and maintenance may affect the value even between identical homes. Few, if any, true comparable sales may exist in the area by which to provide a yardstick of value. In short, too much variability between homes and low sales volumes between dissimilar houses makes accurate pricing problematic in many circumstances. When enough market information is available to make a relatively accurate judgment, individuals may be dealing with a range of $5,000 to $20,000 in legitimate variance – sizeable sums for most people. In more difficult situations, particularly at the luxury mansion end of the market, the variance can be hundreds of thousands of dollars. As a result, knowingly or unknowingly, people rely on the asking price as a reference point from which to start negotiations. It directly affects buyer psychology. Few people have the behavioral discipline to ignore the asking price entirely, assessing the house's value from a totally unrelated perspective.

One influence of reference points is what Richard Thaler characterized as the endowment effect – the increased value of a good to individuals when they perceive it as an endowment, either earned, inherited, gifted, or acquired by accident (Thaler, 1980). People place an extra value on things they already own or perceive that they have some endowed right to no matter how dubious. Strangely, the endowment effect can happen virtually instantaneously. For instance, in a Cornell University experiment students were given a coffee mug or a chocolate bar each with identical value. Experimenters confirmed that half of the students preferred one good to the other. After the items were randomly distributed, the students were allowed to trade. Barely 10 percent of the students chose to trade as the value of ownership in a few short minutes had modified the students' prior preferences. One would expect a trading volume closer to 50 percent, not 10 percent.

Another example of the endowment effect is that people will demand far more community reimbursement in the clean-up of a damaged environment, say an oily beach, if they perceive it as an endowment than they will accept to sell a similar environmental resource for economic development (Camerer, 2004). Put another way, people value environmental resources and open space differently depending on whether they view themselves as owners considering selling, or as potential buyers. If they perceive themselves as having some right to a given resource or program, they place a higher value on it than if they have a desire to acquire the resource or program. Sayman and Onculer summarized 73 separate studies and data sets that showed that selling to buying ratios ranged from 0.67 to 20 or higher, meaning that sellers valued the same resource as much as 20 times higher than buyers due to the endowment effect (Camerer et al., 2004; Sayman & Onculer, 1997). In behavioral economic experiments, the endowment effect ratio between sellers and buyers most often ranges from 2.1 to over 6.0 with a typical effect measured at 2.5 (Kahneman, Knetsch et al., 2004).

There have now been scores of endowment experiments conducted in behavioral economics with consistent results collaborated through the use of contingent valuation studies in other disciplines. The time of possession can be extremely short and yet the effect is still observed. Further, the linkage between endowment and the factors attributed to deserving the endowment can be on the most tenuous grounds. The endowment effect is observed in not only individuals, but in the behavior of firms and governments (Kahneman, Knetsch et al., 2004).

One particular type of endowment effect is loss aversion. People feel the pain of a loss more than the utility of an identical gain. In short, we hate losing more than we enjoy winning, which is why the fear of failure tends to be a stronger motivation for most individuals than the prospect of success. Behavioral economic experiments show an average coefficient of loss aversion of 2.25, or put another way, we dislike losing 2.25 times more than acquiring the same utility (Thaler, 2004). Interestingly, the new field of neuro-economics has shown that the prospect of gains and losses activate different parts of the brain.

While behavioral economists are concerned with reference points, endowment effects and loss aversion in the context of how markets actually perform, they also hold powerful implications for the planner implementing a behavioral management model. The predominant public hearing behavior in development proposals is almost always opposition-based regardless of whether the project is poorly or brilliantly conceived. People often perceive that the vacant open space next door is a personal endowment that is being taken away. Research has shown a direct correlation between proximity and opposition. In one study looking at 45 projects, the probability that a landowner will participate in a public hearing declines by half for every 79 feet that their ownership is from a proposal boundary (Tideman, 1969). The aversion to losing that open space is greater than the value they were willing to pay to acquire the resource and its associated utility because psychologically they already perceive that the open space in question is theirs in a manner of speaking – it is interpreted as an endowment that they expect the government to protect. Its value to them is higher precisely because it is viewed as an endowment, an endowment at risk.

This reaction is all too well known to experienced developers and it affects their decision making. More rural locations with fewer neighbors simply mean less people to contend with in the all too predictable response. The impact of reference points that manifest themselves in the form of endowment effects and loss aversion, say that of an inner-suburban neighborhood, can make a shambles of transportation-oriented development proposals, in-fill strategies, and community development initiatives. The necessity to up-zone older neighborhoods and the political resistance that it evokes, are two of the fundamental hurdles in most statewide growth management schemes, and those hurdles are directly related to issues of loss aversion and endowment effects.

The differential values that loss aversion provokes are also reflected in the public's willingness to actively participate in planning processes. Since we feel the pain of a perceived loss far more than a comparable gain, it is far easier to generate an angry crowd at a project public hearing than it is to get widespread participation in the formulation of a proactive planning program designed to enhance community and personal utility. The endowment effect nearly ensures that we will be motivated more by potential loss than potential gain.

Solutions to this problem are not easy to envision since a sense of endowment is so easily established in people. Attempts to consult with surrounding neighborhoods in the early project design process have met with mixed, but generally disappointing results. No matter how well-conceived a proposal and potentially consistent it is with existing plans and ordinances, and no matter how artful the neighborhood is approached, some individuals will feel a particularly strong sense of both endowment and loss aversion. That small, highly-motivated core, can mobilize broader neighborhoods through emotional appeals to undermine rational public planning objectives, paradoxically in the name of "good planning." They can also provoke the political response of large-lot zoning, or developer behavior in which the tendency is to propose only high-end, low-density developments – both planning scenarios that promote sprawl and exclusivity.

Experiments in loss aversion indicate to overcome the response, positive consequences under the applied behavioral analysis model would have to be on average at least two to six times greater than the perceived loss. Some well-capitalized developers are beginning to play this game in earnest. One national firm in northern Virginia recently offered to absorb the outstanding bond indebtedness of $20 million in recreation improvements for the approval of a high-end project. The town accepted and then found itself married to the marketplace, just like its developer partner, when a decline in the housing market forced the firm to rescind the offer and walk away from the project. Another developer in the San Francisco area basically approaches existing neighborhoods when proposing mixed commercial – residential projects and asks, "What do you want?" and no one is ashamed to place the order in the swap meet that follows.

Attempting to offset loss aversion and capture externalities through financial incentives has its limitations, for example in development related up-zoning. The costs of such inducements are directly or indirectly borne by the future businesses and homeowners in such developments, not the developer. Such an approach has a direct effect on housing affordability and encourages exclusivity and gentrification in development proposals. Only the wealthy need apply. It also further constrains market competition among development interests by further encouraging consolidation within the industry. Only the larger firms have the capitalization to play the game.

An alternative approach to dealing with misguided endowment effects in planning may instead lie in a communications strategy. While direct appeals to conservation oriented public education programs under ABA strategies have generally not yielded encouraging results, an educational approach to managing endowment effects may be different. Only experimentation will answer the question. What we do know by experience is that it is not enough to encourage broad public participation in comprehensive plan and ordinance development to embed expectations, since few truly participate and there is a constant turnover in neighborhood residents. What may be more effective in contending with wayward endowment effects, at least in building some predictability in ordinance administration based on adopted plans, is a combination of early notification of ordinance and plan provisions when properties are first purchased with periodic communication reminders to residents.

At first blush such a strategy may sound like a logistical nightmare, but structured and administered with common sense, it represents a viable option and one that would certainly improve the general public's basic understanding of planning. It would likely also stimulate greater involvement during the policy development process. A bluntly worded one to two page disclosure summary provided for all real estate listed properties that indicated area zoning, by-right and discretionary densities, and the general development outlook under plan provisions, would potentially go a long way toward damping wayward endowment effects and improve predictability for citizens and businesses alike. Periodic re-notification with property tax bills would also reinforce land-use expectations.

A second implication of the endowment effect is how to structure incentives and other provisions in ordinances in order to either maintain future flexibility or to enhance predictability. The question is always the trade-offs between providing increased predictability that influences human behavior and the advantages of maintaining management flexibility. Once programs get developed, even with sunset provisions, they quickly become viewed as endowments and develop constituencies, which is why failed or obsolete government programs are so difficult to politically eliminate. It is also why the automobile manufacturers found it so difficult to wean conditioned consumers off of new car rebate programs.

In one example of how to avoid the endowment effect and preserve future flexibility, employers are increasingly going to annual bonuses rather than salary increases. In a rational economic system employers would be constantly adjusting employee salaries, both up and down, based on market demand, economic cycles, and labor market conditions. This would allow businesses to retain more employees in economic downturns, spreading the pain across the larger workforce. The reason that businesses do not is obvious. The average person, who may have adjusted their standard of living to the higher salary, would consider it patently unfair. So instead certain individuals are fired and the existing workload is heaped on those remaining. An alterative that breaks the endowment expectation is to establish a base salary for different job classifications and then to issue annual bonuses, not permanent salary increases.

In the construction of both planning codes and potential voluntary inducements, careful consideration must be given to the issues of predictability and sense of endowment. In many circumstances public policy is best served by constructing provisions for maximum predictability, even an enhanced sense of endowment. In others where certain behaviors are to be discouraged but choice still offered, construct uncertainty and undermine any sense of endowment.

Reference points and loss aversion also play a role in land-use disputes. When concessions are viewed as losses as opposed to forgone gains by one of the negotiating parties, it is far more difficult to find resolution (Kahneman, Knetsch et al., 2004). As a lobbyist involved in hundreds of legislative policy conflicts, this reality is encountered constantly. True collaborative problem solving among parties was generally only possible when pre-existing programs did not exist. When they did exist, they provided reference points and hence a platform for loss aversion with its depressing effect on creative problem solving.

It is much easier for people in program formulation negotiations to forgo a potential benefit than to concede a benefit they already have. This has real implications for the planner in regards to structuring certain ordinance provisions and engaging in project negotiations. Where flexibility is preferable to predictability, it is important to frame provisions or discussions as early as possible as definable objectives instead of specific standards or hard positions. However, there are no hard and fast rules except one. In encouraging the desired outcome, whatever that might be, consider the likely behavioral response of the other parties to a given approach. Do not approach it from your own perspective or that of interests that you represent.

Happiness Research and Planning

Among all the topics discussed in this chapter, happiness research at its current state of development has perhaps the most obscure behavioral applications to planning. Paradoxically, it may have the greatest strategic importance. Dominated by "positive psychology," and behavioral economics, the topic is introduced to stimulate thinking. As the field expands, it may represent a significant pillar of planning practice.

The Buddhist dominated nation of Bhutan is pursuing a novel national objective: maximize gross domestic happiness. It is hardly a flaky idea challenging the paradigm in the West that happiness equals consumption and our focus on gross domestic product or per capita income as the hallmark of collective national utility. The Bhutan government has developed, and continues to refine, an index of gross domestic happiness as its primary measure of citizen well-being, and a guiding objective in national policy. The concept has attracted economists and other disciplines from around the world in international conferences on how to refine and implement the measure in public policy. In the meantime, Bhutan is marching forward in their international experiment.

Planning for happiness constitutes both a worthy public objective and implies a potential set of behavioral tools for plan implementation. In the former case, there are now isolated examples of jurisdictions planning specifically for happiness objectives. Catherine O'Brien in recent work, cites several examples including Bogotá and child-friendly transportation studies in Canada (O'Brien, June, 2005). During his tenure as mayor of Bogotá, Enrique Penalosa instituted an urban infrastructure and public spaces planning program that gave priority to children and those who did not own an automobile. The primary objective of the program was to enhance happiness.

But what of happiness as the basis for behavioral incentives in plan implementation? Research tells us that beyond a basic level of comfort and security, additional wealth does not improve happiness (Easterbrook, 2003; Easterlin, 2005). This is particularly true when considering the advancement of national prosperity as measured by GDP or other wealth measures. The percentage of Americans who describe themselves as "happy" has not increased since the 1950s, a time period when the average new home had one bath and was less than 1,400 square feet, when less than 15 percent of American families had more than one car and only 4 percent had an automatic dishwasher. In fact by some measures, happiness has declined in America since the 1970s.

The likely reason that individuals do not feel better with growing wealth is habituation – our rapid adjustment to changes in living standards. The effect has also been labeled the "hedonic treadmill" or "hedonic adoption" and is observed in income, career advancements, housing, and even leisure pursuits (McMahon, 2006). Research in psychology, sociology and economics all indicate that people will momentarily be happier with increased wealth and promotions but the effect rapidly fades (Kahneman, Diener, & Schwarz, 1999; Layard, 2003). In numerous surveys a consistent pattern is observed. When individuals are asked what amount of income would make them happy, the average response is double their current income. The response is consistent between individuals that make $40,000 a year and people who make $200,000 a year. With hedonic adaptation we constantly plateau, searching for the next ephemeral thrill that we are sure will bring contentment.

What does make people happy is to be comparatively better off than their neighbors and workmates (Firebaugh & Tach, 2005). In one study that is characteristic of results in this area, students at Harvard University were asked whether they would prefer to earn (a) $50,000 per year while others got half that, or (b) $100,000 per year while others got twice as much (Economist, 2003). A wide margin chose (a). When extraordinary incomes and lavish consumption are constantly portrayed across a broad spectrum of media, they generate a form of pollution envy and unhappiness. In this light, consider the findings of a report done by the U.N. Development Institute in 2006 that the world's richest 2 percent control more than half of all wealth, while the poorest half possesses just 1 percent. Interestingly, there are preliminary indications that this envy factor in income does not exist for leisure time. The implication is that developed societies may be behaviorally driven to overachieve in the pursuit of material wealth at the detriment of other lifestyle factors that bring greater happiness.

So what does make people happiest? One study conducted an exhaustive search of 30 years of data looking at 20,000 working-age Americans and the conclusion was health and a happy marriage (Firebaugh & Tach, 2005). Other studies consistently show socializing, strong social networks, significant time with family and friends, flexibility and control of personal work activities in the workplace, and a short commute.

Among routine daily activities what is least enjoyed? Hands-down, it is the morning and evening commute, in that order (Kahneman, Krueger, Schkade, Schwarz, & Stone, 2004; Stutzer & Frey, 2004). Given the adaptability of humans this conclusion is surprising, but it is the lack of control in commuting that induces stress. Weather, accidents, back-ups, and the seeming inability to do anything about the traffic except endure – each commute is an unpredictable event in many urban environments.

Given that most humans find long daily commutes to be so unpleasant, one would think that it would serve as a powerful motivation in household location decisions. Economic theory suggests that people will find equilibrium between a housing market (i.e. location, quality, expense, and size), and a labor market (i.e. salary, employment opportunities, quality of workplace and position), that reflects the tility for the individual. However, studies indicate that people often miscalculate, resulting in a combined package that significantly sub-optimizes their well-being as they themselves define it (Stutzer & Frey, 2004). By far the most common error is to accept a longer commute that may maximize house and land for the money, but that results in significantly lower reported well-being.

There are several explanations for this miscalculation. Home purchases are often an emotional decision that offers immediate gratification with postponed costs. New homes are specifically designed to show well on first impression, evoking strong emotional responses that overwhelm other considerations. Paradoxically, the features that show well at first, contribute to the structure's lack of intimacy and hominess for residents later, although homeowners have a difficult time identifying the connection (Susanka, 2001). The immediate reward (consequence) of that exurban home with a 50-minute commute is that it is larger, newer, and far more alluring than the house you get for the same money closer to your job. It delivers an immediate emotional rush. The negative consequence of that daily commute is postponed by enough time to encourage a miscalculation of maximum utility by the purchaser.

A second explanation is that assessing the true costs of commuting is not an intuitively easy calculation when attempting to maximize well-being. It is difficult for people to measure the future cumulative costs of added stress, less time for family and friends and more direct expense, in the decision-making process. Finally, once the decision is made, if the homeowner comes to understand that a miscalculation has occurred and their true preferences have not been met, rectifying the situation requires substantial energy and expense to either change jobs or house locations.

Knowing what we do, planning strategies could conceivably be devised, primarily communication and education, to help housing consumers avoid committing the commuting paradox. Preferences already lean in the direction of desirable planning behavior – shorter commutes. By framing the options to remind the buyer of the true costs and benefits to well-being, hopefully before the house search even begins, a long-term outlook in decision-making may be encouraged.

Behavior-Based Land Planning

SECTION Three

CBIP in Application

CHAPTER Seven

Private Forestlands and Community Planning

The following chapter is intended as an example of CBIP's basic principles in field application. The U.S. Forest Service and Virginia Department of Forestry have a continuing concern over private forestland fragmentation trends. As part of their outreach activities to support local government planning efforts in the forestland regions of the Southeast, the agencies contracted with Virginia Tech to develop a CBIP based analysis with accompanying recommendations for remedial action. What follows is a portion of that study and associated ordinance recommendations.

While it may seem strange that an issue such as forestland fragmentation was selected as a case example, it was done for several reasons. The general principles of CBIP, with its behavioral orientation and public-agent model of incentive construction, are universally applicable to a broad range of planning issues. CBIP is a general framework by which to approach planning problem analysis and program design, not a specific tool designed for a given fact pattern. As a format for problem analysis and the engineering of implementation programs, it can just as easily be applied to issues of suburban development patterns, as to the design of a better sign ordinance. By selecting an example of CBIP in practice that topically is outside the familiarity of many planners, it is hoped that the principles of CBIP in application will be more sharply displayed. A second reason for the selection of forestland fragmentation is that program development conducted under the CBIP philosophy can generate fundamentally different strategies than those in common practice. Rural planning issues beyond the urbanizing fringe receive little focus in the profession but may be of paramount importance, both in terms of urban containment and in maintaining some semblance of rural landscapes for future generations of Americans. Where current command-and-control suburban containment strategies have generally failed to maintain metropolitan area separation, clever rural planning strategies that rely on behavioral analysis may provide an effective alternative. This implies that the relationship between suburban and rural planners may need to change institutionally, with a greater sense of collaboration and strategic coordination to achieve the traditional objectives that typically exist in each sector.

How to achieve the objectives of conserving rural landscapes where appropriate, and providing some sense of separation between growing metropolitan complexes, raises a fundamental question for every rural and suburban planner. Is it possible to construct an effective and enduring rural land growth management scheme suitable for the American culture? To do so requires satisfying the five performance tests stipulated in the CBIP model.

The example that follows integrates these considerations. It also illustrates the type of nuanced relationships that have to be considered when designing a CBIP behavioral-based planning program (Illustration no. 7).

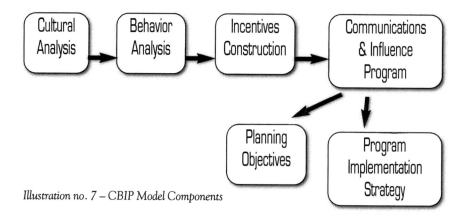

Illustration no. 7 – CBIP Model Components

The process requires a planner to recognize cultural tendencies, be they political, lifestyle, social, or economic in the strategic formulation of planning objectives and strategies. Within this cultural framework, existing behavioral incentives are identified that both support and undermine planning program objectives. The planner must then attempt to eliminate or modify incentives that are encouraging counterproductive behavior to the planning objective, and engineer a new incentive program that stimulates desired behaviors for implementation. Ultimately, the final incentive regime that is engineered must be implemented using the behavioral tools of influence and applied persuasion in our advocacy-based society.

CBIP does not dictate a rigid sequence of compartmentalized steps to be followed in a planning intervention, since as Illustration no. 7 implies, there are interrelationships and natural feedback loops between cultural analysis, applied behavioral analysis, incentive construction, and persuasion-based implementation that prevent purely linear thinking. But, as has been previously described, it does suggest a basic framework and progression of considerations. Each practitioner engaging in a CBIP-oriented approach will undoubtedly devise their own customized analysis and design sequence, depending on the nature of the problem and their mental preferences. In other words, in application think conceptually about how you intend to capture the elements of a behavioral-based practice given the individual circumstances. If it works for you personally and for your specific institutional setting, while capturing all the necessary behavioral elements, then you have at least designed one viable approach. The application of CBIP is certainly more professional art and judgment than programmatic procedure.

In the example that follows, the public-agent model created to guide incentive program design is employed to structure the analysis (Illustration no. 8). We start by first delineating the objective of a forestland planning intervention. It is done by backing into the issue by combining a cultural analysis of the current and evolving circumstances associated with forestland fragmentation with a review of current planning programs associated with the issue. By testing current interventions such as exclusive-use zoning against the five tests of performance, insight is gained into cultural considerations. This makes possible the integrated development of a specific program objective, which in turn leads to ensuing steps in the public-agent model. These next steps are to identify the principal-agent relationships, conduct an ABI analysis, and eventually design a specific incentive package, which may include potential institutional changes.

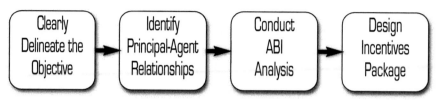

Illustration no. 8 – Public-Agent Format

Forest Fragmentation – Trends and Implications

Forest fragmentation is the division of private forestland into parcels of smaller size. Fragmentation is a long-term trend in every region of the United States, and it is a trend that is accelerating (Birch, 1996; Birch, Hodge, & Thompson, 1998; Sampson & DeCoster, 2000). Between 1978 and 1994, the amount of forestland in small parcels between 10 and 50 acres in size nearly doubled to 60 million acres, as did the number of owners in that size class – 4 million individuals.

In the Lake States region, more than 70 percent of forestland occurs in stands of less than 40 acres (Schmidt & Raile, 1998). In the South, non-industrial forestland owners have always been the dominant ownership class by total numbers and acreage. In Virginia, for instance, 70 percent of forestlands are in the control of private non-industrial owners. In the 16 years between 1978 and 1994, the southern forestland base increased by over 1 million acres, primarily as a result of agricultural land conversion, while the percentage of forestland owners increased by 28 percent from 3.85 million to 4.95 million owners.

The fragmentation trend occurring in forestland is driven by powerful demographic and economic factors. Since 1970, the nation's population has grown 45 percent and is projected to double in the first half of this century. Developed areas are projected to increase 79 percent over the next 25 years, raising the proportion of the nation's total land base that is developed from 5.2 to 9.2 percent (Alig, Kline, & Lichtenstein, 2004). Exurban areas, and in particular, counties high in natural resource amenities, are the fastest growing regions of the nation (Crump, 2003a; Johnson & Beale, 1995). Residential preference studies and other forms of analysis have identified consumer preferences for rural or small town locations, and natural area amenities in residential choice (Austin, 2004; Crump, 2003a; Kaplan & Austin, 2004; Vogt & Marans, 2004). The retirement of 78 million baby boomers looms on the horizon and many of these individuals, an estimated 20 to 30 percent, will seek to relocate, often into rural forested locations.

In addition to the factors just mentioned, the market globalization of commodities is also contributing to fragmentation pressures. Many of the largest forest corporations are electing to sell their forestland base after retaining large block ownerships for more than a century. While companies have historically engaged in massive land sales and exchanges among themselves and with the U.S.D.A. Forest Service in efforts to consolidate or shift ownership patterns for management efficiency, the new trend is something fundamentally different. Large forest product corporations are reverting to the open market to purchase fiber from private sources outside their own companies as a more rational business model. With a long-term glut of wood fiber available on the world market, combined with corporate tax implications, it is now far more rational to purchase raw materials on the open market than to retain their own private fiber supply. In the past, local planners in forested regions could generally count on large corporate forest resources being retained within the industry. This is no longer the case. When combined, all of these factors point to a trend where the rate of forest fragmentation will continue to quicken in America.

In a planning context, it is important to understand that the issue of forestland fragmentation is not one of looming national fiber shortages. The larger issue is, instead, one of management convenience and practices, economies of scale, landowner motivations, and the implications of public goods such as recreational access and regional landscape importance. While the distinction is somewhat subtle, it is important.

Forest product corporations would not be selling their timberland base if there were a timber supply shortage now or projected in the future. Nor would they have banded together for decades in the bitter fight to politically restrict timber imports from Canada, or be engaged in the current painful reduction of capacity in the pulp and paper business due to oversupply. Basic fiber supply is not the issue, although independent mills that have been heavily dependent on the availability of logs from public lands have suffered from serious regional supply problems resulting in local economic dislocations. Advances in intensive forest management and product utilization technologies, as seen in the agricultural industry, continue to encourage the trend of supply outstripping demand.

Moreover, in the last century, not only has standing stumpage increased, so has the domestic forestland base. Between 1907 and 1997 the Northeast regained almost 26 million acres of forest. In 1880, New York was only 25 percent forested but today it is 66 percent forested. Vermont is 80 percent forested and New Hampshire has a tree cover of 90 percent - all dramatic increases over the past 80 years. By the time of the Civil War, many Eastern states had lost 70 percent of their forestland, while today 70 percent of the land that was forested in 1600 is again forested. Most of these gains in the forestland base have come from the conversion of marginal agricultural lands and small subsistence farms back into forests, and are also a result of the educational and technical assistance outreach activities of the forestry profession. Today, forestland is the predominant landform in many states, constituting more than 60 percent of the land base of most eastern states.

The Cultural Matrix Associated with Forestland Fragmentation

Public attitudes and social values tend to be different for forests from other landforms, and they tend to be culture specific. While the general public would never suggest that farmers not harvest their crop at maturity, forest harvesting and associated management activities in America often provoke controversy and local governmental response despite the renewable nature of the resource. This is not the case in many other cultures where landscape sensitive, intensive timber management and harvesting practices are routinely accepted in national parks and immediately adjacent to village boundaries such as in Germany, Austria, and England. In England, land conversion to forest cover types continues to be socially controversial in some settings largely due to a public preference for the aesthetics of open moorlands. Clearly, attitudes toward forestland are shaped by the larger culture and they vary within a culture between cultural and socio-economic subsets.

Most forested regions in the nation today have become communities in transition and conflict as once homogenous rural cultures, largely based on traditional natural resource utilization, have become increasingly diluted with the motivations of urban expatriates. In addition, however, this tension extends far beyond a clash of behavioral motivations within forested rural communities to a broader conflict between entire regions – rural and urban.

The origin of this tension is the ability of forested landscapes to provide a rich mixture of both market and non-market benefits that is highly valued by society. The list of such attributes includes: watershed benefits, habitat, recreation, regional landscape aesthetics, a sense of rural character, and economic returns associated with a plethora of goods and services critical to a modern society.

Aesthetics, recreation, and rural landscape character dominate forestland disputes, although such issues are often professed in terms of ecological values such as the loss of habitat or appeals to maintaining the viability of the commercial forest base. This likely occurs because people believe that issues of open space, aesthetics, and rural character have less legitimacy in public debate so they offer other justifications to support their true interests. Mature forests evoke strong emotions in many people that range from a spiritual appreciation of the resource to the simple enjoyment of their intrinsic beauty. While not necessarily unique to forests, no other classification of privately held landform generates such a strongly held emotional response from an environmental attributes perspective.

Objections to commercial forestry are at their base largely aesthetic, particularly clearcutting, which the untrained eye finds counterintuitive to basic principles of land stewardship. How can something so ugly not be the ultimate affront in soil erosion, habitat loss and general destruction of the environment? Foresters have not been successful in communicating the research realities of their science to the general public, or in many cases, to policy-makers. Moreover, the profession has not fully appreciated that the real issue is one of human landscape values. Forests may be a renewable resource but from the perspective of the short human time frame, the harvesting of a mature forest has a sense of permanency. Within these observations, lies one of the principal problems facing every forester and forest landowner, and by extension, every rural land planner dealing with forestlands within their jurisdiction. Forests are capable of producing a broad range of public benefits, but who pays and how are the various resource values allocated?

On public forestlands the policy debate about the appropriate mix of benefits to be generated by management practice has shifted constantly, and continues as a perpetual point of contention within the various branches of the forestry profession. As difficult as these public discussions are, they are at least not complicated with issues of equity and who pays. Regarding publicly owned lands, we all collectively pay in one fashion or another for the benefit mix that government policy ultimately generates, whether it be for fiber, recreation, habitat or aesthetics.

On private forestlands the issue is far more complicated. Forest fragmentation trends on private lands have a direct relationship to issues of which resource values are most likely to be produced and in what configuration. To what extent, if any, is it appropriate to use government regulatory powers in local planning to force economic burdens on a private forest landowner for the purpose of providing free open space benefits to the general public, particularly given the thin margins or negative returns associated with forestland ownership? What unintended consequences might such public policies have in distorting the decision making of forestland owners in counterproductive ways?

In a recent study conducted by the Virginia Department of Forestry for the State legislature, it was determined that 379 local government ordinances in the state affected 10 percent to 33 percent of operable forested areas within their jurisdictions to some degree (Mortimer, Prisley, Daversa, & Stull, 2005). Despite Virginia's Right to Practice Forestry Law that attempts to encourage forestry through standardization of silvicultural regulations through the State Department of Forestry, local governments' efforts to preserve forest resources often create a perverse economic and psychological incentive for private landowners to convert such lands prematurely.

Serious issues of environmental justice arise when the political power of majority urban interests imposes significant economic hardships on rural forest landowners in order to derive such desired public goods as open space and rural character. The issue is not whether the objective of maintaining rural character is somehow unworthy. As will be argued shortly, it is of paramount importance among forestland management objectives in today's society. The real question is how best to achieve these public management objectives in an equitable and realistic way? Heretofore, most attempts have been through command-and-control regulations such as forest practices legislation, best management programs, and the application of various zoning tools. An alternative solution that may have greater authority in a culture dominated by competitive individualism is the institutional design of a public-agent approach whereby private interests are more closely aligned through incentives with public motivations.

Under CBIP's public-agent model for incentive construction, the delineation of the planning objective should reflect cultural sensitivity. Part of that cultural analysis is an understanding of the perspectives of the various audiences concerned with the issue of fragmentation. Within the forest management and forest landowner communities those perspectives vary. The issue of fragmentation for many procurement-oriented foresters is the potential loss of commercial timber management potential, which is a different concern than that of reduction in forestlands in general, or the loss of rural character.

For other foresters involved in the promotion of conservation, it is the concern of how to deliver basic land stewardship education and services to large blocks of small landowners. Traditional commercial timber harvesting techniques benefit from economies of scale. Below parcel sizes of about 40 acres, current industrial harvesting practices, and in particular the transport and set-up of heavy logging equipment, tend to become uneconomic. From a management perspective, it is also simply harder to deal with hundreds of small forestland owners as opposed to a smaller population of large-tract owners.

The demographic characteristics and motivations of non-industrial forestland owners are also an issue and they are shifting. Ownership trends are moving from older, less educated individuals of moderate incomes who were more prone to engage in commercial harvesting, to well educated early retirees of substantial means. Lifestyle concerns are becoming the motive for small-tract forest owners with wildlife, recreation and aesthetics constituting their primary interests (Angelina,

2003; Campbell & Kittredge, 1996; Gobster & Rickenbach, 2004). Forest management interests in this demographic group are shifting to landscape forestry or what some foresters are describing as "woodscaping" where country estate management is the underlying objective.

These shifts in ownership profiles are beginning to stimulate experimentation in management regimes such as the establishment of cooperative forest banks, cluster development formats, landowner incentive programs, and small scale harvesting technologies (Campbell & Kittredge, 1996; Dedrick, Hall, Hull, & Johnson, 2000). Landscape forestry and woodscaping, which are the desired aesthetics of many of today's small-tract owners, still produce forest harvesting and commercial potential. One difference, however, is that the landowner partially pays for the landscape objective, since the commercial harvesting aspects of the management regime tend to be uneconomic under today's market conditions and harvesting systems. All these considerations suggest that in the future, new institutions in both forest management and planning may have to evolve to accommodate this new mix of objectives.

Existing Programs and the Tests of Performance Under CBIP

One effective way to back into a CBIP-based analysis of forest fragmentation, or of any other planning issue, is to review existing program approaches from the perspective of the five tests of performance that have been previously described. By considering current program approaches against such tests, insight is gained into the behavioral dynamics surrounding the current planning regimes. Such an exercise also helps to point a spotlight on the underlying objectives. Are the objectives clear? Do current programs really address the underlying objective(s)? And most fundamentally, has the right objective(s) been delineated in the first place?

Local government forestland planning is an endeavor that spans two different disciplines – forestry with its base in the natural and physical sciences, and the profession of land planning. The practice of regulatory-based forestland planning on private land, utilizing the traditional planning and ordinance tools of local governments, falls on the outer periphery of both professions. Neither foresters nor local government land planners typically receive substantial academic training or engage professionally on a routine basis in this unique area. What activity that does occur in this area is often an afterthought associated with some other project or program responsibility.

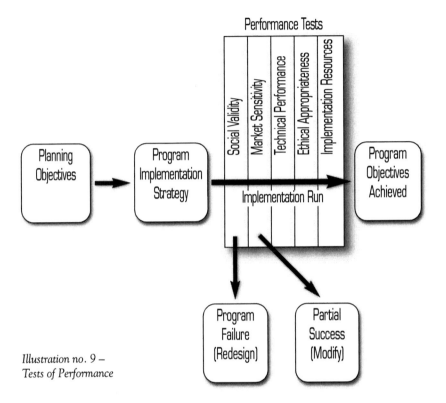

Illustration no. 9 – Tests of Performance

There is a strong tendency in the planning literature, the classroom, and the profession to both literally and figuratively lump forest planning considerations with agriculture. It's a poor fit that dismisses the unique circumstances associated with forestland economics and culture, and diminishes the ability to effectively plan for a landform that dominates in many rural jurisdictions. It also results in a muted vision of underlying planning objectives. Are the circumstances and objectives of the planning intervention the same as those for agricultural land in the jurisdiction? Are the underlying objectives those of the non-industrial forest landowner community, commercial forestry interests, or individuals with an urban outlook?

Very little has been written or researched specifically in the area of private forestland planning from a local government planner's perspective in contrast to volumes about agricultural land planning issues. It is rare to find dedicated zoning districts and other planning mechanisms solely developed for forestry. The primary planning tools now in widespread application for forestry (exclusive-use zoning districts, large-lot or rural residential zoning districts, and purchase of development rights programs) all provide valuable insight into the design of a CBIP-based intervention. These various planning programs are considered below as the next step in the design of a culturally-sensitive, behavioral-based approach to forest fragmentation.

Exclusive-Use Districts

Exclusive-use natural resource zoning districts theoretically restrict permitted uses to only agricultural and forestry applications, including accessory uses like farm dwellings. Residential density restrictions range from a typical 20-acre minimum lot size in the eastern United States to as much as a 640-acre minimum lot size in one Colorado county. These districts are employed in some cases by local governments in attempts to stabilize the resource land base, while in other circumstances the districts are essentially viewed as long-term holding zones with individual parcels reclassified as demand rises.

Unfortunately, the technique suffers from a variety of weaknesses in practice. It is politically unstable over time as the motivations and circumstances of individual landowners and elected officials change. In their development and adoption, the district designs often pit resource landowners against each other, generating significant controversy and opposition in some quarters. While certain owners may want to preserve their development options into the future, others may hold a different set of objectives whereby they gain personal advantage if neighboring tracts have been stripped of any development potential. As a technique, it is politically unpopular in many rural jurisdictions, and it has rarely been employed in a fashion that is effective and stable over time. In fact, the record is one of aggravating land conversion trends as noted below (Diaz & Green, 2001; Esparza & Carruthers, 2000). The technique can also be highly inequitable for area landowners stripped of any meaningful development potential, particularly when imposed by state mandates driven by urban interests to preserve rural character or open space.

To be effective, the minimum lot size requirement has to be established at a very low density, but to achieve political consensus in most rural areas the average density is set at a 10 to 40 acre minimum, which is far too high for traditional commercial forestry. At these density thresholds, there is a surprisingly high level of demand for country estates and so-called hobby tree farms that results in the fragmentation of forestland at accelerated rates since lot size requirements are so large. I have witnessed excessive conversion rates even with lot size requirements of 40 acres or larger. At development densities ranging from 10 to 40 acres, rural character is quickly lost unless mandatory clustering is imposed. The technique, in only accommodating rural residential demand at very low densities, also has the tendency to shift market demand across jurisdictional lines where the zoning may be more accommodative. The result is that rural sprawl is encouraged on a regional basis into other forested areas.

Most exclusive-use districts are riddled with administrative loopholes. Landowners in such areas are often conflicted in their interests when considering such zoning proposals. They may like the idea of restricting another person's ability to subdivide today, but may want to maintain some development flexibility for their own circumstances in the future. As a result such districts routinely have family member exemptions, occasional lot sale provisions, and a variety of other loopholes that inevitably undermine the original intent of the zoning district. Rigorous consistency in zoning administration is another key to the effectiveness of exclusive-use districts, and in most rural environments the long-term political support required to make such zoning work for traditional approaches to commercial forestry is lacking.

A final limitation associated with exclusive-use districts is the potential economic impact on the community. There is often an assumption that very low-density, exclusive-use districts provide an important economic benefit to natural-resource-dependent communities by reserving the land base for commercial forestry or farming in support of processing facilities nearby. But there is strong field evidence that the inverse may be true under many market situations. Many communities in the Pacific Northwest that have historically been dependent on commercial forestry and related processing facilities, have been routinely devastated as market conditions in the industry have declined and mills have closed. This same pattern has been observed in the Upper Great Lakes states, Maine and areas of the Southeast.

Exclusive-Use Districts		
Performance		
High	Low	
	◆	Social Validity
	◆	Market Sensitivity
◆		Technical Performance
	◆	Ethical Appropriateness
◆		Implementation Resources

In those few areas where exclusive-use zoning has been applied and administered rigorously enough to freeze the rural land base into only commercial forestry or farming applications, an interesting pattern is observed. In eastern Oregon where state planning mandates of minimum lot sizes as large as 160 acres have largely achieved the exclusive-use objective, many timber and agriculture-dependent communities have been suffering a slow, agonizing decline despite some outstanding natural environment attributes surrounding them – places like John Day, Vale, Baker, La Grande and Enterprise. Cross the state line into Idaho, and a different pattern emerges in very similar natural-resource-dependent communities. Many of the Idaho resource-dependent communities, where exclusive-use zoning is not widely employed, are regaining or expanding economic health due to rural residential demand as a result of their recreational attributes and rural character. Old Idaho timber-dependent communities such as Sandpoint, Coeur d' Alene, McCall and Salmon have either been successful in maintaining their basic economic health or in radically transforming themselves into modern, rural culture-based centers. Exclusive-use zoning, if politically maintained over long time periods, which is unlikely to happen, can maintain the commercial forest base by freezing it in place, but the technique cannot ensure the economic vitality of the enterprise.

Large-Lot Rural Residential Districts

The second and most prevalent regulatory planning approach applied to private forestlands is large-lot, rural residential zoning districts. Rural residential uses are generally permitted by-right at established densities that range from 2 acres to 10 acres. Densities are routinely established based on minimum lot size requirements, not gross or net density calculations that might permit lot size averaging or clustering.

The districts serve limited planning benefit and are certainly counterproductive to many planning objectives, whether to maintain commercial timber viability or a sense of rural character, but they are popular with the rural public and in the marketplace. As Randall Arendt has famously quoted, "The lots are too small to farm and too big to mow"(Arendt, 1994). The initial popularity of the district type in many rural settings is because it is perceived to provide three benefits depending on individual perspectives. The first is that most people mistakenly believe that under a 2 to 10-acre-minimum lot size requirement, rural character will be maintained. What occurs, in fact, is an exurban rural sprawl appearance - a systemic suburban development pattern on large lots. The most critical element to how humans perceive rural character disappears - irregular but sizeable expanses of open space that are devoid of buildings. Most people cannot judge the size of 2, 5 or 10-acre lots in their minds. When shown physical examples of what such minimum lot size requirements look like at full build-out, they are surprised at how suburban, not rural, it appears. The key is how residential density is established, lot size requirement or gross density on the tract, and how it is placed on the land

Large-Lot Rural Residential Districts		
Performance		
High	Low	
◆		Social Validity
◆		Market Sensitivity
	◆	Technical Performance
Variable		Ethical Appropriateness
◆		Implementation Resources

A second perceived advantage in some community circles is that such densities are assumed to be economically exclusive - a way to create a gated community without a gate. Exclusionary zoning can be a local government strategy to encourage large, expensive homes filled with wealthy retirees without children, a format for maximizing net property tax revenue. It can also be a community technique to exclude housing diversity for all economic classes - a breach of ethical standards for professional planners. It should be noted that large-lot zoning is not exclusionary on its face. It depends on the circumstances. When applied on the fringe of growing metropolitan areas where land values may be high, it tends to have an exclusionary effect or motive. But when applied in the deep rural regions of some forestland areas where land costs are relatively low, the effect may not occur.

The third advantage perceived by the public for large-lot zoning is that of "having your cake and eating it too." If you believe that it will maintain rural character, a strongly stated goal of most residents in these areas, but you want to maintain your financial flexibility to benefit from your property's development potential, then large-lot zoning looks like the perfect solution to the mixed objectives. It is also a handy political compromise.

From a regional market perspective in areas of growing rural housing demand, the smaller the lot size requirement, the less forestland will be converted. Ten-acre-minimum lot size requirements in robust rural housing markets have the counterintuitive effect of converting more land than a five acre or one acre requirement. But none of these densities will maintain rural character or the viability of other forestland attributes such as wildlife corridors or commercial timber potential. We will explore a technique that will in an ensuing section.

Transfer of Development Right Programs (TDR)

TDR programs are a planning innovation that allow the transfer and sale of development rights from one parcel of land to another. Under normal practice, a local government establishes a "sending area," for instance a region of forestland that it wishes to protect from development, and a "receiving area" where development is encouraged. Landowners in the receiving area who want to build to full residential density or to receive bonus density for their development proposal, purchase and transfer development rights from a willing seller in the sending area. Theoretically, the open marketplace establishes the value of a development right, although to make such systems work, local governments have been forced to create an artificial market floor.

TDR Programs		
Performance		
High	Low	
◆		Social Validity
	◆	Market Sensitivity
	◆	Technical Performance
◆ When functioning		Ethical Appropriateness
	◆	Implementation Resources

The concept, which requires local governments to establish an artificial market for the sale and transfer of development rights, was an innovation to create equity between landowners – a potential solution to the "windfalls and wipeout" problem of zoning. Conceptually it was brilliant, and many of us held out high hopes for the technique 20 or 30 years ago. If successful, it would have solved the age-old problem of compensating landowners at fair market value for the restriction or complete loss of development rights on their land so that society could benefit from the rural character and preserved open space. It also was a mechanism to price and allocate the public goods involved.

TDR programs, of which there are only a handful of successful ones in the nation after nearly three decades of attempts, are complicated to establish and difficult to administer. They require substantial local government resources, which are often beyond the financial and manpower capabilities of most forest dominated rural jurisdictions. Most of the successful programs were forced to establish TDR banks with significant public funding to enable the market to operate. TDR programs also require active real estate markets under steady growth, principally suburban counties with a high level of growth pressure. For all these reasons, TDR programs are generally poorly suited for rural forestland protection schemes except in the most select of circumstances.

Conservation Easements and Purchase of Development Rights Programs

A conservation easement is a legal agreement between a landowner and a government agency or non-profit organization that limits development rights. Conservation easements are often charitable grants by landowners, partially stimulated by the associated tax benefit of making such a contribution under federal and state tax laws. The economic inducement provided by existing tax programs, however, is generally small in relation to the economic value contributed, and hence the technique relies heavily on altruistic behavior. As a technique, one of its principal weaknesses is in the area of market sensitivity. Few individuals in American society, particularly rural landowners, can afford to donate substantial monetary resources on the magnitude of a sizeable conservation easement. Nor are most people behaviorally so altruistic, and even when they may be, many are subject to a sense of family obligation and social pressure in regards to their potential heirs.

Conservation easements, however, can also be established through monetary transactions where development rights are directly purchased by a non-profit or government entity. Purchase of development rights programs (PDRs) are most often the mechanism by which such sales occur. Both state and local governments have been active in the passage of bond issues or the establishment of other funding sources to finance PDR programs.

Conservation easements and PDR programs can be valuable planning tools, but they have significant limitations in a technical performance and resource availability context, as well as the market limitations previously mentioned. The techniques are most effective when concentrated on specific, high-value open space and public access objectives. High-value objectives might include greenway corridors, waterfront access, strategic parcels of open space in suburbanizing areas, and for the protection of wetlands or unique stands of old growth timber.

As a tool to maintain rural character or commercial forestland potential, PDR and conservation easement programs are, however, generally ineffective. The resource base requiring protection is simply too large. Depending on definition, the U.S. has approximately 1.5 billion acres of private rural land constituting 65 percent of the nation's land base. Scattered conservation easements that have been donated are not sufficient to protect the broad land resources necessary if the objective is to maintain rural character or commercial forestry potential under current commercial timber management regimes.

Conservation Easement Programs		
Performance		
High	Low	
◆		Social Validity
	◆	Market Sensitivity
	◆	Technical Performance
Can be subject to system abuse		Ethical Appropriateness
	◆	Implementation Resources

By way of example, consider that the Virginia Outdoors Foundation, a state agency, is the recipient of most conservation easements in the state. Its total conservation easement holdings as of 2005 were 329,800 acres, generated by the aggressive activities of conservation land trusts around Virginia. While an impressive number, it is only 515 square miles, or slightly more than 1 percent of a state that is 64 percent forested. PDR program funding will never be large enough to accomplish the objective of preserving rural character or commercial forestry resources in a jurisdiction. Such limited funding is best directed to more specific, high-value resource objectives in suburbanizing locations.

Rural Clustering and Conservation Design Ordinances

Rural clustering and conservation design ordinances were the final general classification of planning techniques in practice today that were analyzed under the fragmentation study. Under the considerations of CBIP, they offer the greatest promise for improvement in planning performance among existing tools described in the exemplar. The remainder of this section will describe the basic attributes of rural clustering and conservation design ordinances that make them an attractive implementation tool under CBIP analysis.

Land planners have been using the concept of clustering since the advent of organized civilization. Knossos, the ancient capital of the Minoan civilization on the Greek island of Crete was a highly complex cluster design dating from 1900 B.C., nearly 4,000 years ago. Ancient Akrotiri on the Greek Island of Thira, the likely home of the lost city of Atlantis, was also a cluster design. The Norman Doomsday Book, a comprehensive survey of English property in the year 1086, along with substantial documentation from current-day landscape archeologists and planning historians, affirm the common use of rural clustering in field, forest, and hamlet patterns throughout the Middle Ages (Williamson & Bellamy, 1987). These practices are still widely employed in Western Europe and Great Britain today, and are the very basis of their national planning policies in natural resource areas where rural landscape character and land conservation goals dominate far more than in America (Cullingworth & Nadin, 2006).

In the context of modern-day America, rural clustering has been actively advocated in cluster zoning provisions for more than 35 years. William Whyte in 1968 advanced cluster zoning for the purpose of preserving rural character in his watershed work, *The Last Landscape* (Whyte, 1968). During the same time period, Ian McHarg pursued a parallel course of ecological site analysis and design principles as did Palmer (McHarg, 1969; Palmer, 1981). Most recently, Randall Arendt, drawing upon his early English planning exposure and the work of others before him, has been the most publicized advocate of an improved format of rural clustering commonly referred to as conservation zoning and subdivision design (Arendt, 1994, 1996, 1999, 2004).

Cluster zoning formats allow or require the density transfer of residential lots internally on a site for the express purpose of maintaining open space, rural character, and/or natural resource management potentials. These zoning districts function by allowing smaller lot sizes on a tract where larger lots are normally required. Under cluster zoning anywhere from 50 percent to as much as 90 percent of the land is set aside as conservation land, open space, or may be retained for traditional forest practices.

Rural cluster zoning as a tool to cope with forest fragmentation trends has a considerable constructive potential under the fundamental tests of a CBIP-based outlook, unlike many of the other common planning approaches to forestlands now in practice that contain basic flaws that are difficult, if not impossible, to realistically overcome. While the potential of rural clustering has not been broadly realized in field practice, the techniques of a behavioral–based, incentives-oriented approach could dramatically unleash its latent potential.

Rural clustering is capable of preserving and enhancing rural character, open space, pedestrian linked access, and even commercial resource potential over large regions, while still accommodating rural residential housing demand. It can do so without causing substantial market distortions or creating serious economic impositions on rural landowners. Other current planning techniques cannot do this due to a variety of technical, monetary, or political limitations.

Rural Clustering and Conservation Design Ordinances	
Performance High　　　　　　Low	
◆ (Under CBIP practice)	Social Validity
◆ (Under CBIP practice)	Market Sensitivity
◆	Technical Performance
◆	Ethical Appropriateness
◆	Implementation Resources

The technique does not require peak performance to generate substantial benefits. Even when projects are designed or approved in less than an ideal manner, the accumulative results are far superior to the typical development patterns now being generated in most rural communities. When designed with finesse, the technique tends to be more sensitive to rural values and American culture, offering a higher level of social validity and political acceptance in rural communities where rigorous command-and-control regulatory formats have historically been divisive and politically unstable.

Moreover, the concept of rural clustering is easily adaptable to a variety of different community objectives and circumstances. It is also relatively convenient to retrofit most existing comprehensive plans and land-use ordinances under the technique without substantial public expense or effort. And the technique can be administered within the constraints of a typical rural planning office.

Among those factors that have restricted the full potential of the tool are a lack of market familiarity, a perception of market recalcitrance, and a weak or often unintentionally distorted incentive regime. All are factors that a CBIP-based practice is capable of remedying. Consider the following research conclusions. Rural clustering projects, while still not common in the marketplace, are well received where they have been introduced. Lot sale premiums range from 30 percent to 50 percent higher per acre than in traditional subdivisions, and lot sales occur 20 percent to 30 percent faster (Mohamed, 2006a). Lot/home resale values from the homeowner's perspective have been 15 percent to 25 percent higher in rural clusters than comparable lots/homes in standard projects in the same marketplace (Lacy, 1990). Development costs for the lots are 15 percent to 54 percent less expensive due to a reduction in infrastructure runs, primarily in road lengths and power line extensions (Mohamed, 2006a). The sense of community and neighborhood satisfaction is higher for homeowners in cluster or conservation designed developments (Austin, 2004; Kaplan & Austin, 2004; Kim & Kaplan, 2004; Vogt & Marans, 2004). Finally, public preference research in rural areas indicates that rural residents support and prefer conservation design subdivisions (rural clustering) as more compatible and more effective in maintaining rural character (Ryan, 2006).

From the perspective of a CBIP-based analysis, summarized momentarily, rural clustering provides the best prospects among current planning tools to meet the unique cultural and behavioral circumstances associated with forest fragmentation. But that conclusion is unique to the objective that the above analysis generates. As is characterized in the CBIP model, it is important to remember that the elements of CBIP not only assist in the design of a behavioral-based implementation regime for improved performance, but they also help to define the underlying objectives (see Illustration no. 1).

Delineation of the Planning Objective and Public–Agent Relationships

As with all land planning processes, CBIP requires that a fundamental question be answered when undertaking a potential planning intervention. What are the true public management objectives? The standard planning approaches for forestland just discussed, particularly the most common tools of large-lot rural residential zoning and exclusive-use zoning, tend to be applied in local practice under poorly defined objectives. Is the objective to enhance or protect private interests or to generate certain public goods? What are the private and public goods in question, and in what combination and quantity are they to be generated under the stated objective? One of the advantages of the CBIP process is that it tends to force a greater degree of specificity in the delineation of program objectives since behavior analysis and incentive design must be focused on specific behavior outcomes, not broad platitudes of intent.

Every community, when considering its planning approach to private forestlands, must consider its individual circumstances. Their individual circumstances may dictate a different goal orientation than that which is about to be suggested. But for the vast majority of communities with substantial forestlands under potential development pressure, the strategic objectives about to be suggested offer one rational advocacy position given the cultural and behavioral dynamics of the issue. Here in summary are the elements of that logic.

Commercial forestry, even more so than small-scale agriculture, is at the very margin of economic justification. Local government policy implemented through planning ordinance provisions can only encourage, but not ensure or dictate, the continuance of traditionally practiced commercial forestry as the principal activity on private forestlands in areas under rural development pressure. Moreover, the narrowly focused objective to preserve commercial forestry potential assumes that it is a pubic good in high demand, and a public good of such importance, scarcity, or fragility as to justify government intervention. The analysis surrounding commercial forestry does not suggest that to be the case.

In addition, a number of powerful economic and demographic trends, along with cultural preferences, are exerting pressure on forestlands that overwhelm the traditional control strategies of local governments to preserve commercial forestry as it has historically been practiced. While traditional control strategies may be marginally effective in the short term in some applications, commercial forest management is not a short-term enterprise, nor is it one immune from global market pressures. Any public planning interventions aimed at private forestland should reflect these realities, while avoiding creating unintended adverse incentives to either prematurely convert land or to convert land in ways that fail to conserve strategically important public goods that are truly of high value and at high risk.

When all the potential public planning goals associated with private forestlands are considered, including commercial timber viability, habitat protection, watershed management, recreation, and suburban containment, the most pressing public concern is most likely the landscape objective of preserving a picturesque form of rural character. Note that it is possible for an area to remain rural, but to lose its rural character. It is also possible to make a distinction in quality. The public good in demand is arguably the community and landscape experience of Norman Rockwell. This, in fact, is the heart of the landscape management regime practiced in the English national parks and on America's Blue Ridge Parkway.

The issue of maintaining and enhancing picturesque rural character has ramifications in strongly expressed public preferences, both in rural and urban populations (Bliss, Nepal, Brooks, & Larsen, 1994; Gobster, 2004; Kaplan & Austin, 2004; Kaplan, Kaplan, & Ryan, 1998; Ryan, 2006; Tilt, Kearney, & Bradley, 2006). It is a resource attribute that is rapidly disappearing in the American landscape, as population growth and certain prevalent rural development practices march forward (Crump, 2003b; Esrza & Carruthers, 2000; Fulton et al., 2001). As an issue, it is also center stage in many rural community economic strategies and in larger regional considerations of urban containment.

As an attribute of the natural and man-made environment, rural character in the landscape is highly sensitive to certain development practices that can quickly transform an area. How to define rural character has always been an interesting discussion among rural planners. Recent research has begun to isolate these factors that most influence human impressions and preferences in rural landscapes (Austin, 2004; Kaplan & Austin, 2004; Kaplan et al., 1998; Ryan, 2006; Tilt et al., 2006). Humans perceive rural character as large uninterrupted viewscapes, particularly irregular field and forest stands adjacent to roads, interspersed with small, irregular clusters of residents or individual homes. Open space views devoid of structures in the foreground, along with other commonly associated rural culture attributes such as farm fencing or agricultural buildings, combine to create the landscape vernacular in the public's mind. It is also not so much about the presence or density of structures, as their configuration, design, and location on the landscape.

It is suspected that a major consideration in rural character is the visual illusion of accessibility. In America with our conditioning to certain landscape vernaculars, rural development patterns that communicate to the mind exclusivity and private property, that is, development patterns that we equate with suburban lots where we would feel quite uncomfortable violating someone's private space, look more urban than rural to the American eye. Large-lot rural sprawl patterns, even at very large lot sizes of 20 or 40 acres, increase this sense of exclusivity (land out-of-bounds), and a sense of creeping urbanism that doesn't permit people to visually imagine a landscape as substantial, quasi-public domain. Rural character isn't so much tied to the concept of public land access in America, unlike England where rural public pedestrian access is widespread, as it is to the visual illusion of quasi-public open space.

The loss of these visual traits is particularly likely under common rural land development practices where roadside viewscapes become dominated or interspersed with rural residential development that has the appearance of low-density suburban development patterns and architecture that is out of place. Humans, by visual and cultural conditioning, equate certain landscape appearances with certain values that become landscape vernaculars in a society. For instance, today's suburban home buyers expect to see closely mowed lawns and certain highly structured and neat landscaping styles in suburban projects, and they equate certain traits to the owners of such lots – responsibility, success and being a good neighbor among others. Research has shown that farmers develop such farm appearance vernacular stereotypes as to who is a good versus a poor farmer, and that these vernacular views can change slowly over time as accepted farming practices change (Ulrich, 1983, 1986). Similar observations in public responses to forest practices has also been observed (Bradley, 1995). These landscape vernaculars develop by both organic forces and by specific design.

What people interpret as rural character can be retained by certain design techniques that accommodate rural housing demand while simultaneously maintaining important viewscape characteristics (Arendt, 1994, 1996, 1999). The key to encouraging such development formats is the proper construction of land-use codes, particularly as they relate to development in forested areas where public residential demands are higher, and where aesthetic management is easier to achieve than open field locations. This is a circumstance where forest landowner economic options can be maintained and public objectives achieved in a way that is fair to all parties. It is capitalism mated with conservation.

The issue of rural landscape character is also directly tied to the economic health of high-amenity rural jurisdictions that are increasingly dependent on recreation, tourism and the immigration of affluent retirees (Green, Marcouiller, Deller, Erkkila, & Sumathi, 1996; Power, 2000). Over the last 30 years as forest-based communities have suffered serious economic impacts with the decline of traditional natural resource industries and the demise of local manufacturing, the lifeblood of their economic futures has become attractive landscape characteristics which support a broad range of service sector, supplier, and construction industry classifications. It is also enriching the local landowner community directly as land values rise.

While the economic return from forestry, farming, and ranching has traditionally determined rural land prices, ranging from several hundred dollars to several thousand dollars an acre, recreational demand in many areas is redefining rural land markets at far higher prices. These prices range as high as $10,000 to $30,000 per acre for parcels in the 20 to 40-acre range. This is having a significant wealth effect on traditionally depressed rural economies, and while some may bemoan the ability of commercial operations to compete, the rural landowner community generally delights in the dramatically increased value of their retirement, investment, or inheritance legacy. Paradoxically, the very activities and development that are the result of people being attracted to these resource values can also threaten the underlying attributes. The planning objective, it is argued, should be to sustain and expand this important element of many rural economies while simultaneously conserving the resource values that drive the sector.

Finally, maintaining rural character has a direct connection with the nation's single largest land use dilemma – the containment of exurban development and maintaining separation between growing metropolitan areas. Clever construction of forestland planning programs may hold the best hope for urban containment and separation. Where suburban and urban jurisdictions have been unable to achieve important societal planning objectives, their rural counterparts may offer key long-term solutions.

Public–Agent Relationships

Under CBIP, once an objective is clearly defined, in this case the retention of rural character, it allows a better definition of the public–agent relationships that are central to the engineering of a behavior-based incentive program. Again, under incentive theory and the principal–agent relationship, the objective is to design incentive-based programs that align the interests of the agent with those of the principal. In some cases this may require the redesign of existing planning institutions or the invention of entirely new institutions to provide a framework for the structuring of incentives between principal and agent. CBIP, with its focus on planning interventions, is most often concerned with the production of public goods and the management of externalities. Hence, in many circumstances the principal is some element or aspect of the general public, which is why CBIP's incentive-based approach could be described as a modified public–agent model.

In the current example of forest fragmentation with the objective of retaining rural character, there are several sets of public–agent relationships. They include:

Public/Principal	Agent
Rural Community	Forest Landowner/ Landowner Developer
Rural Community	Rural Residential Consumer (home purchaser)
Urban Culture	Forest Landowner/Landowner Developer
Urban Culture	Rural Residential Consumer (home purchaser)
Forest Products - Producers/Consumers	Forest Landowner/Cluster project homeowners

In this particular case, the motivations of the rural community and an outlying urban culture are similar, but not necessarily identical. Both may want to retain and enhance rural character, and subsequently design incentives to encourage certain behaviors among individual forest landowners. However, the rural community has specific motivations, such as enhancing rural economic vitality that the urban public does not. This implies that collaboration between the two would be ideal in aligning objectives for the design of incentives for forest landowners, for without it, a secondary competition will likely result between rural and urban public interests as to who is in the role of principal. State-based growth management schemes that attempt to impose an urban outlook on rural communities at their local expense, is an example of the friction that can be generated, often in the form of legislative opposition or lack of local government cooperation. Rural government policies that ignore issues of high-value, urban public goods, such as rural character, are an inverse example.

In the case of rural character it can also be seen that any incentive program has to be concerned with multiple principal–agent relationships. These multiple incentive relationships exist for most complex planning issues. In this particular instance, incentives have to be aligned to encourage certain behaviors for not only forest landowners, but also to direct consumer preference in rural housing choice, and in cluster project land management to retain commercial resource utilization capabilities. Cluster forest projects are fully capable of maintaining commercial forestry potential after development, albeit under different management regimes, but to do so requires the right kind of incentives for project developers and future owners. With principal–agent relationships identified, along with the management objectives that define those relationships, it is now possible to engage in an antecedents-behavior-incentives analysis (ABI) and the construction of the incentives-based implementation program.

Incentive Program Design and ABI Analysis

In developing specific incentive strategies to accomplish the stated public objective of enhancing rural character, it is important to consider the behavioral incentive landscape for forestland owners. One way to structure that analysis is the construction of an ABI grid (antecedents-behavior-incentives table) where the elements of current behavior are outlined for a given issue, and then an alternative set of incentives is proposed for the intervention. The technique is a convenient way to summarize a number of involved behavioral considerations. In the previous chapter an example of an ABI grid was presented related to developer acceptance of rural cluster ordinance options.

An alternative to the ABI grid is the development of a written narrative format. By way of example, the remainder of this chapter presents a written narrative for the same issue – the encouragement by code of rural conservation clusters as the dominant development format in forested regions. That example is then carried to one more level of detail by presenting in the appendix model zoning and subdivision ordinance language that specifically implements a CBIP-based incentive strategy.

ABI Narrative

Landowners who are concerned with commercial forestry potentials face one set of realities that drives incentive-based behavior. Small, non-industrial landowners unconcerned with commercial forestry potentials are driven by a second set of factors. As a general statement, no land-based economic activity has a longer investment horizon than commercial forestry, lower return on investment, and in some regards, greater risk that is economically uninsurable. These very long investment time horizons associated with commercial forest management have a dominant impact on commercially oriented landowners along with issues of taxation and land conversion.

The majority of the cost associated with commercial forest management occurs in the early years of forest-stand establishment – site preparation, planting, and pre-commercial thinning. The landowner then waits substantial time periods for a potential return on investment, while at the same time he or she is considering the original purchase price of the forestland along with annual property taxes. In the softwood forests of the Pacific Northwest primarily composed of conifers, the rotation length is typically 40 to 50 years under intensive management. In the eastern hardwood forests, rotation lengths are typically 100 years or longer. The shortest rotations of around 25 to 35 years can be achieved in the southern coastal plain and piedmont pine plantations.

When an investor discounts management investments back to current-day dollars, he or she is likely facing a return of less than 6 percent on an investment that will not generate a positive cash flow for 40 to 100 years. From a behavioral economics viewpoint, these are traits that are highly unattractive to human psychology, particularly for individuals as opposed to larger institutions. Humans are risk adverse and like rewards sooner than later. Forestry represents the exact opposite in comparison to other investment options. Consider that the meager return on investment for non-industrial forest landowners engaged in commercial management will go to their children or their grandchildren, but certainly not to them. This consideration plays on the investment psychology of many landowners.

What every local planner concerned with conserving forest resources has to remember is that virtually any other viable economic activity to which forestland can be converted pays more than commercial forest management, often substantially more. Even isolated rural lots at densities as low as one house per 40 acres, pay an economic return higher than that of commercial forestry in many circumstances after the conductance of a landscape-oriented timber harvest in which most of the commercial forest value is removed. An individual or company cannot pay more than several hundred dollars per acre in many forestland settings for "bare land value" (i.e. bare land that has been recently harvested) and hope to make the investment pencil for long-term commercial forestry.

Low return on investment has historically made large forest products companies with substantial land bases susceptible to corporate raiders. Many forestry firms with substantial land assets have been ripped apart in leveraged buyouts and unfriendly takeovers, or have chosen voluntarily as a rational business decision to sell off their land base in bulk or through real estate development subsidiaries. In the former case, such was the demise of such venerable firms as Scott Paper, Diamond International, Crown Zellerbach and others. This fact has ramifications for local government planners.

In a private conversation with the chief economist of arguably the nation's, and probably the world's, best run forest products firm the question was asked, "Why does company *xyz* stay in the forestry business instead of divesting into other more profitable realms?" The cheeky answer, "Because we don't know how to make pantyhose." His point was that its not necessarily rational economic behavior, which can also be said for the motivations of many non-industrial forestland owners.

Surveys repeatedly indicate that non-industrial forestland owners as a class are subject to the same behavioral dynamics. In general, these are often individuals who enjoy the intangible benefits of owning and managing forestland even though it is not rational economic behavior, or they inherited or acquired the land in some other fashion and have limited options in ownership.

The long investment horizons for forestry also inject a higher level of uncertainty and risk for the owners of this land class. Risks from natural disasters such as fire, ice and wind related weather events, wildlife damage, and insect outbreaks are extensive over an investment time horizon that may exceed a century. In agriculture when you suffer a catastrophic loss, you have generally lost one year of investment and can hopefully regain a positive cash flow the next growing season. In forestry, you may lose decades of unrealized investment with no prospect of a positive cash flow for decades to come.

The long investment time horizons in forestry also inject greater market risk, such as substitution to non-wood products, international competition, and market shifts. An area related specifically to local governments is the regulatory risk of being prohibited from engaging in harvest and management activities such as slash burns and herbicide or pesticide use as urban encroachment slowly surrounds a forest stand nurtured over 60 years of investment. Partially due to this later risk and because forestland sitting on the rural/urban interface almost always reflects a better investment if converted from forest to rural residential, forest landowners routinely evaluate their land holdings on the "fringe" for possible conversion. Regulatory risk and public relations considerations are a major concern at the time of harvest of a mature forest stand anywhere near an expanding urban area or in areas of rural recreational development potential.

Forestland planning is the ultimate long-range planning exercise. Where urban planners may think in terms of a 20-year comprehensive plan vision, forest planners must think in terms of the length of a timber rotation (40 to 100 years) when staring at a recently harvested tract. Taking regulatory and public relations risks into consideration, they ask themselves, "If I reinvest in this tract today for forest purposes will I be allowed to harvest this investment 60 years from now or will I likely be surrounded by some form of residential development?" You can guess the rational answer that is often rendered, with the tract converted for either exurban or recreational land development.

The long time horizons associated with forestry have one more perverse effect impacting local planning and policy that is unique to the land classification - the effect of property taxes. Decades of research and practical experience have shown that the retention of forestlands is hypersensitive to the impact of property tax structures and rates in comparison to other land types. Even at the low rates associated with most forestland, property taxes can quickly become confiscatory when you have to contend with the realities of forest economics.

By way of example, the majority of forestland that comprises the national forests of the eastern United States, was acquired during the Depression, much of it as tax delinquent land. The landownership patterns of the eastern national forests typically follow the north to south ridgelines of the Appalachian Mountains with the intervening valleys retained in private ownership. A common practice during the Depression in an act of economic triage was for a landowner to take his most unproductive land (mountain ridges), harvest all of its timber, and then hopefully sell it to the Forest Service before the land was lost to delinquent property taxes. As Lippke states from the experiences in the Northwest, "Regulators have ironically found the surest way to eliminate much of the habitat they were intending to support – by taxing it! The forced preservation of stands of diverse characteristics becomes a potential tax liability that motivates investors to avoid creating those types of characteristics" (Lippke, 1996).

Given the cultural environment and diversity of behavioral incentives just described, what is required is a rural planning format that aligns public objectives (the retention of picturesque rural character on a sustainable basis) with private sector realities and motivations. As has been previously described, rural clustering and conservation design ordinances have that potential. However, the question has to be asked, if the techniques of rural clustering and conservation development are so advantageous in accommodating rural residential demand, a myriad of landowner objectives, and the production of desired public goods in a format with high social validity, then why aren't the practices more widespread?

There are at least three factors, the first being the lack of attractive rural conservation district options. Sometimes the code option is nonexistent, while in other circumstances ordinance language serves as a strong behavioral disincentive to landowners/developers. Currently, many rural local government planning ordinances have the perverse effect of inadvertently encouraging development patterns that are counterproductive, while discouraging practices that would be desirable. With advances in ordinance construction and the employment of behavioral techniques, the incentives can be reversed.

Most model ordinances for rural clustering are found in growing exurban areas where land values are high. These higher land values finance increased sophistication in the development sector, influence market thinking, and allow local governments to be more rigorous in a regulatory command-and-control approach. Conservation design normally requires the services of a design oriented environmental planner or landscape architect. In most rural forested areas where land values are lower, development design is little more than the local surveyor laying out a large-lot design under the inherent incentives of by-right development provisions. Clustering options, if they exist in an ordinance, almost always require greater landowner approval risk, design expense, and procedural steps that are highly unattractive to the novice rural developer.

Ordinance language and associated incentives have to be adjusted for the circumstances of the rural culture. Tradition in practice also plays a role in why certain advancements are slow to catch on in application, particularly in rural environments where less money is available to fuel innovation and development. More often than not, rural planners and development professionals are forced to utilize urban models ill-suited to their particular needs and circumstances. Incentive-based models that are designed specifically for the cultures of deep rural environments as opposed to exurban jurisdictions, are one solution.

A second explanation for why such ordinance provisions and development formats are not widespread is that in rural residential land markets, the consumer preference is assumed to be for large lots. Market research and project experience indicate a window of opportunity for alternative formats, but there is no denying that an advocacy-based, "market making" planning intervention would be required under the CBIP philosophy. Research studies have consistently shown that today anywhere from a quarter to a third of potential buyers desire the characteristics and advantages of cluster design (Audirac & Smith, 1992;

Austin, 2004; Heath, 2001; Kaplan, Austin, & Kaplan, 2004; Senior et al., 2004; Settle, 2005). This market segment will almost certainly increase as the buying public has both more experience with conservation developments and access to them as a purchasing option.

In the early 1990s, there were only a handful of neo-traditional neighborhood developments in the country. Today the major players in the urban and suburban development industry see new urbanist design, pushed by growing market demand, constituting as much as 50 percent of all new projects in the future. The driving force has been publicity, model projects, and market availability.

The same experience can be expected with rural conservation designs. Very few rural housing consumers have ever seen conservation developments or understand how such developments can deliver more rural estate satisfaction. Robust markets are often created from unfulfilled consumer interests. The public didn't know they couldn't live without copy machines, personal computers, cell phones or bottled water until they were introduced and gained market penetration over time. The fact that rural development today is dominated by large-lot formats is not necessarily a reflection of market preference. It is just as likely to be a reflection of the lack of product availability, regulatory disincentives, and little public familiarity with what will be a superior product for many, but not all, rural housing consumers.

Public officials tend to relate to such design formats from the perspective of the benefits that they generate for public planning goals. But just as important, conservation subdivisions offer superior lifestyle benefits to a large market segment. The latent market demand from active retirees, the market segment that poses the primary issue in future rural growth, is for a rural estate experience with substantial natural area access wrapped in a strong sense of community. Much of that market segment doesn't necessary want the physical work involved with maintaining a large rural estate, nor can it afford to acquire an estate large enough to satisfy their dreams. Marketers just haven't gone to work yet. Conservation cluster designs give people more of the experience they are seeking for less money. But it is a landscape vernacular that is yet to be created in the public's mind.

Will conservation project design and rural clustering satisfy all facets of rural housing demand? No. There will always be a significant market segment that has a strong desire for independent, large parcel estates in forested areas. But development of the conservation design market to its full potential would make a dramatic impact in conserving rural character and natural resource management options.

A third explanation for why rural conservation clusters have not become more prevalent may be the potential lack of cradle-to-grave analysis of available planning options and their likely performance under the five tests of performance. Some critics of rural clustering describe it as green sprawl. Even some supporters of conservation subdivisions make a distinction between the substantial environmental benefits associated with them and their use as a growth management tool in natural resource districts (Belansky & Justus, 2000). A CBIP orientation generates a different characterization.

A robust demand for certain types of rural living experiences has always existed and is growing. As a planner in a culture strongly committed to the principles of a market economy, personal freedom, consumer choice, and private property rights, you play the hand that is dealt as skillfully as you can. Attempts to treat rural housing demand as somehow illegitimate, assumes that there are socially valid and politically stable tools available that are effective in the American culture to achieve a purely rational, and some would say utopian land-use vision, whereby the vast majority of population is restricted to only urban or suburban living experiences. It also implies in practice that the interests of rural property owners and the economic vitality of rural American communities should be subservient to urban interests if there is a conflict between public and private goods.

The CBIP philosophy does not reject the vision of conservation and rationality in land-use policy – quite to the contrary – but it does acknowledge the general ineffectiveness of approaches that are culturally insensitive and that fail to align incentives for desired outcomes. It acknowledges – in fact – embraces, the inherent and sometimes painful tradeoffs that must be made to achieve the best results possible in an imperfect world.

Advanced techniques in rural cluster ordinances hold the political and technical potential to become standard practice in conservative regions of rural America, where other more regulatory-oriented approaches do not. If achieved, they would largely preserve rural character and resource management potentials, albeit in a different form than traditionally practiced in the past. If unsuccessful in becoming widely implemented as the rural development option of first choice, the resource values in question will almost certainly be largely lost in many areas over the next several decades.

Incentive Design

The narrative just concluded is CBIP analysis in practice, laying the foundation for the final step in a behavioral-based planning intervention – an engineered incentive package. The final section of this chapter summarizes nine techniques in incentive construction that were recommended for the intervention in forest fragmentation out of a larger universe of CBIP-related tools. Those that apply to code construction are incorporated into model ordinance language that is included in Appendix A. The model code language is annotated for the convenience of the reader so that the connection between incentive principle and the specific ordinance application becomes obvious.

- Risk aversion is a strong behavioral trait in most individuals. Currently, most rural zoning codes make large-lot development by-right at the underlying district density. Where they exist, rural clustering options are normally established as discretionary approvals, even in the current generation of advanced conservation development codes. Conditional use formats or floating zone mechanisms, such as those for planned unit developments that require that applicants go through the rezone process, constitute major disincentives to landowners considering conservation developments. It is recommended that code language reverse the incentive. Specifically, conservation subdivision options should be by-right and large-lot formats discretionary. This can be accomplished without any change in zoning district density or zoning map designations.

- Ordinances should be drafted so that they offer choice with consequences. Americans respond poorly to government authority in land-use controls. As a culture steeped in consumer choice and personal freedom, individuals are conditioned to respond better to choices that offer trade-offs. This is particularly true in rural regions where landowners are less accustomed to having to deal with the land-use restrictions associated with suburban or urban settings.

Some rural conservation development ordinances completely eliminate the large-lot option, permitting only advanced design clustering. In many rural jurisdictions this is likely to provoke unnecessary political opposition in ordinance adoption, and it restricts market expression. Allow both choices, but provide strong incentives for the conservation development option through process advantages, standards flexibility, and technical assistance. Create negative consequences associated with standard, large-lot subdivision options.

- Early concept approval reduces applicant risk and potential expense. Under the Growing Greener/Arendt model of conservation developments, two general purpose, inexpensive concept plans must be prepared and submitted for preliminary review and approval – a base plan indicating lot yield under the ordinance's basic large-lot provisions and a concept plan for a conservation development. After approval of the concept plan, second phase approvals should be reduced to the technical review of detailed site plan considerations, not issues of land-use or density. To empower the technique, it should be restricted to only the conservation subdivision option in an ordinance, not the large-lot options. Further, the formal subdivision review process should be largely administrative in character since the basic land-use and density issues have already been answered.

- Current conservation development code provisions have the decided disadvantage of being lengthy, complex and intimidating to novice rural landowners/developers. Communicating advanced design visions has never been easy in ordinance form. In the attempt to direct and achieve the design benefits of conservation-oriented development, ordinance complexity has become a major disincentive. For the rural landowner clientele group – the target audience - simplicity trumps flexibility.

Research in behavioral economics has shown that if you want to increase the psychological impact of costs in human decision making, which can be defined as any perceived disincentive, break them into smaller components or amounts and list them next to each other. If you want to de-emphasize the impact, combine the costs. The current construction of most rural clustering provisions and conservation development codes has the effect of emphasizing process costs and design requirements.

There are two potential answers for the dilemma. The first is to substitute a design assistance incentive into the code as is discussed later. The second solution is to reduce the complexity of the ordinance provisions down to what is truly necessary. Economy of process is the behavioral incentive goal. As planners, we see the tremendous potential of conservation design formats, and often attempt to maximize the benefits in every aspect of the tool. Ordinance construction often reflects that enthusiasm combined with a mistrust of the applicant. But consider what is better, an ironclad conservation development format that few will use due to behavioral disincentives resulting in the accelerating pattern of large-lot rural sprawl, or conservation design formats that are user-friendly and routinely embraced by landowners/developers? The latter may result in the occasional mediocre or poor project, but it will achieve the larger goal of preserving regional rural landscape character and natural resource potentials. Achieving volume is more important than high-end product quality in this particular application. Market competition will ultimately drive project quality, as will technical design assistance programs that set a high market standard.

- Rural planners know by experience that the majority of forestland development applicants encountered beyond the urban fringe are one-time novice developers, often non-industrial forest landowners headed toward retirement. They are under-capitalized and probably incapable of financing an experienced planning and design team. They are also generally unaware of the development process, and certainly have no background in sophisticated project schemes or value-added approaches to development that maximize returns.

Even the most basic conservation subdivisions require the design orientation of a competent landscape architect or design-oriented environmental planner, which is normally only associated with larger scale suburban or urban developments. Such expertise can be difficult to find in rural locations and represents an additional expense. Current conservation development code models put the burden of advanced design on the backs of these novice developers. The result is that most rural development design is contracted to local surveyors under the least complicated and most destructive format – large-lot design.

A basic and extremely powerful incentive in this case is technical assistance creatively and appropriately administered. While some may initially find such a suggestion provocative, consider the following. It is in every community's public interest to promote advanced development practices and design – everyone benefits from the outcome – the community at-large, adjacent neighbors, the future homeowners in the development and the landowner/developer. You are not going to have advanced conservation development in most rural communities under current code practices and landowner limitations unless assistance is provided in a format that offers a powerful enough incentive.

Further, the tool of public-private partnerships in land planning and development is widely employed in some of the most successful planning schemes in the world, but historically at scales far larger than rural conservation developments. When planning truly becomes collaborative it ceases to be a purely regulatory function at the local government level. It takes on the characteristics of a mutually beneficial partnership. This is a case where the design of a new planning institution may be required to accomplish the stated objectives.

Many rural planners and planning commissions already find themselves in the role of trying to indirectly coach inexperienced applicants in order to improve results. This is normally done in a fashion that both planners and applicants find to be highly inefficient - pre-submission conferences, informal design reviews, plan rejections, and slow processing times. One side tries to communicate what it wants, often afraid to express it directly for fear of overstepping regulatory prerogative, while the other side struggles to understand and comply. Regulatory roles can still be maintained under design assistance regimes.

Finally, as a society we routinely provide technical assistance to private interests to achieve public goals in hundreds of programs. These programs currently include forestry and agricultural cost-share and extension activities for conservation, free forest management plans, manufacturing technology assistance in pollution control and prevention, and small business incubators. Plan assistance to advance the goals of resource land conservation would not be setting a new precedent.

Public design assistance incentives should be offered as an option, not mandatory requirement, and should be restricted to development formats that the community desires to promote. Assistance programs can be established under any number of arrangements and criteria, both in terms of the services delivered and cost-share criteria and mechanisms.

The most powerful incentive is for a jurisdiction to offer such a program as entirely free given available resources, and to potentially link utilization of the service to an expedited review process. Other mechanisms include granting a bonus lot above the base density that is to be conveyed to the jurisdiction upon project approval to pay for either direct or contracted design services. The jurisdiction should make a handsome return, both monetarily and in a public interest context. The jurisdiction could establish a rotating design fund from public moneys or grants to be reimbursed. University planning or landscape architecture outreach programs could also be established as a basis for advanced studios, or state extension service programs established to offer free or cost-share services. However the program is designed, the key is that it has to be a persuasive enough incentive to strongly influence landowner/developer behavior. If a program is not getting the desired results, it has not been structured with enough incentive power.

■ When faced with uncertainty, individuals have a strong tendency to go with the default option. It eliminates the need to make a choice and assumes a heuristic response, that is, we tend to assume that the default option is the most logical choice. Conservation design ordinances should be drafted so that at any decision juncture for the applicant, the default option is the most desirable for public planning goals. The default option should also automatically include several positive process incentives. Selection of the non-default option should require a formal action to request the change.

- A variety of research studies conducted on the attitudes of forestland owners, large-lot residents, and homeowners in conservation subdivisions provide valuable framing effect clues in the selection of ordinance language. A number of behavioral framing effect techniques are applied in the model ordinance provisions that follow.

Research in the Tennessee Valley, Alabama and Pennsylvania have all shown forest landowner attitudes are similar to those of the general public (Bliss et al., 1994). Forestland owners are conflicted over strongly held environmental values and private property rights, but the great majority favor a balance that ensures conservation of the resource over freedom from regulatory restraints. Put another way, faced with the value choice of environment first with a bias toward limiting property rights as opposed to a strident property rights orientation as the more important consideration, they choose the former. But note that we are talking about values, not actual decisions.

Applied behavior analysts have known for decades that values are not a good prediction of behavior. Consequences and incentives that are specific to the individual are far more determinate in the action taken. That's why we can appear to be a nation of environmental hypocrites. Conservation development formats allow forest landowners to reconcile personal environmental values with behavioral incentives such as the desire to make money. In short, the planning format allows someone to do well while doing good. But that nexus needs to be pervasively communicated for it to be recognized. Appropriate appeals to landowners should not just emphasize the environmental sanctity of the technique, but should also tactfully suggest a consistency with more base human motivations such as the profit motive.

Research into the motivations of people who choose a rural lifestyle and perceptions of conservation development also provides guidance in framing effect applications. The principal motivators of people who search out forest living environments is a desire for rural character, natural views from the home, and privacy (Crump, 2003a; Ryan, 2006). Existing large-lot purchasers are far more likely to complain about rural development pressures than homeowners in conservation subdivisions (Kaplan et al., 2004). The explanation likely lies in their respective experiences. Homeowners in well-designed conservation subdivisions have achieved a sense of rural character with a combination of buffered borders, significant open spaces within the community and protected viewsheds from the house. It may be an illusionary oasis surrounded by large-lot sprawl outside the development, but for the many hours that are spent at home each day, a sense of rural character prevails.

Large-lot owners, who believed that low density, large-lot formats would achieve the same objectives, recognize that their sense of rural character is impacted when others around them engage in the same large-lot development practice. Basically, large-lot development threatens the attributes desired by existing large-lot owners. This rural design reality has communication and education implications for planners that extend into framing effects.

There are indications that the terms *cluster* and *open space* have different meanings or provoke different images from the general public and professional planners. While planners relate to clustering as a body of land-use techniques, a concept both applicable in urban or rural settings, the general public is more likely to equate it with density, loss of privacy and urban environments. While the term clustering has been widely used in this report since it is aimed at a professional audience, it is not used in the model ordinance provisions. Rural planning practitioners may want to avoid its use in general public application.

Research is also showing a potential disconnect with the term open space (Kaplan et al., 2004). As Kaplan and Austin comment in their research, the term is being loosely interpreted by different groups to represent different experiences, and has become too imprecise to describe the benefits of rural clustering over large-lot formats. Golf courses and large-lot development patterns create open space, but they destroy rural character. What the general public really wants is rural character, not the rural sprawl of 10-acre minimum lot sizes. While Randall Arendt makes a distinction between rural clustering ordinances and conservation design ordinances when attempting to distinguish between various technical ordinance provisions, I would suggest using the terms rural conservation or rural character for their framing effect values with the general public. Terms like *forest conservation* are likely to be interpreted as exclusive-use forest preservation districts, and zoning district titles like *rural residential* will simply communicate the status quo.

■ To assist in driving consumer preferences toward rural cluster formats and away from scattered large-lot configurations, local jurisdictions should actively promote the development of marquee demonstration projects of both large and small scale. Demonstration projects of sufficient sophistication serve multiple benefits. They can set the standard for planning and development quality in the marketplace, driving competition. They can serve to encourage development-minded landowners to pursue similar models of success. Most importantly, demonstration projects can spark shifts in consumer preferences – they can serve as "market makers." Publicly accepted landscape vernaculars and ownership preferences can be changed over time with active marketing and persuasion-based programs. Demonstration projects are an effective tool in that strategy, and one that is likely required to drive market preferences toward desired development formats.

■ A recommendation that is institutional in nature is the technical training of a new class of professional planner – the entrepreneurial planner/developer. Instead of attempting to regulate for results, plan and build them directly as a profession. Rural land markets provide an ideal setting for smaller-scale development ventures that thrive on professional planning and development talent without the requirement for massive capital outlays. The incentive formulae for rural planners are currently weak – modest public sector compensation associated with social controversy regardless of the outcomes generated, outcomes often largely outside their control. By approaching an institutional redefinition of the profession, or at least a segment of the profession, through academic training and field experience, it is possible to fundamentally modify the incentive package to generate better outcomes. It is also possible to change the paradigm of the rural development sector, driven by a new business model with a public goods orientation of professional rewards. The culture of development need not be driven by competitive individualism. It can just as easily be dominated by individuals with a communitarian and traditionalist orientation, motivated by a somewhat different set of personal incentives.

The exemplar just presented illustrates a range of CBIP principles. To summarize, CBIP as a model of planning practice is a form of social engineering that incorporates the behavioral tools of soft paternalism in a culturally sensitive format. It operates at two levels, strategic and tactical, but the distinction can become blurred in an actual planning intervention. In the example of forest fragmentation, the strategic objective of preserving rural character was blended into longer-range formulae for metropolitan growth management by relying on three behavioral principles: 1) people will make more deliberative planning decisions when the majority of costs and benefits extends into a distant time horizon; 2) people quickly develop a sense of entitlement; and 3) loss aversion is a powerful human motivator.

Once build-out has largely occurred under rural clustering, the open space and rural character preserved will likely be stable from conversion. Owner opposition within conservation developments combined with the legal mechanisms employed to protect the forestland set-asides at the time of project approval, will provide social, political, and legal obstructions to conversion – a pattern for which there is substantial evidence. Outlying rural jurisdictions that adopt such planning formats as by-right standard practice, will eventually constitute greenbelt barriers to further exurban and suburban expansion. Where current attempts to maintain metropolitan area separation and urban containment have nearly all failed at the exurban county level, rural conservation zoning and development strategies may succeed since they move implementation far ahead on the urban development curve. The strategy does so by taking advantage of human time discounting tendencies whereby we make more deliberative decisions if the majority of costs and benefits extend into a distant time horizon. It tactically implements the strategy through the application of a number of behavioral techniques that are sensitive to the underlying culture.

Some may argue, particularly individuals who adhere strictly to a market-based model of planning, that attempts to control future outcomes, as in the current example, are not advised. But the nature of public goods and their production, and the management of externalities require some form of reasoned intervention. When planning is truly deliberative it must make a distinction between those circumstances where the ability to make flexible adjustments is a key design criteria, such as the ability of urban areas to transform themselves, and those circumstances where resource values or public goods are of such a nature that once lost, they can not be re-established without almost insurmountable obstacles. In both instances, planning institutions and associated practices should accommodate cultural traits and behavioral tendencies for sustainable results. This is the intent of the CBIP model of implementation practice.

Conclusion

America's dominant culture of competitive individualism favors personal flexibility over social discipline - a contrast to most European societies. Our institutional embodiment of self-interest over community obligation is reflected in how we view and manage market forces and private property rights in our political, legal, and planning institutions. Property rights are normally interpreted in America as the right to exclude. In European and British cultures, they are just as likely to be interpreted as a communal right not to be excluded. American planning is primarily concerned with protecting private property interests, whereas European and British planning have a far greater focus on proactive management and visioning (Cullingworth, 1993, 1999).

American planning practices are currently off code, that is, they do not connect with cultural underpinnings, nor do they tend to align self-interest through the use of various incentive strategies with the production of public goods or the management of externalities. The result is land-use development patterns that are neither efficient nor environmentally sound or socially desirable.

The over-reliance on planning institutions and regulatory approaches that tend not to align self-interest and freedom of choice to public objectives is, in retrospect, a near guarantee for underperformance when matched to societal traits. Even the European and British experiences, which accept far more rigorous regulatory regimes than our own, match regulatory programs with elements of economic subsidization and public education almost inconceivable to Americans, to achieve their results. To assume that the current strategy of straightforward, command-and-control regulation will be effective is to assume that planners will be successful in overpowering American culture, including transforming market, legal, and political institutions that reflect these cultural traits. We haven't been successful in this quest in the last half-century and it is unlikely we will have any greater success in the future if we continue to rely on the same outlook.

This book has identified a significant number of principles from the disciplines of behavioral and experimental economics, psychology, and the broad field of persuasion that offer a culturally sensitive alternative to planners. Those principles can be applied in three categories of incentives – economic, social, and behavioral. What has been discussed is a sample of incentive-based schemes, not an exhaustive list. Will these principles of incentive-based planning work? They certainly should offer an enhancement to existing tools. They also present the opportunity for entirely new non-regulatory approaches to advance planning objectives. But CBIP as a behavioral-based approach to planning is in its infancy. While these principles are being applied in many other management arenas with startling success, experimentation in planning is just beginning. Will they work? Almost certainly. Will there be failures requiring adjustment along the way as greater experience is gained in their application? Without question.

Bibliography

Alig, R., Kline, J., & Lichtenstein, M. (2004). Urbanization on the US Landscape: Looking Ahead in the 22st Century. *Landscape and Urban Planning, 69*(2-3), 219-234.

Allison, P. D. (1992). The Cultural Evolution of Beneficent Norms. *Journal of Experimental Psychology, 71,* 279-301.

Altshuler, A., & Behn, R. (1997). *Innovation in American Government.* Washington DC: Brookings Institution Press.

Altshuler, A. (1965). *The City Planning Process.* Ithaca, N.Y.: Cornell University Press.

Altshuler, A., Wolman, M., Morrill, Wolman, & Mitchell (Eds.). (1999). *Governance and Opportunity in Metropolitan America, National Resource Council.* Washington DC: National Academy Press.

Andreoni, J. (1995). Warm-Glow Versus Cold-Prickly: The effects of positive and negative framing on cooperation in experiments. *Quarterly Journal of Economics, 110*(1), 1-21.

Angelina, K. (2003). *New Landowners in Virginia's Forest: A Study of Motivations, Management Activities, and Perceived Obstacles.* Virginia Tech, Blacksburg.

Anthony, J. (2004). Do State Growth Management Regulations Reduce Sprawl/. *Urban Affairs Review, 39*(3), 376-397.

APA. (2002). *Planning for Smart Growth: 2002 State of the States.* www.planning.org/growingsmart.

Arendt, R. (1994). *Rural by Design.* Chicago, Washington, D.C.: Planners Press.

Arendt, R. (1996). *Conservation Design for Subdivisions:* Island Press.

Arendt, R. (1999). *Growing Greener: Putting Conservation into Practice:* Island Press.

Arendt, R. (2004). *Crossroads, Hamlet, Village, Town design* (Vol. PAS 523/524): American Planning Association.

Ashley, R., Ball, S., & Eckel, C. (2004). *Analysis of Public Goods Experiments Using Dynamic Panel Regression Models.*Unpublished manuscript.

Audirac, I., & Smith, M. (1992). Urban Form and Residential Choice: Preference for Urban Density in Florida. *Journal of Architectural and Planning Research,* 9(1).

Austin, M. (2004). Resident Perspectives of the Open Space Conservation Subdivision in Hamburg Township, Michigan. *Landscape and Urban Planning,* 69(2-3), 245-253.

Axelrod, R. (1984). *The Evolution of Cooperation.* New York: Basic Books.

Axelrod, R., & Hamilton, W. D. (1981). The Evolution of Cooperation. *Science, 211,* 1390-1396.

Babcock, L., & Loewenstein, G. (2004). Explaining Bargaining Impasse: The Role of Self-Serving Biases. In M. Rabin (Ed.), *Advances in Behavioral Economics.* New York: Princeton University Press.

Baer, D. (1987). *A Behavior-Analytic Query into Early Intervention.* Paper presented at the Banff International Conference on Behavioral Science, Banff, Canada.

Baer, D., Wolf, M., & Risley, T. (1968). Some Current Dimensions of Applied Behavior Analysis. *Journal of Applied Behavior Analysis, 1,* 91-97.

Baerwald, T. (1981). The Site Selection Process of Suburban Residential Builders. *Urban Geography,* 2(4), 339-357.

Baldwin, R., & Cave, M. (1999). *Understanding Regulation; Theory, Strategy and Practice.* Oxford, England: Oxford University Press.

Barker, K. (2006). *Barker Review of Land Use Planning:* HM Treasury.

Barnard, C. (1938). *Functions of the Executive.* Cambridge, Mass.: Harvard University Press.

Baumhart, R. (1968). *An Honest Profit.* New York: Prentice-Hall.

Belansky, E., & Justus, S. (2000). *The Conservation Subdivision Design Project: Booklet for Developing a Local Bylaw.* Boston: Metropolitan Area Planning Council.

Bell, P., Greene, T., Fisher, J., & Baum, A. (2001). *Environmental Psychology, Fifth Edition.* New York: Harcourt College Publishers.

Benartzi, S., Rapoport, A., & Yagil, J. (1989). Discount Rates Inferred from Decisions: An Experimental Study. *Marketing Science, 35,* 270-284.

Benedict, R. (1934). *Patterns of Culture.* Boston: Houghton Mifflin.

Berkman, H. a. L., Sirgy. (1996). *Consumer Behavior:* NTC Publishing Group.

Birch, T. (1996). *Private Forest-land Owners of the United States*, 1994 (Resource Bulletin NE-134): USDA Forest Service, Northeast Forest Expermiment Station.

Birch, T., Hodge, S. S., & Thompson, M. T. (1998). *Characterizing Virginia's private forest owners and their forest lands.* (NE-707): USDA Forest Service, NE Research Station.

Bliss, J., Nepal, S., Brooks, R., & Larsen, M. (1994). Forest Community or Granfalloon. *Journal of Forestry, 92*(9), 6-11.

Blundell, J., & Robinson, C. (2000). *Regulation without the State; The Debate Continues; Readings 52:* The Institute of Economic Affairs.

Bolton, G., & Ockenfels, A. (2000). A Theory of Equity, Reciprocity and Competition. *The American Economic Review, 90*(1), 166-193.

Bolton, P., & Dewatripont, M. (2005). *Contract Theory.* Cambridge, Mass.: The MIT Press.

Bradley, G. (1995). *Urban Forest Landscapes.* Seattle: University of Washington Press.

Buchanan, J., & Tullock, G. (1965). *The Calculus of Consent:* University of Michigan Press.

Burby, R., & May, P. (1997). *Making Governments Plan: State Experiments in Managing Land Use.* Baltimore and London: John Hopkins University Press.

Callies, D. (1992). Dealing with Scarcity: Land Use and Planning. In Z. Smith (Ed.), *Politics and Public Policy in Hawaii:* University of New York Press.

Camerer, C. (2003). *Behavioral Game Theory: Experiments in Strategic Interaction.* New York: Princeton University Press.

Camerer, C. (2004). Prospect Theory in the Wild: Evidence from the Field. In G. Loewenstein (Ed.), *Advances in Behavioral Economics.* New York: Princeton University Press.

Camerer, C., & Loewenstein, G. (2004). Behavioral Economics: Past, Present, and Future. In M. Rabin (Ed.), *Advances in Behavioral Economics.* New York: Princeton University Press.

Camerer, C., Loewenstein, G., & Rabin, M. (Eds.). (2004). *Advances in Behavioral Economics.* New York: Princeton University Press.

Campbell, S., & Kittredge, D. (1996). Econsystem-Based Management on Multiple NIPF Ownerships. *Journal of Forestry, 94*(2), 24-29.

Carlton, J. (2006, March 8, 2006). *It Takes a Village to Lure Buyers Back to Town.* Wall Street Journal.

Carnegie, D. (1936). *How to Win Friends and Influence People.* New York: Simon and Schuster.

Carruthers, J. (2002). The Impacts of State Growth Management Programs: A Comparative Analysis. *Urban Studies, 39*(11), 1959-1982.

Center, P. E. R. (2000). *The Lone Mountain Compact: Principles for Preserving Freedom and Livability in America's Cities and Suburbs.* Big SKy: PERC.

Chaiken, S. (1987). The Heuristic Model of Persuasion. In C. P. Herman (Ed.), *Social Influence: The Ontario Symposium* (Vol. Vol. 5). Hillsdale, N.J.: Lawrence Erlbaum.

Chamberland, S. (1972). *Aspects of Developer Behavior in the Land Development Process. Research Report No. 56.* Toronto: Centre for Urban and Community Studies, University of Toronto.

Churchman, A. (2002). Environmental Psychology and Urban Planning: Where Can the Twain Meet? In A. Churchman (Ed.), *Handbook of Environmental Psychology* (pp. 191-199). New York: John Wiley.

Cialdini, R. (1993). *Influence: Science and Practice* (third ed.): Harper Collins College Publishers.

Coughlin, R., & Lockhart, C. (1998). Grid-group theory and ideology: A consideration of their relative strengths and weaknesses for explaining the strucuture of mass belief systems. *Journal of Theoretical Politics, 10,* 33-58.

Crump, J. (2003a). Finding a Place in the Country. *Envrionment and Behavior, 35*(2), 187-202.

Crump, J. (2003b). Finding a Place in the Country: Exurban and Suburban Development in Sonoma County, California. *Environment and Behavior, 35*(2), 187-202.

Cullingworth, B. (1993). *The Political Culture of Planning: American Land Use Planning in Comparative Perspective.* New York and London: Routledge.

Cullingworth, B. (Ed.). (1999). *British Planning: 50 Years of Urban and Regional Policy.* London, New Brunswick: The Athlone Press.

Cullingworth, B., & Nadin, V. (2006). *Town and Country Planning in the U.K, 14th Edition.* London and New York: Routledge.

Dalton, L., & Burby, R. (1994). Mandates, Plans, and Planners: Building Local Commitment to Development Management. *Journal of the American Planning Association, 60*(4), 444-457.

Daniels, A. C. (1989). *Performance Managment.* Tucker, Ga: Performance Management Publications.

Danielsen, K., Lang, R., & Fulton, W. (1999). Retracting Suburbia:Smart Growth and the Future of Housing. *Housing Policy Debate, 10*(3), 513-553.

Davidoff, P. (1965). Advocacy and Pluralism in Planning. *Journal of the American Institute of Planners, 31*(4), 331-338.

Davis, D., & Holt, C. (1993). *Experimental Economics.* Princeton, New Jersey: Princeton University Press.

Dedrick, J., Hall, T., Hull, B., & Johnson, J. (2000). An Experiment in Managing Fragmentation. *Journal of Forestry, 98*(3), 22-24.

DeGrove, J. (1984). *Land, Growth and Politics*. Washington D.C.: Planners Press, American Planning Association.

Devine, D. (1972). *The Political Culture of the United States: The Influence of Member Values on Regime Maintenance*. Boston: Little, Brown.

Deyle, R., & Smith, R. (1998). Local Government Compliance with State Planning Mandates. *Journal of the American Planning Association*, 64(4), 457-468.

Diaz, D., & Green, G. P. (2001). Growth Management and Agriculture: An Examination of Local Efforts to Manage Growth and Preserve Farmland in Wisconsin Cities, Villages, and Towns. *Rural Sociology*, 66(3), 317-341.

Dolsak, N., & Ostrom, E. (Eds.). (2003). *The Commons in the New Millennium*. Cambridge, Mass.: The MIT Press.

Douglas, M. (1978). *Cultural Bias*. London: Royal Anthropological Society.

Douglas, M. (1982). *In the Active Voice*. London: Routledge and Kegan.

Douglas, M. (1996). *Thought Styles*. Thousand Oaks, CA: Sage.

Downs, A. (1989). *The Need for a New Vision for the Development of Large U.S. Metropolitan Areas*. New York: Salomon Brothers.

Downs, A. (1991). The Advisory Commission on Regulatory Barriers to Affordable Housing: Its Behavior and Accomplishments. *Housing Policy Debate*, 2(4), 1101-1161.

Duany, A., Plater, Zyberk, & Speck. (2000). *Suburban Nation:* North Point Press.

Easterbrook, G. (2003). *The Progress Paradox: How Life Gets Better while People Feel Worse:* Random House.

Easterlin, R. (2005). Feeding the Illusion of Growth and Happiness: A Reply to Hagerty and Veenhoven. *Social Indicators Research*, 74(3), 429-443.

Economist. (2003, August 9, 2003). Chasing the Dream. *The Economist*.

Economist, T. (March 27, 2004). Save, save, save. *The Economist*.

Ellis, R. (1993). *American Political Cultures*. New York, Oxford: Oxford University Press.

EPA. (2000a). *A Guide to Selected National Environmental Statistics in the U.S. Government*. Washington D.C.: U.S. Environmental Protection Agency.

EPA. (2000b). *Municipal Solid Waste Generation, Recycling and Disposal in the United States: Fact and Figures for 1998*. Washington D.C.: U.S. Environmental Protection Agency.

EPA. (2000c). *National Air Quality and Emmissions Trends*. Washington D.C.: U.S. Environmental Protection Agency.

Esparza, A., & Carruthers, J. (2000). Land Use Planning and Exurbanization in the Rural Mountain West: Evidence from Arizona. *Journal of Planning, Education, and Research*, 20, 23-36.

Esrza, A., & Carruthers, J. (2000). Land Use Planning and Exurbanization in the Rural Mountain West: Evidence from Arizonia. *Journal of Planning, Education, and Research, 20*, 23-36.

Etzioni, A. (1988). *The Moral Dimension:* The Free Press.

Fehr, E., & Gachter, S. (2000). Cooperation and Punishment in public goods experiments. *American Economic Review, 90*, 980-994.

Fehr, E., & Schmidt, K. (1999). A Theory of Fairness, Competition, and Cooperation. *The Quarterly Journal of Economics, August.*

Fehr, E., & Schmidt, K. (2004). A Theory of Fairness, Competition and Cooperation. In M. Rabin (Ed.), *Advances in Behavioral Economics.* New York: Princeton University Press.

Firebaugh, G., & Tach, L. (2005). Money Can Buy (Some) Happiness. *Science, 309*(5739), 1322.

Fischel, W. (1985). *The Economics of Zoning Laws: A Property Rights Approach to American Land Use Controls.* Baltimore: John Hokins Press.

Fischel, W. (1995). *Regulatory Takings: Law, Economics, and Politics.* Cambridge, Mass.: Harvard University Press.

Fischel, W. (2001). *The Homevoter Hypothesis.* Cambridge, Massachusetts: Harvard University Press.

Fischel, W. A. (1990). *Do Growth Controls Matter? :* Lincoln Institute of Land Policy.

Fischhoff, B., Slovic, P., & Lichtenstein, S. (1978). Fault trees: Sensitivity of estimated failure probabilities to problem representation. *Jouranl of Experimental Psychology: Human Perception and Performance, 4*, 330-344.

Fishchel, W. (2005). Politics in a Dynamic View of Land-Use Regulations: Of Interest Groups and Homevoters. *The Journal of Real Estate Finance and Economics, 31*(4), 397-403.

Forester, J. (1989). *Planning in the Face of Power.* Berkeley: University of California Press.

Frederick, S., & Loewenstein, G. (2002). The Psychology of Sequence Preferences. *Working paper, Sloan School, MIT, MA.*

Frederick, S., Loewenstein, G., & Odonoghue, T. (2004). Time Discounting and Time Preference: A Critical Review. In M. Rabin (Ed.), *Advances in Behavioral Economics.* New York: Princeton University Press.

Friedmann, J. (1987). *Planning in the Public Domain:* Princeton University Press.

Friedmann, J. (1997). *Planning Theory Revisited.* Paper presented at the Nijmegen Academic Lecture.

Fulton, W., Pendall, R., Nguyen, M., & Harrison, A. (2001). *Who Sprawls Most? How Growth Patterns Differ Across the U.S.* (Survey Series). Washington, D.C.: The Brookings Institution.

Garreau, J. (1995). Ten Commandments for Planners. *Whole Earth Review*(Winter 1995).

Geller, S. (1976). Behavioral Approaches to Environmental Problem Solving: Littering and Recycling, *Conference Proceedings of the Association for the Advancement of Behavior Therapy*, New York, (1976).

Geller, S. (1981). Evaluating Energy Conservation Programs: Is verbl report enought? *Journal of Consumer Research*, 8, 331-335.

Geller, S. (1987). Applied behavior analysis and environmental psychology: From strange bed fellos to a productive marriage. In I. Altman (Ed.), *Handbook of Environmental Psychology* (Vol. 1, pp. 361-388). New York: John Wiley & Son.

Geller, S. (2001a). Behavior-based safety in Industry: Realizing the large-scale potential of psychology to promote human welfare. *Applied and Preventive Psychology*, 10, 87-105.

Geller, S. (2001b). *Psychology of Safety Handbook*. Boca Raton, Fl.: CRC Press.

Geller, S. (2002). *The Psychology of Safety*. Unpublished manuscript, Blacksburg, Va.

Genesove, D., & Mayer, C. (2004). Loss-Aversion and Seller Behavior: Evidence from the Housing Market. In M. Rabin (Ed.), *Advances in Behavioral Economics*. New York: Princeton University Press.

Glaeser, E. (2006). *Paternalism and Psychology*. Chicago Law Review, 1.

Glenwick, D., & Jason, L. (1980). *Behavioral Community Psychology*. New York: Praeger Publishers.

Glenwick, D., & Jason, L. (1993). *Promoting Health and Mental Health: Behavioral Approachs to Prevention*. New York: Springer.

Gobster, P., & Rickenbach, M. (2004). Private Forestland Parcelizatin and Development in Wisconsin's Northwoods: Perceptions of Resource-Oriented Stakeholders. *Landscape and Urban Planning*, 69(2-3), 165-182.

Goldstein, A. P., & Krasner, L. (1983). *Modern Applied Psychology*. New York: Pergamon Press.

Goodman, R. (1971). *After the Planners:* Simon and Schuster.

Gourville, J., & Dilip, S. (1998). Payment Depreciation: The Effects of Temporally Separating Payments from Consumption. *Journal of Consumer Research*.

Green, G., Marcouiller, D., Deller, S., Erkkila, D., & Sumathi, N. (1996). Local Dependency, Land Use Attitudes, and Economic Development" Comparisons between Seasonal and Permanent Residents. *Rural Sociology*, 61(3), 427-445.

Hancher, L., & Moran, M. (Eds.). (1989). *Capitalism, Culture, and Regulation*. Oxford: Clarendon Press.

Harrison, L. (2007). *The Central Liberal Truth: How Politics Can Change a Culture and Save It from Itself*.: Oxford University Press.

Harrison, R. (2008). *Prefurbia – Redesigning the Suburbs: From Disdainable to Sustainable*. Dubuque, IA.: Sustainable Land Development International.

Healey, P. (1997). *Collaborative Planning: Shaping Places in Fragmented Socieities:* UBC Press.

Heath, T. (2001). Revitalizing Cities: Attitudes Toward City-Center Living in the United Kingdom. *Journal of Planning, Education, and Research, 20,* 464-475.

Heckelman, J., & Coates, D. (Eds.). (2003). *Collective Choice: Essays in Honor of Manucur Olson:* Springer.

Hepner, G. (1983). An Analysis of Residential Developer Location Factors in a Fast Growth Urban Region. *Urban Geography, 4*(4), 355-365.

Hogarth, R., & Einhorn, H. (1992). Order Effects in Belief Updating: The Belief-Adjustment Model. *Cognitive Psychology, 24*(1), 1-55.

Huber, J., Payne, J., & Puto, C. (1982). Adding Asymmetrically Dominated Alternatives: Violations of Regularity and the Similarity Hypothesis. *Journal of Consumer Research, 9*(1), 90-98.

Hudson, B. (1979). Comparison of Current Planning Theories: Counterparts and Contradictions. *American Planning Association Journal, October 1979,* 387-406.

Huntington, S. (1981). *American Politics: The Promise of Disharmony.* Cambridge: Harvard University Press.

Inglehart, R. (1990). *1990 World Values Survey.* Ann Arbor: Institute for Social Research.

Jacobs, J. (1961). *The Death and Life of Great American Cities.* New York: Vintage Books.

Jarvis, H. (2003). Dispelling the Myth that Preference makes Practice in Residential Location and Transport Behaviour. *Housing Studies, 18*(4), 587-606.

Jensen, M. (1998). *Foundation of Organizational Strategy.* Cambridge, Mass.: Havard University Press.

Jensen, M. (2000). *The Theory of the Firm; Governance, Residual Claims, and Organizational Forms.* Cambridge, Mass.: Harvard University Press.

Johnson, E., Hershey, J., Meszaros, J., & Kunreuther, H. (1993). Framing, Probability Distortions, and Insurance Decisions. *Journal of Risk and Uncertainty, 7,* 35-51.

Johnson, K. M., & Beale, C. (1995). The Rural Rebound Revisited. *American Demographer, 17,* 46-49.

Jones, A. (1996). The Psychology of Sustainability: What Planners Can Learn from Attitude Research. *Journal of Planning, Education, and Research, 16,* 56-65.

Kachelmeir, S., & Shehata, M. (1992). Examing Risk Preferences Under High Monetary Incentives: Experimental Evidence from the People's Republic of China. *The American Economic Review, 82*(5), 1120-1141.

Kagel, J., & Roth, A. (Eds.). (1995). *The Handbook of Experimental Economics.* Princeton, New Jersey: Princeton University Press.

Kahneman, D., Diener, E., & Schwarz, N. (Eds.). (1999). *Well-Being: The Foundation of Hedonic Psychology.* New York: Russell Sage Foundation.

Kahneman, D., Knetsch, J., & Thaler, R. (2004). Experimental Tests of the Endowment Effect and the Coase Theorem. In M. Rabin (Ed.), *Advances in Behavioral Economics*. Ney York: Princeton University Press.

Kahneman, D., Krueger, A., Schkade, D., Schwarz, N., & Stone, A. (2004). A Survey Method for Characterizing Daily Life: The Day Reconstruction Method. *American Economic Review*, 94(2), 429-439.

Kahneman, D., Slovic, P., & Tversky, A. (1982). *Judgement Under Uncertainty: Heuristics and Biases*. New York: Cambridge University Press.

Kaplan, R., & Austin, M. (2004). Out in the Country: Sprawl and the Quest of Nature Nearly. *Landscape and Urban Planning*, 69(2-3), 235-243.

Kaplan, R., Austin, M., & Kaplan, S. (2004). Open Space Communities. *Journal of the Amerian Planning Association*, 70(3).

Kaplan, R., Kaplan, S., & Ryan, R. (1998). *With People in Mind*. Washington, D.C: Island Press.

Kaplan, S. (1992). Environmental preference in a knowledge-seeking, knowledge-using organism. In J. Tooby (Ed.), *The Adapted Mind*. New York: Oxford University Press.

Kaplan, S., & Kaplan, R. (1982). *Cognition and environment: Functioning in an uncertain world*. New York: Praeger.

Katz, L. (1964). Effects of Different Monetary Gain and Loss on Sequential Two-Choice Behavior. *Journal of Experimental Psychology*, 68, 245-249.

Katz, L., & Rosen, K. (1987). The Interjurisdictional Effects of Growth Controls on Housing Prices. *Journal of Law and Economics*, 30(April 1987), 149-160.

Kelly, E. (1993). *Managing Community Growth*: Praeger.

Kelly, E. (2004). *Managing Community Growth (2nd edition)*. Westport: Praeger.

Kendig, L., Connor, S., Byrd, C., & Heyman, J. (1980). *Performance Zoning*. Washington D.C.: Planners Press.

Kenney, K. (1972). *The Residential Land Developer and his Land Purchase Decision*. University of North Carolina.

Kim, J., & Kaplan, R. (2004). Physical and Psychological Factors in Sense of Community. *Environment and Behavior*, 36(3), 313-340.

Kleindorfer, P. (2002). Understanding Individuals Environmental Decisions: A Decision Sciences Approach. In T. Burkhardt (Ed.), *Better Environmental Decisions*. Washington D.C.: Island Press.

Knaap, G. (1985). The Effects of Urban Growth Boundaries in Metropolitan Portland, Oregon. *Land Economics*, 61, 28-35.

Knaap, G., & Nelson, A. (1992). *The Regulated Landscape: Lessons on State Land Use Planning from Oregon*. Cambridge, Mass.: Lincoln Institute of Land Policy.

Koebel, C. T. (1990). *The Impact of Zoning on Housing Costs*: Virginia Center for Housing Research.

Lacy, J. (1990). *An Examinatino of Market Appreciation for Clustered Housing with Permanent Open Space*. Amherst: Center for Rural Massachusetts.

Laffont, J.-J., & Martimort, D. (2002). *The Theory of Incentives*. Princeton and Oxford: Princeton University Press.

Landis, J. (1992). Do Growth Controls Work? - A New Assessment. *Journal of the American Planning Association, 58*(4).

Layard, R. (2003). Happiness - Has Social Science a Clue? : Lionel Robbins Memorial Lectures, Center for Economic Performance, London School of Economics.

Leclerc, F., Schmidt, B., & Dube, L. (1995). Decision Making and Waiting Time: Is Time like Money? *Journal of Consumer Research, 22*, 110-119.

Lehman, P., & Geller, S. (2004). Behavior Analysis and Environmental Protection: Accomplishments and Potential for More. *Behavior and Social Issues, 13*, 13-32.

Leopold, A. (1933). *Game Management*. New York: Scribner's Sons.

Leung, H. L. (1987). Developer Behaviour and Development Control. *Land Development Studies, 4*, 17-34.

Levin, I., & Gaeth, G. (1988). How Consumers are Affected by the Framing of Attribute Information before and after Consuming the Product. *Journal of Consumer Research, 15*, 374-378.

Levine, J. (2006). *Zoned Out; Regulation, Markets and Choices in Transportation and Metropolitan Land-Use*. Washington DC: Resources for the Future.

Levine, N. (1999). The Effects of Local Growth Controls on Regional Housing Production and Population Redistribution in California. *Urban Studies, 36*(1), 2047-2068.

Levitt, S., & Dubner, S. (2005). *Freakonomics*: William Morrow.

Levitt, S., & Syverson, C. (2005). *Market Distortions when Agents and Better Informed: A Theoretical and Empirical Exploration of the Value of Information in Real-Estate Transations*: National Bureau of Economic Research working paper.

Lichtenstein, S., & Slovic, P. (Eds.). (2006). *The Construction of Preference*: Cambridge University Press.

Lindblom, C. (1959). The Science of Muddling Through. *Public Administration Review, 19*.

Lippke, B. (1996). Incentives for Managing Landscpaes to Meet Non-Timber Goals: Lessons from the Washington Landscape Management Project. In B. Adamowicz, Luchert, Phillips and White (Ed.), *Forestry, Economics, and the Environment*: CAB International.

Lockhart, C. (1999). Cultural Contributions to Explaining Institutional Form, Political Change, and Rational Decisions. *Comparative Political Studies, 32*(7), 862-893.

Loewenstein, G. (1988). Frames of Mind in Intertemporal Choice. *Marketing Science, 34*, 200-214.

Loewenstein, G., & Prelec, D. (1993). Preferences for Sequences of Outcomes. *Psychological Review, 100*(1), 91-108.

Loewenstein, G., Thompson, L., & Bazerman, M. (1989). Social Utility and Decision Making in Interpersonal Context. *Journal of Personality and Social Psychology, 47*, 1231-1243.

Lomborg, B. (2001). *The Skeptical Environmentalist: Measuring the Real State of the World*: Cambridge Press.

Lopez, R., & Haynes, H. P. (2003). Sprawl in the 1990s: Measurement, Distribution, and Trends. *Urban Affairs Review, 38*(3), 325-355.

Lucy, W. (1996). APA's Ethical Principles Include Simplistic Planning Theories. In C. a. Fainstein (Ed.), *Readings in Planning Theory*: Blackwell.

Luger, M., & Temkin, K. (2000). *Red Tape and Housing Costs*. New Brunswick: Center for Urban Policy Research.

Malott, R. (1992). A Theory of Rule-Governed Behavior and Organizational Behavior Management. *Journal of Organizational Behavior Management, 12*(2), 45-65.

Malott, R. (2000). Occupational Safety and Response Maintenance - An alterView. *Journal of Organizational Behavior Management, 21*(1), 85-101.

Malott, R. (2002). What OMB Needs is More Jesiwh Mothers. *Journal of Organizational Behavior Management, 22*(2).

Malpezzi, S. (1996). Housing Prices, Externalities, and Regulation in U.S. Metropolitan Areas. *Journal of Housing Research, 7*(2), 209-241.

Marris, P. (1994). Advocacy Planning as a Bridge Between the Professional and the Political. *American Planning Association Journal, 60*(2), 143-146.

McCrummen, S. (2006, April 16, 2006). *Redefining Property Values*. Washington Post.

Mcharg, I. (1969). *Design with Nature*. Garden City, New York: The Natural History Press.

McKenzie-Mohr, D. (2000). Fostering Sustainable Behavior Through Comminuty-Based Social Marketing. *American Psycholist, 55*(5), 531-537.

McMahon, D. (2006). *Happiness: A History*: Atlantic Monthly Press.

McNutt, P. (2002). *The Economics of Public Choice*. Cheltenham, U.K: Edward Elgar.

Mishel, L., & Bernstein, J. (2001). *The State of Working America 2002/2003*. Paris: OECD.

Mitnick, B. (1980). *The Political Economy of Regulation : creating, designing, and removing regulatory forms*. New York: Columbia University Press.

Mohamed, R. (2006a). The Economics of Conservation Subdivisions: Price Premiums, Improvements Costs, and Absorption Rates. *Urban Affairs Review, 41*(3), 376-399.

Mohamed, R. (2006b). The Psychology of Residential Developers. *Journal of Planning Education and Research, 26*, 28-37.

Mortimer, D. M., Prisley, D. S., Daversa, D., & Stull, L. (2005). *A Report of the Prevalence and Effects of Local-Related Ordinances in the Commonwealth of Virginia*. Charlottesville: Virginia Department of Forestry.

Nassauer, J. I. (1992). The Appearance of Ecological Systems as a Matter of Policy. *Landscape Ecology, 6*, 239-250.

Nassauer, R. I. (1995). Culture and Changing Landscape Structure. *Landscape Ecology, 10*(4), 229-237.

National, S. (1997). *General Household Survey*: www.statistics.gov.uk.

NCSL. (2006). *Eminent Domain Legislative Data Base*. National Conference of State Legislatures, www.ncsl.org.

Nelson, A. (1988). An Empirical Note on How Regional Urban Containment Policy Influences an Interaction between Greenbelt and Exurban Land Markets. *American Planning Association Journal, 54*(Spring 1988), 178-184.

Nelson, A., & Dawkins, C. (2005). *Urban Containment in the United States: History, Models, and Techniques for Regional and Metropolitan Growth Management* (PAS 520): American Planning Association.

Newman, P., & Kenworthy, J. (1989). *Cities and Automobile Dependence: A Sourcebook*. Aldershot, U.K. and Brookfield, VT: Gower Publishing Co.

NOP, R. G. (1997). *House Beautiful, New Home Awards*. London: NOP Research Group.

Norton, R. (2005). Local Commitment to State-Mandated Planning in Coastal North Carolina. *Journal of Planning, Education, and Research, 25*, 149-171.

O'Brien, C. (June, 2005). *Planning for Sustainable Happiness: Harmonizing OUr Internal and External Landscapes*. Paper presented at the 2nd International Conference on Gross National Happiness, Antigonish, Nova Scotia.

Odean, T. (1998). Are Investors Reluctant to Realize Their Losses. *Journal of Finance*.

O'Donoghue, T., & Rabin, M. (2004). Doing it Now or Later. In M. Rabin (Ed.), *Advances in Behavioral Economics*. Princeton and Oxford: Princeton University Press.

OECD. (1997). *Co-operative Approaches to Regulation and Public Management - Occasional Papers No. 18*: Organization for Economic Co-Operation and Development.

Olson, M. (1965). *The Logic of Collective Action*: Harvard University Press.

Orfield, M. (2002). *American Metro Politics: The New Suburban Reality*. Washington, D.C.: Brookings Institution Press.

Orians, G. (1980). Habitat Selection: General Theory and Applications to Human Behavior. In J. Lockard (Ed.), *The Evolution of Human Social Behavior*. New York: Elsevier.

Orians, G. (1986). An Ecological and Evolutionary Approach to Landscape Aesthetics. In D. Lowenthal (Ed.), *Landscape Meanings and Values*. London: Allen and Unwin.

Palmer, A. (1981). *Toward Eden*. Winterville, North Carolina: Creative Resouce Systems Inc.

Payne, J., Bettman, J., & Johnson, E. (1992). Behavioral Decision Research: A Constructive Processing Perspective. *Annual Review of Psychology, 43*, 87-131.

Peattie, L. (1994). Communities and Interests in Advocacy Planning. *American Planning Association Journal, 60*(2), 151-153.

Peltzman, S. (1976). Towards a More General Theory of Regulation. *Journal of Land and Economics, 19*.

Pendall, R. (1999). Do Land-Use Controls Cause Sprawl? *Environment and Planning B., 26*, 555-571.

Pendall, R. (2001). Municipal Plans, State Mandates and Property Rights; Lessons from Maine. *Journal of Planning, Education, and Research, 21*, 154-165.

PERC. (2000). *The Lone Mountain Compact: Principles for Preserving Freedom and Livability in America's Cities and Suburbs*. Big Sky: Poltical Economy Research Center.

Phillips, J., & Goodstein, E. (2000). Growth Management and Housing Prices: The Case of Portland, Oregon. *Contemporary Economic Policy, 18*(No. 3), 334-344.

Platt, J. (1973). Social Traps. *American Psychologist, 28*, 641-651.

Poling, A., & Braatz, D. (2001). *Principles of learning: Respondent and operant conditioning and human behavior*. New York: The Haworth Press.

Pollakowski, H., & Wachter, S. (1990). The Effects of Land Use Constraints on Land Values. *Land Economics, 66*(August 1990), 315-324.

Popper, F. (1981). *The Politics of Land Use Reform*: The University of Wisconsin Press.

Power, T. (2000). *Lost Landscaptes and Failed Economies: The search for a value of place*. Washington: Island Press.

Prelec, D., & Loewenstein, G. (1991). Decison Making over Time and Under Uncertainty: A common approach. *Marketing Science, 37*, 770-786.

Prelec, D., & Loewenstein, G. (1998). the Red and the Black: Mental Accounting of Savings and Debt. *Marketing Science, 17*, 4-28.

Rabin, M. (1998). Psychology and Economics. *Journal of Economic Literature, 36*(March), 11-46.

Ramblers, A. (2006). *Walking is the most sustainable means of transport*. www.ramblers.org.uk/info/factsandfigures.

Rapoport, A. (1982). *The Meaning of the Built Environment*. Beverly Hills, Ca.: Sage Publications.

Ray, P., & Anderson, S. R. (2000). *The Cultural Creatives*. New York: Three Rivers Press.

Redelmeier, D., & Heller, D. (1993). Time Preference in Medical Decision Making and Cost-Effectiveness Analysis. *Medical Decision Making, 13*(2), 212-217.

Rettig, S., & Pasamanick, B. (1964). Differential Judgement of Ethical Risk by Cheaters and Non-cheaters. *Journal of Abnormal and Social Psychology, 69*, 109-113.

Richardson, J. (2000). *Does Smart Growth Protect Open Space and/or Farmland.* St. Louis: Annual Educational Symposium of the American Agricultural Law Association.

Rifkin, J. (2005a). *The European Dream.* New York: Jeremy P. Tarcher/Penguin.

Rifkin, J. (2005b). *The European Dream: How Europe's Vision of the Future is Quietly Eclipsing the American Dream.* New York: Jeremy P. Tarcher/Penguin.

Rippl, S. (2002). Cultural theory and risk perception: a proposal for a better measurement. *Journal of Risk Research, 5*(2), 147-165.

Rusk, D. (1999). *Inside Game Outside Game: Winning Strategies for Saving Urban America.* Washington, D.C.: Brookings Institution Press.

Ryan, R. (2006). Comparing the Attitudes of Local Residents, Planners, and Developers about Preserving Rural Character in New England. *Landscape and Urban Planning, 75*(1-2), 5-22.

Sager, T. (1999). Manipulation in Planning: The Social Choice Perspective. *Journal of Planning, Education, and Research, 19*(2).

Saint, C. G. (2006). *The Saint Index: The Annual Measure of the Politics of Land Development.* www.tscg.biz.

Sampson, N., & DeCoster, L. (2000). Forest Fragmentation. *Journal of Forestry, 98*(3).

Samuelson, W., & Zeckhauser, R. (1988). Status Quo Bias in Decision Making. *Journal of Risk and Uncertainty, 1*, 7-59.

Sandercock, L. (1998). *Towards Cosmopolis.* Chichester, New York: John Wiley & Son.

Sayman, S., & Onculer, A. (1997). A Meta Analysis of Willingness to Accept and Willingness to pay Disparity. *Working paper, Wharton School, Univerisity of Pennsylvania. available at http://home.ku.edu.tr/~ssay,am/research/meta.pdf.*

Schmidt, T., & Raile, G. (1998, Sept. 19-23, 1998). *Forest Fragmentation in the Lake States.* Paper presented at the Great Lakes - Great Forests, Traverse City, Michigan.

Schon, D. (1983). *The Reflective Practitioner.* New York: Basic Books, Inc.

Schwartz, S., Hansen, D., & Green, R. (1984). The Effect of Growth Control on the Production of Moderate Priced Housing. *Land Economics, 60*(February 1984), 110-114.

Schwartz, S., & Zorn, P. (1988). a Critique of Quasiexperimental and Statistical Controls for Measuring Program Effects: Application to Urban Growth Control. *Journal of Policy Analysis and Management, 7*(No. 3, 1988), 491-505.

Segal, D., & Srinivasan, P. (1985). The Impact of Suburban Growth Restrictions on U.S. Housing Price Inflation, 1975-1978. *Urban Geography*, 6(January-March 1985), 14-26.

Senior, M. L., Webster, J. J., & Blank, N. E. (2004). Residential preferences versus sustainable cities: quantitiative and quantitative evidence from a survey of relocating owner-occupiers. *Town Planning Review*, 75(3).

Shaw, J., & Utt, R. (2000). *A Guide to Smart Growth: Shattering Myths, Providing Solutions*: The Heritage Foundation.

Shefrin, H., & Statman, M. (1988). The Disposition to Sell Winners too Early and Ride Losers too Long. *Journal of Finance*, 40, 777-790.

Shilling, J., Sirmans, C. F., & Guidry, K. (1991). The Impact of State Land-use Controls on Residential Land Values. *Journal of Regional Science*, 31(1), 83-92.

Simonson, I., & Tversky, A. (1992). Choice in Context: Tradeoff Contrast and Extremeness Aversion. *Journal of Marketing Research*, 29, 281-295.

Sirgy, J. (2001). *Handbook of Quality-of-Life Research: An Ethical Marketing Perspective*: Kluwer Academic Publishers.

Skinner, B. F. (1974). *About Behaviorism*. New York: Alfred A. Knopf.

Skinner, B. F. (1990). Can Psychology be a Science of Mind. *American Psychologist*, 45, 1206-1210.

Skinner, B. F. (2001). The Design of Cultures. *Behavior and Social Issues*, 11(4), 4-13.

Slovic, P. (1995). The Construction of Preferences. *American Psychologist*, 50, 364-371.

Slovic, P., Finucane, M., & Peters, E. (2006). The Affect Heuristic. In P. Slovic (Ed.), *The Construction of Preferences*: Cambridge University Press.

Slovic, R., & Lichtenstein, S. (1968). Relative Importance of Probabilities and Payoffs in Risk Taking. *Journal of Experimental Psychology*, 78, 1-18.

Staley, S. (2001). *Market-oriented Approaches to Growth: Outsmarting Sprawl*. Reason Public Policy Institute.

Stern, P. (2000). Psychology and the Science of Human-Environment Interactions. *American Psychologist*, 55(5), 523-530.

Stigler, G. J. (1971). The Theory of Economic Regulation. *Bell Journal of Economics*, 2, 3-21.

Stutzer, A., & Frey, B. S. (2004). *Stress That Doesn't Pay: The Commuting Paradox*. Zurich: Institute for the Study of Labor, University of Zurich.

Sunstein, C., & Thaler, R. (2003). Libertarian Paternalism is Not an Oxymoron. *University of Chicago Law Review*, 4.

Susanka, S. (2001). *The Not so Big House: A Blueprint for the Way We Really Live*. Newtown, Ct: Taunton Press.

Svenson, O. (1981). Are We all Less Risky and More Skillful Than Our Fellow Drivers? *Acta Psychologica*, 9, 143-148.

Thaler, R. (1980). Toward a Positive theory of Consumer Choice. *Journal of Economic Behavior and Organization, 1*, 39-60.

Thaler, R. (2004). Mental Accounting Matters. In M. Rabin (Ed.), *Advances in Behavioral Economics*. New York: Princeton University Press.

Thompson, M., Ellis, R., & Wildavsky, A. (1990). *Cultural Theory*. Boulder, San Francisco, and Oxford: Westview Press.

Tideman, N. (1969). *Three Approaches to Improving Urban Land Use - Doctoral Dissertation*. University of Chicago, Chicago.

Tiebout, C. (1956). A Pure Theory of Local Expenditures. *Journal of Political Economy, 64*(5).

Tilt, J., Kearney, A., & Bradley, G. (2006). Understanding Rural Character: Cognitive and visual perceptions. *Journal of Landscape and Urban Planning, 10*.

Turnbull, G. (2005). The Investment Incentive Effects of Land Use Regulations. *The Journal of Real Estate Finance and Economics, 31*(4), 357-395.

Tversky, A., & Kahneman, D. (1971). Belief in the Law of Small Numbers. *Psychology Bulletin, 76*(2), 105-110.

Tversky, A., & Kahneman, D. (1981). The Framing of Decisions and the Rationality of Choice. *Science, 211*, 453-458.

Tversky, A., & Kahneman, D. (1986). Rational Choice and the Framing of Decisions. *Journal of Business, 59*, 251-278.

U.S. Department of Housing and Urban Development. (1991). *Not in My Backyard, Removing Barriers to Affordable Housing*: U.S. Government Printing Office.

Ulrich, R. (1983). Aesthetic and Affective Response to Natural Environment. In J. F. Wohlwill (Ed.), *Behavior and the Natural Environment*. New York: Plenum.

Ulrich, R. (1986). Human Response to vegetation and Landscapes. *Landscape and Urban Planning, 13*, 29-44.

Urban Land Institute. (1999). *Smart Growth: Myth and Fact*. Washington, D.C.: Urban Land Institute.

Vaillancourt, F., & Luc, M. (1985). The Effect of Agricultural Zoning on Land Prices, Quebec, 1975-1981. *Land Economics, 61*, 36-42.

Vogt, C., & Marans, R. (2004). Natural Resources and Open Space in the Residential Decision Process: A study of recent movers to fringe counties in southeast Michigan. *Landscape and Urban Planning, 69*(2-3), 255-269.

Washington, P., Kaiser, F., & Harvard, U. (2005). *Survey of Teens in the Greater Washington, D.C. Area*: www.kff.org.

Washington, P., Kaiser, F. F., & Harvard, U. (1998). *American Values: 1998 A survey of American Values*. www.kff.org.

Weber, E., Blais, A.-R., & Betz, N. (2002). A Domain-Specific Risk-Attitude Scale: Measuring Risk Perceptions and Risk Behaviors. *Journal of Behavioral Decision Making, 15*.

Webster, C., & Wai-Chung, L. (2003). *Property Rights, Planning and Markets*. Cheltenham: Edward Elgar.

Weinstein, N. (1980). Unrealistic Optimism about Future Life Events. *Journal of Personality and Social Psychology*(39), 806-820.

Whyte, W. H. (1968). *The Last Landscape*. New York: Doubleday (Reprinted by University of Pennsylvania Press, 2002).

Wildavsky, A. (1994). Why self-interest means less outside of a social context: Cultural contributions to a theory of rational choice. *Journal of Theoretical Politics, 6*, 131-159.

Williams, R. (1960). *American Society: A Sociological Interpretation*. New York: Knopf.

Williamson, T., & Bellamy, L. (1987). *Property and Landscape: A Social History of Land Ownership and the English Countryside*. Frome and London: Butler and Tanner Ltd.

Winett, R., Moore, J., & Anderson, E. (1991). Extending the Concept of Social Validity: Behavior Analysis for Disease Prevention and Health Promotion. *Journal of Applied Behavior Analysis, 24*(2), 189-249.

Wingo, L. (1973). The Quality of Life: Toward a Micro-Economic Definition. *Urban Studies, 10*(3).

Woodward, G., & Denton, R. (2000). *Persuasion & Influence in American Life* (Fourth ed.): Waveland Press Inc.

Young, R. (1993). Changing Behavior and Making it Stick : The Conceptualization and Managment of Conservation Behavior. *Environment and Behavior, 25*(4).